What people say about CRYO KID ...

"*Corinne Copnick has done a remarkable job of demystifying the increasingly common experience of using a sperm donor. Her warm, caring account of her own daughter's story provides a compelling introduction into the possibilities and responsibilities incumbent on both the industry and the parents-to-be as the field of assisted reproduction technology grows. California Cryobank is proud to have provided a helping hand in making her grandchildren possible. We applaud her well researched efforts and are grateful for the care and respect she shows in protecting the privacy of the other individuals involved in her story.*"
    —California Cryobank, Los Angeles

"*A highly literate, courageous, and masterly account of the changing ways children—and families—are brought into being. CRYO KID is a compelling read from start to finish. It is both educational and thought-provoking. I couldn't put it down.*"
    —Jeannette Moscovitch, BA, MA
    Founder, Canadian Cultural Programmes, Montreal, QC

"*Corinne Copnick has written a thoughtful, funny, and very timely book describing her own experiences as a hip seventy-one-year-old grandmother caught up in her family's struggles to deal with unexpected fertility problems, and the varied and surprising solutions available today to those who missed their opportunity to birth a child.*"
    —Trudi Alexy
    Author of the *Mezuzah in the Madonna's Foot*, Los Angeles

"*An exciting, joyful, true story about a wondrous new age involving fertility and multiple births, all at different times and places geographically disparate. Yet all events and their participants are very much related to each other. This is also a story of active curiosity, of trust and risk, and above all, of generosity of spirit. Kudos to this brave story! It must be told for the benefit of the many*

[children] who already exist, and for the many more who will join us in the future.
—Dr. Fern Waterman, MD, MSc
Physician and Psychotherapist, Toronto, Canada

"Corinne Copnick is a terrific author, and she allows us to share, not only her memories of her family life, but also that of her daughters and granddaughter, Samantha. It is a fascinating story which is not only informative and educational but also warmly personal. I was captivated throughout."
—Anita Genest
Former *Radio Canada* (CBC) Television Producer, Montreal, QC

"Groundbreaking! Heartwarming! Seventy-one years of experience captured in a terrific book. I laughed until I cried, and I cried until I laughed."
—Wendy Spiegel
Founder, GenPlus, Los Angeles

It is California's good luck to have attracted a writer of Corinne Copnick's astonishing caliber. As a publisher for the last twenty-five years, I have rarely come across a literary talent that can pack so many desirable qualities—societal vision, dedicated research, humor, and deeply felt honesty—into the top-drawer telling of a terrific true story. It's topical, controversial, courageous, and, above all, loving. Welcome to the Western States, Cryo Kid!
—David Epstein
Publisher, *Western States Jewish History*

CRYO KID

CRYO KID

Drawing a New Map

Corinne Heather Copnick

iUniverse, Inc.
New York Lincoln Shanghai

CRYO KID
Drawing a New Map

Copyright © 2008 by Corinne Heather Copnick

iUniverse books may be ordered through booksellers or by contacting:

iUniverse
2021 Pine Lake Road, Suite 100
Lincoln, NE 68512
www.iuniverse.com
1-800-Authors (1-800-288-4677)

Because of the dynamic nature of the Internet, any Web addresses or links contained in this book may have changed since publication and may no longer be valid.

The views expressed in this work are solely those of the author and do not necessarily reflect the views of the publisher, and the publisher hereby disclaims any responsibility for them.

Although the events recorded in this book are factual, the names of some individuals, their locations, and other details have been changed to protect their privacy.

ISBN: 978-0-595-47834-7

Printed in the United States of America

For all my grandchildren
with love, pride, and faith
in the maps my little explorers will draw for their future.

ACKNOWLEDGMENTS

This book is an exploration inspired by a true story, the personal experiences of my family and myself. I have written it with the intention of sharing as much as I can, as honestly as I can. How much to reveal of our lives and identities and how much to conceal has been an ongoing dilemma. Should I use a pseudonym? Finally, in consultation with my family and friends, I decided to use my own name and the real names of my children and grandchildren. Also, where they are a matter of record, I have used authentic events, names, locations, and descriptions. In most other instances, I have disguised the identities and locations of the people encountered in this book, including "the Sibs," in order to protect their privacy. The thoughts and feelings of Adam, while based on written records, an audiotape, photographs, and e-mails, are, in large part, imagined. The contact with him described is authentic, but I have changed his name and donor number.

I would like to thank my family and friends for reading this manuscript prior to publication and offering their useful comments. In particular, I want to thank my four daughters: Janet, for allowing me to tell her story and encouraging me for the full year it took me to write it. Laura went through the entire manuscript in its different versions, offering very helpful suggestions by e-mail. Shelley burned the midnight oil to read the book through in one sitting and then read it through again before making her recommendations. When I began this book, I had not intended to include Susan's experience with *in vitro* fertilization because it had not yet taken place. We are both grateful that it has been possible to describe it while *Cryo Kid* was still in progress. Loving thanks to my grandchild, Samantha, for her many keen observations, often shared with me from the back seat of my car as I drove her back and forth to school. Thank you to the California Cryobank and to the California doctors whose incredible knowledge and dedication helped bring Samantha into being. And, of course, to Samantha's biological father, Adam, and to my exhusband, Bert, for his part as progenitor of my children and grandchildren. Many thanks to the Donor Sibling Registry, instrumental in helping us contact Samantha's half-siblings.

A heartfelt thank you to the friends who have also helped *Cryo Kid* along with their appreciation and suggestions: to Edith Sobel who devotedly read every chapter as I wrote it; to Anita Genest for her useful candor and keen eye; and to Mirjam Rosenfeld, whose daughter also gave birth to a beautiful, talented, cryo kid.

And very special thanks to my dog, Daisy Mae, herself an astonishing mix of unknown canine breeds, for sitting by my side for countless hours at the computer, and for pushing my hands off the keys when she considered it enough for one sitting.

Finally, thank you to my readers, whose interest will help continue this account, for the story has just begun.

◆

Contents

PROLOGUE

Los Angeles, 2008

A few years ago, I bought the "watch part" of a gold watch at a Los Angeles consignment shop that sold vintage objects at reasonable prices and donated the profits to help senior citizens. The watch was white gold, rectangular, with little diamond chips, and fastened with a silk ribbon band in the manner of models popular in 1925.

As a precaution, I removed the excellent antique movement and fragile silk ribbon and put them in my safety deposit box in case I ever wanted to resell the watch. Then I replaced the movement with a battery. The watch was now updated in time but still needed a band. Alas, it didn't have a pin to hold a modern watch band, only a slot on each side where the ribbon had been inserted. Temporarily, I "made do" with a sturdy, black leather band that an innovative jeweler pasted into place.

Despite a search of antique and watch shops, finding a matching white gold band was fruitless in Los Angeles. While a bracelet could be modified to fit the watch, the gold color of modern bracelets didn't match, and antique bracelets were very costly. It was the same story everywhere I went, even surf-side Carmel, where an antique shop owner produced a triple strand, pearl band that could be made to fit for an astronomical price. Surprisingly, I couldn't find anything in New York either.

But then I discovered Newberry Street in Boston, and at the very first antique store I entered, there it was—my white gold watch-bracelet. Filigreed, inlaid with onyx and moonstone, and circa 1925, it was the right color and could be made into a band. It was more than twice what I hoped to pay. The jeweler wouldn't bargain but threw in the labor. He was shocked when I bought it in one minute flat. But hadn't I shopped around, even on the Internet? For two years? Hadn't I tried, way back in my college days, to make sense of Samuel Beckett's play, *Waiting for Godot*, with its inescapable message, "Don't Wait"?

Practically speaking, I can buy the things I need, but I really can't afford to splurge like this on luxury items. Like so many seniors in their seventies, my financial resources are limited.

"I am not retired." I told myself in the minute before I bought the gold bracelet. "I can *still* work to buy the things I *don't* need. I want to have a gold watch with a matching gold band *before* I retire." And a minute later, I did. Then I left it at the antique shop, so that the bracelet could be modified and sent to me in Los Angeles.

That is how it happened that when I strolled on the broad, alphabetical avenues in Boston, I was watchless. My left wrist, where I normally wear a watch, was completely unadorned. I stopped a friendly-looking young man. "Do you have the time?" I asked him, smiling. "Yes, indeed," he replied, taking the cell phone off his belt. "It's just noon."

That's when I began to notice that time had changed all around me. Boston, with its close proximity to Harvard, was full of young people—lots of twenty-somethings. I had a little time to kill before meeting my then forty-five-year-old-daughter-who-still-wears-a-wrist-watch for lunch. So I asked a few more "youngsters" for the time. All of them referred to their cell phones. Some were already holding them, a call obviously just completed or about to be initiated. Some reached into a jacket, others into a purse. No one was wearing a wrist watch.

Of course. Who needs to wear a wrist watch? There's a clock on the bedside table, a clock in the kitchen, a clock in the car, in the office, on the computer. And the multi-tasking, ubiquitous cell phone—already the blackberry has succeeded it—always knows the time of day or night.

Suddenly, I felt young. I had no watch, but I had a cell phone in my purse. Why had I asked for the time when all along I had it with me? All of a sudden, time was on my side.

When my beautiful watch arrived in Los Angeles, I decided to wear it only on "dress" occasions, as a curiosity, something from the past. I smiled when I looked at the wrists of my chronological contemporaries who are still wearing wrist watches. They couldn't tell from looking at me that I had stepped forward in time. But I knew. Psychologically, I had changed generations.

It's a good thing I did, because the generations have certainly changed all around me. Both in the generations of my growing up, and the one in which I raised my family, it would have been impossible for me—and probably for my children—to imagine the variations within my family today, and the ways in which those variations have come about.

What is different from past centuries is the astonishing speed at which these variations have occurred. As futurist Alvin Toffler points out, families in pre-industrial times were multi-generational, and life, work, schooling, and care of the elderly were all home-centered. The shrunken nuclear family came about as a result of the disruptive industrial revolution, which scattered the family in the workplace and geographically. With the information revolution and globalization, the family is evolving once again. "Now we see not the death of the family, but the diversification of family formats...."[1]

This is not the future. This is now. Over the last several decades, my own family's formats have most certainly diversified. It was hard to change, to transition. Each of us struggled with our values as we transformed ourselves, as individuals and as a family that remains close-knit. We are a family transformed.

This book, the story of that transformation, is a voyage into unexplored territory.

◆

PART I

FERTILITY FOREVER

"A student of anthropology once told me that human beings are the only species who can look each other in the eye when they have sexual relations."

—Rabbi David Woznica
Stephen S. Wise Temple, Los Angeles

1

THE BOOK of JANET

It is probably four to six thousand years since an unknown Neolithic couple died, their skeletal remains believed to be that of a man and woman forever locked in eternal embrace.[1] When I viewed the enlarged image of these hugging human skeletons on the Internet, it struck me as undeniably unique and universal at the same time, so poignant in its tender visual statement of love that it took my breath away.[2] According to a newspaper report,[3] archeologists discovered the young lovers, their teeth still intact and their flint tools close by, at a construction site outside of Mantua, the setting for Shakespeare's famous play. Like Romeo and Juliet, the image of their romanticism survives.[4]

Another kind of love, a mother's love for her child—one of the strongest human bonds known—is equally timeless.

♦

That is why I want to start this Book of Janet, my first-born daughter, with the loving image of six little, seven-year-old girls enjoying a sleep-over in sleeping bags on two large air mattresses, placed on the floor, in a prosperous middle class neighborhood in Los Angeles County. Most of the people who live in this area are professionals or business people who take great interest in their children. The little girls are in their sleeping bags, with six pairs of eyes focused on a *Sponge Bob* DVD as a movie treat conclusion to the celebration of their friend's birthday party. They have all brushed their teeth after the birthday cake, gone to the bathroom, and climbed into their pajamas with little girl giggles. They are cozy and warm as they watch the movie together, and soon they will fall asleep with satisfied sighs after the mother of the birthday girl reads them a funny story with a happy ending. They still very much enjoy the bedtime story, although these smart girls have nearly finished Grade One now, and all of them are proud that they can read and write several grades beyond their level.

Four of the six girls have a father and a mother living in the same house. One of the girl's parents were divorced recently, so she has a mother most of the time and a father every second weekend. The sixth little girl is called Samantha. She was born to a single mother by artificial insemination. She lives with her Mom and Grandma in this pretty little bungalow in Southern California, with rose bushes lining the front lawn and herbs (lavender, mint, tarragon, rosemary, basil) and fruit trees—you can pluck oranges, grapefruit, lemons, plums and peaches from them—in the back garden.

Her mother is beaming with happiness as she kisses each of the children good night with a special hug and kiss for Samantha. Her name is Janet, and she would do anything for Samantha. It has been a long, hard-working, courageous, and to add an overused word, soul-searching, route to get to this sleep-over. The Grandma is me.

When I look at Janet caring for her child, the image flashes before my eyes of Baby Janet, only thirteen months old as she crawls to the bottom shelf of the bath table where the diapers are kept in the children's room, extracts a folded diaper, and crawls back to hand it to me; I am in the rocking chair, where I sit feeding newborn Baby Shelley, her sister, and her junior by just a year. Even as a baby, Janet was a helper, a caregiver, a role she has continued to play all her life.

I am seventy-one years old, and whenever I think about my now forty-seven-year-old daughter, I also think of Janet wearing a cornflower blue dress to match her eyes at her fourth birthday party. The dress was hand-sewn by my mother and featured elaborate, intricate hand-smocking (an almost lost art, as it is usually done now by machine) on the bodice. It endured well and was subsequently worn by Shelley, when *she* reached four years of age, and then by Susan, one of my twins who, together with her sister Laura (who wore a matching yellow dress crafted by my mother), was born four years after Shelley. And, some forty years later, my grandchild, Samantha, Janet's daughter, wore the same blue dress at her own four-year-old birthday party.

*   *   *   *

The artistic influence of my mother, Gertrude, was very prevalent in our lives. (My kids, living in the *milieu* of a French language city, called her *Grand'mère*; by the time I got to be a grandmother, I was living, at least most of the time, in Los Angeles, and I was referred to as just plain Grandma.) From the ages of three and four, I transported my first set of little girls, Janet and Shelley, to ballet school twice a week at Miss Eleanor's in the Town of Mount Royal, a posh area of Montreal. It was *Grand'mère* who sewed their costumes for the big show at the end of each year. I also took them once weekly for art classes at the Museum of Fine Art's School for Children, until my belly was so swollen with my not yet emergent twins that I couldn't fit behind a wheel to drive them downtown. At one of the last classes to which I was able to drive the children (parents were not allowed to stay during the class), Dr. Arthur Lismer—the school's founder and one of the internationally renowned Group of Seven artists[5]—took pity on me and invited me (holding my belly) up the many stairs to his office. There he proceeded to blow the considerable dust off a teacup and offer me a cup of tea.

My mother's artistry continued to exert a profound effect on all my girls at a young age. My twins, Laura and Susan, were more attracted to athletics than the arts, although grown-up Laura exhibits a decided streak of mysticism. I switched them both from ballet classes to gymnastics at an early age. As a matter of fact, they first manifested their athleticism by rocking their cribs together from opposite sides to the middle of the room, screaming with laughter, and climbing out of them in unison. Sometimes they fell on their heads, so we had to take them out of their cribs and put them on mattresses on the floor at the advanced age of nine months.

My mother taught my older girls to knit, crochet, sew, and a multitude of other crafts. She encouraged them to draw and paint and taught them how colors work together. The twins didn't have as much of this influence on their lives, partly because she kept the older girls busy when she came to visit, so that I could concentrate on the twins. When they were born, I had four children under five. That's how I had them: boom, boom, and boom-boom.

Not only was Janet an accomplished artist and craft person by the time she entered kindergarten at five years old (she proudly wore the dark blue and light blue poncho she had crocheted with *Grand'mère's* help), but she could also read and write very well. So after her first month of kindergarten, where she was very, very happy, recounting all the details of her morning class to me when she returned home to eat her lunch with gusto, the principal decided (with the permission of my husband and me) to "skip" her to first grade as part of a school "experiment" with bright children. We agreed because Janet had spent her mornings for the previous year at an excellent, cooperative Pre-school (lots of creative imagination exercised there, along with the paint spills). At that time, not every child had the advantage of Pre-school before kindergarten, and we thought the experience probably replaced kindergarten.

It was a big mistake to move her from kindergarten, though. My happy little girl now spent a full day instead of a half day in school. When she was advanced to first grade, she was also advanced to wearing a school uniform and to carrying a lunch, which she didn't eat. For a while, she seemed sad, but before too long, she bounced back to being my happy little Janet. Although she did extremely well academically, "skipping" put her at a disadvantage socially, because now she was the youngest child in the class and would remain so throughout elementary school. She especially suffered the embarrassment athletically (as I had before her, because I was also "skipped" to first grade) of always being the last person chosen for a sports team ... or else being paired with the teacher. As I look back, I think being advanced ahead of her age group put her into the mindset of trying too hard. All of her life, she has tried harder than most people would in order to please others. Like her mother before her, she tries to please everyone.

Although Janet loved the twins, their arrival also placed a burden on her: instead of simply being mother's "big girl" (Shelley was a year younger), as she had been before, she was now "mother's helper." Now I tried to find opportunities to spend time alone with my "two big girls," sometimes hiring a babysitter, so that I could enjoy activities with Janet and Shelley. In a way, it was like having two sets of twins: Janet and Shelley, and Susan and Laura. Each "set" has been wonderful friends with one another, and all of them got along beautifully and still do. They have been, and continue to be, each other's support group through all the highs and lows of living.

Janet and Shelley loved dramatic arts from an early age, probably accentuated by my own love of theater, and by the drama classes I taught to one hundred children in back-to-back classes to "enrich" the curriculum at Glencoe School. This was the public school they attended when we lived in New Bordeaux, a then new "development" of single family houses north of the Town of Mount Royal. One of the highlights of the drama classes was a production of "Little Moon," a play set in China, for which we also created the sets and costumes in cooperation with the art class. It was a splendidly ambitious, visually beautiful (and exhausting) endeavor, and one that my two older girls and I still remember with great pleasure.

*   *   *   *

I am glad that their early years were spent in a neighborhood with a diverse population made up mostly of people of Greek, Italian, and Jewish derivation. Everyone got along in this ethnic neighborhood, and the children played together and walked to school together. I didn't have to drive them to play with their friends or make "play dates," as the mothers do here in Los Angeles. They could find playmates next door or on the next block or two. I encouraged my kids to bring their friends home (so that I knew where they were), and with four kids already there to play with, our house was usually filled with other children as well, all of them enjoying cookies and cocoa after school and then playing in the "rec" room (as these rooms were called before the terminology changed to "family rooms"), the garden, or "out in front," depending on the weather.

Glencoe School, an English-language school run by the Protestant School Board, was, in the 1960s, a sparkling new building situated on a beautiful grassy site surrounded by flower beds and a far cry from the plain, if not ugly, buildings and chain link fences that surround most public schools in Los Angeles in 2007. In Montreal, at that time, the public schools were either under the aegis of the Protestant or the Catholic School Board, and there were language divisions (French/English) as well.

My husband and I were active on the Executive of the Home and School Association. I produced a monthly newsletter, and Bert was President of the Ski Club that we organized as an extra-curricular activity. Winters were severe in Montreal, and either you shivered and resented the cold weather for seven months of the year, or you engaged in winter sports and enjoyed it. So we decided that our family would all become skiers and look forward to snow on the weekend. Instead of saying, "Ugh, it's snowing," we would exult, "Wow, we'll have great snow on the slopes!"

It took a bit of doing. I am not a natural athlete, but nevertheless we wound up with six skiers in our family. Laura and Susan were already doing well on skis at six years old. Every Saturday morning from mid-November to the end of March, I became a volunteer bus mother on the transport that took sixty kids, including my own four children, up to the Laurentian Mountains and back for a day of skiing. My sister-in-law accompanied another sixty kids—we had to recruit one hundred kids each season in order to have the popular ski school contract to teach our little skiers—on a second bus, and the two of us took ski lessons (our bonus for being bus mothers) together while the kids were getting theirs. The kids encouraged me every time I fell down while I was learning to control my skis in a very wide snow plow.

"It's okay, Mrs. Corinne," they would call, as they whizzed by high above me on their chair lifts, "You'll be able to get up. You're doing fine. Just lean a little more on your ski pole." They were great confidence-builders.

Although I always enjoyed the cocoa in the ski "shack" (what we called the very pleasant cafeteria/lounge at the base of the ski slopes) more than the actual skiing, eventually I learned how to ski to the point where I could negotiate the moguls on intermediate hills, while my kids whizzed down expert hills that should have been marked "Death;" they did "hot dog" tricks like skiing backwards on one leg. Skiing is all confidence. The turning point in my skiing came about when an inspired instructor tried to explain the rhythm of skiing to me by comparing it to dancing. Prior instructors had exhorted me to "attack the hill." I didn't want to attack anything. But once I understood that I could dance on my now parallel skis, I zoomed down the gladed slopes, vocalizing to the trees with the kind of singing people usually do in the shower.

"We always knew when Corinne was jumping the moguls," a skier friend at Sutton confided to me, laughing. "We could hear the opera all over the mountain." I had never thought about the echoes that carried my exultant voice from the bunny slopes to the expert trails.

By the time I was singing through skiing, we had "graduated" from the children's ski school and the Laurentian Mountains to the Eastern Townships, specifically to the town of Sutton, about eight miles from the Vermont border and about an hour away from Jay Peak. For a couple of years, we rented a ski chalet. Then, deciding we liked it (despite one year when we were all laid up with a case of flu at the same time a guest came to visit—bearing her skis, a bouquet of flowers, and much good will—while we all took turns throwing up), we decided to purchase our very own "Swiss" chalet at the summit of the Number One ski lift atop Mount Sutton. What a marvelous view of the slopes and the valley we had!

When I sold the home years later, after my divorce, I was amazed when the purchasers said, "We almost didn't buy the house because there's no view." I looked around and saw with their eyes that the developers had been at work on the mountain all around us. While we were the only home for miles around at the top of *rue Boulanger* when we purchased the house, construction had taken over the territory. I used to leave my door open when we went skiing and, later, when I was alone in the house, with an ex-husband and four kids busy with their own activities in the city, I still did not lock the door at night. When friends asked me, "Aren't you afraid to be alone up there at night?" I would laugh and respond, "Who's there?"

We had such happy times as a family, very child-centered at Mount Sutton. It was an idyllic setting with ski friends dropping in, friends from the city, and easy, country entertaining. We did all the traditional country ski things— bought apple cider from Vermont and heated it with cinnamon sticks on the stove. The tantalizing aroma of the after-ski, cider brew permeated the house throughout the late afternoon and evening. A poem I wrote at that time entitled "Sutton" and later published in my book of bilingual poems, *Embrace/Etreinte*, captures the feeling of our ski house.

> *I have made my house*
> *into a fireplace ...*
> *where goodnight guitars*
> *link reddening cheeks*
> *in soft-chanted dreams,*
>
> *where flickering chords*
> *blow hot chocolate*
> *children marshmallow kisses,*
>
> *where footprints in snow*
> *melt your treebark face*
> *rough against my heart.*[6]

*   *   *   *

By that time, Janet was a senior at Mount Royal High School. We had moved from our split-level on *rue Capitaine Bernier* (named after a famous explorer) in ethnic New Bordeaux to a larger home in the Town of Mount Royal (an affluent area of Montreal) when she first started high school. All our kids were truly sorry to leave our cozy house because the basement recreation room featured a paneled library wall that was my husband's pride and joy—he had built it with his own hands—and that turned around at the touch of a button (just like in the story books) to reveal a secret wet bar. Janet and her sisters had a great time playing hide and seek in this alcove when their friends came over to play. Fortunately, I knew where to look for them.

At Mount Royal High, Janet completed the French-immersion program (her studies were almost completely in French, so that she could perfect her oral and written knowledge of that language) and was busily engaged in being the social director of her school grade. It was no surprise that Janet would be arranging social activities, such as dances and outings, for her peers. When she was only six months old—and this is not an exaggeration aggrandized by the fallibility of senior memory; it is perhaps unbelievable, but it is accurate: she would sit up in her finely-made, English baby carriage, that had first converted into a car bed and now into a stroller, and call out "Hi" to all the neighbors.

Now, at the age of sixteen, she had met her very first love, a brilliant, dark-haired, dark-eyed young man called Lawrence, who wanted to follow his father's footsteps into a prominent and noteworthy medical career and eventually did. Had they met at a later time, perhaps they would have married. At this stage in their lives, it was premature, but they loved each other with the playfulness and intensity of a first love that can rarely be recaptured in any other love. At any rate, for a couple of years they were inseparable, and Lawrence spent a great deal of time both at our ski place in Sutton and at our home in the Town of Mount Royal (later referred to as *Ville Mont Royal*).

Our gracious Lethbridge Avenue home might not quite qualify for the McMansions that proliferate all over Los Angeles, where I live now, but it came pretty close. It was a two-story, red-brick, colonial with imposing, but graceful, white columns and a beautiful, mature garden in the back. The front featured bay windows that looked into a dream kitchen that we had also added to the house. It had ample cupboards in white, "French provincial" style, with gold moldings, a magnificently patterned ceramic floor in shades of blue and white, a double stainless steel sink, in-counter burners (an innovation at the time), and a double oven and indoor barbecue (both also stainless steel) purchased from the United States because nothing like this was yet available in Canada. A mud room (with lockers for the kids to keep their snow gear, skis, and exercise equipment, as well as hopefully hang up their wet clothes) led from the kitchen into the back garden. There was a large entry way with a cross-hall dining room and living room on either side. The hallway led to a grand staircase that opened at the top into a hallway with five, very roomy bedrooms and two bathrooms. There was a guest bathroom downstairs.

This was the house where Janet was living when she met Lawrence in high school. His family also lived in the Town of Mount Royal where, although we held her Sweet Sixteen party in our knotty-pine-paneled recreation room, other kids were just as likely to have theirs on a yacht or take their friends on a three-day vacation to classy Stowe, Vermont. Lawrence spent so much time cuddling with Janet on the sofas of our homes that I began to think he also lived with us. They parted when his mother intervened. She felt they were too young to be serious and wanted to make sure that Lawrence finished his studies and followed the path predestined for him by his family. She was probably right, but I remember both kids feeling crushed at the time. Most of the men Janet has been attracted to ever since have had a little bit of Lawrence in them. At least, they look a little bit like her high school sweetheart.

But through all the happy remembrances I still hold in my mind of the time when I lived for fifty years in Montreal, the French part of Canada—and then for more than a dozen years in Toronto, once a predominantly Anglo-Saxon part of Canada, whose streets now speak of ethnic diversity—it never once occurred to me that my first granddaughter would be born to her mother, the same young girl that was once in love with Lawrence, with the assistance of an unknown donor from a California sperm bank.

*   *   *   *

Between Lawrence and the birth of Samantha, Janet went on to other loves, of course. Her early attraction to theater, her love of people, and her innate gift for communication led her, after a stint at Vanier College, to McGill University's film and communications program. In the years before she graduated with a bachelor of arts degree, she was very active at McGill, just as she had been in high school. One of her major involvements was with the Tuesday Night *Café*, where she both acted in and directed some astoundingly good plays (a few were astoundingly bad as well) and forged a long-lasting friendship with Jacqueline, who came from the French stream of Quebec students. McGill University—from which I had graduated with two degrees, as had my father before me, while my mother became a teacher at McGill's Macdonald College—was long a bastion of English language education in Quebec. Now, for political and economic reasons, it had become a bilingual university. In any case, although they came from diverse situations and had opposing political views, for Jacqueline and Janet, their love of theater has remained a bond

· 15 ·

between them through the years, even though they have largely been separated by distance and circumstance.

I was aghast when, like so many young people craving independence, they took a seedy apartment in McGill's "ghetto," the name for a "bohemian" student area close to the university. They were both heterosexual, but, at that time, it wasn't something you would think of mentioning. We lived in a gorgeous house, as I have described, and I couldn't understand why, at only nineteen years old, my daughter would want to live in a crumbling place where you had to climb narrow stairs to get into the apartment, and, when you did, you were faced with a long, long wall that ran at either end into a run-down living room and an equally decrepit bedroom. But it was theirs. I visited only once, but left when I found neither Jacqueline nor Janet at home. Instead, a young man and woman, whom I presumed my daughter knew, were using the living room to "make out." I understood why Janet wanted her own apartment, and from then on I left it to her to visit us, which she did frequently.

*　　*　　*　　*

This was the seventies. When I was at McGill for the first time twenty years earlier, it was a different era with a different set of mores. In the fifties, a girl who studied at McGill was expected to live with her family. If she came from out-of-town, she was required to live in residence at Royal Victoria College. She had to have passes to come back to the residence later than 10:00 PM on week nights, and, depending on her year at college, the passes were given out on the weekend for 11:00 PM, 12:00 PM, and 1:00 PM, if I recall correctly. Young men were known not to want to date RVC women for this reason. If you went, say, to a movie, you had to rush through a snack afterwards in order to get back to the residence on time. No time left for smooching. Also, a young man had to wait in a reception room at the college until the lady of his choice was contacted and came downstairs to greet him. He was very visible if he was unwise enough to date several RVC girls at the same time.

I remember being invited to dinner at RVC by a sorority sister (sororities were "out" in the 1970s when Janet was studying) from New Brunswick. It was a "white glove" Friday night, which meant that we had to eat wearing white gloves so delicately that we did not stain them. On another occasion, we had a surprise Chinese dinner. The food was Chinese style, and so was the cutlery—chopsticks. No other cutlery was allowed. Either you had to learn to eat with chopsticks that very night, or else you went hungry. I learned fast. I always thought that RVC was part residence, part finishing school. We were, after all, at McGill, the Harvard of Canada.

There was the sad case of Marla, a member of the McGill Players Club, who stayed out all night with Rudolph, reputed to be from an Austrian baronial family, a fact he admitted to with modesty when questioned. When Marla tried to get home to RVC at three in the morning, she found the doors were locked. The second time this happened, she was expelled. No more Players' Club for Marla. No more McGill.

During Janet's years at McGill, however, the rules had changed, and many girls had their own apartments. Some girls even shared apartments with boys. Janet did not share an apartment with a boy, but she did date a number of young men. Notable among them was Frankie, who was bestowed with such remarkable male beauty that it took one's breath away. He looked like a Grecian god. Although Frankie had some personal problems that worried Janet, he was very much in love with her and she with him. Frankie was serious about their relationship and wanted to get married, but, at twenty, Janet felt that they were too young to consider marriage. I often wondered if she ever regretted not marrying Frankie.

When I was in college, a girl was supposed to have snared her beau by the time she graduated. Most of my college friends were engaged between the ages of eighteen and twenty. I was considered "old" when my parents announced my engagement at the age of twenty-two. By Janet's college days, after the advent of "the pill," no one seemed in a rush to get married any more.

I hoped that a long-term, platonic friendship with one very bright, articulate young man, blessed with an almost patrician presence, would develop into something more, but it didn't. Interestingly, one young fellow who did not interest her romantically became a journalist, as he had dreamed, and, in recent years looked her up on the Internet. "I've never forgotten you, Janet," he said. Although he is married, a father, and still in Montreal, they carry on a friendly e-mail correspondence from time to time. And, among the variety of young men that Janet did not want to marry, there was Bob, splendidly gentile, an adventurous sportsman, and a technological genius, but more about Bob later.

*   *   *   *

Between 1963 and 1970, political problems intensified in Quebec. A series of terrorist acts that involved letter bombs, kidnappings, explosives (the Montreal Stock Exchange was bombed in 1969, when Janet was ten years old, Shelley was nine, and the twins were only five), and murders—all prompted by extreme Quebec nationalism—culminated in the October Crisis of 1970.[7] As events worsened, I would caution my young children not to go near mail boxes, because the letter bombs usually targeted English-language areas of Montreal. After the British Trade Minister, James Cross, was kidnapped, hooded, and held—and the Vice-Premier and Minister of Labour of the Province of Quebec, Pierre Laporte, was "executed" by strangling with his own gold cross, his body found stuffed in the trunk of an abandoned car—Prime Minister Pierre Elliot Trudeau invoked the controversial War Measures Act. When the Canadian army intervened in Quebec, preventing the build-up of a separatist revolution, the general public was vastly relieved, but, in later years, the federal government was accused by French nationalists of over-reacting.

It was no overreaction, in my opinion. Having lived through it, I firmly believe that Trudeau's strong response saved Canada from a civil war. At the time, I walked my children to school past the troops, rifles at the ready, lining the streets of our affluent Town of Mount Royal, with its mixed population of French- and English-speaking people who had always gotten along very well. The Premier of Quebec's sister lived a few blocks from us, and troops were stationed at her driveway. My children were later to attend the high school named in Pierre Laporte's memory.

Meanwhile a series of language laws that Quebec introduced in the mid-seventies created havoc for the English-speaking population and pleased no one.[8] When the people of Quebec voted the separatist *Parti Quebecois* into office in 1976, there were shock waves as the separatist party passed the *Charte de la langue française* (Bill 101) a year later. This prescriptive, sweeping Charter, which has been greatly softened and amended in the following decades by court challenges, proclaimed that French would be Quebec's official language for almost everything one could think of in daily life: government, the judicial system, education, advertising, business, contracts, and more.

As I read reports of this legislation from today's perspective, those sympathetic to the French-language position present the imposition of these restrictive laws as an effort to protect the endangered French-language and culture in North America and to protect the "rights" of "Francophones" in Quebec. As an "Anglophone," however—it was only after these laws were imposed that we suddenly were divided into "Anglophones" and "Francophones"—I know that most English-speaking residents of Quebec felt harassed and reduced to the status of second class citizens. The government of Quebec even tried to create another category, "Allophones" (those whose first language was neither

French nor English), but public adverse reaction was too great. In my view, language was merely a mask for a power grab.

Certainly, Bill 101 created dissension in almost every facet of life in Quebec, and there was bitter division in the social services. Since francisation programs (making French the official language of business) applied to businesses of more than fifty employees, corporations and major banks moved their head offices out of Quebec in droves. They weren't going to print costly separate catalogues in French and change all their advertising. Their executives from across Canada didn't want to be forced to place their English-language kids in French-language schools. The Bank of Montreal considered changing its name but didn't. At a much later date, even the Montreal Expos would relocate. After all the good feeling and tremendous pride generated by the wonders of Expo 67, which attracted people from all over the world to the gracious hospitality of Montreal, it was an utter shame.

It was shameful, especially if you were a fluently bilingual "Anglophone," to walk through the streets of Montreal and look at street signs with big black marks slashed through the English names. It was shameful to have huge machines scrape the English names off the cement faces of schools and replace them with French ones. It was shameful to be obliged to sign a request in order to have a business contract written in English, or if you wanted your children to attend an English-language school. It was shameful to go to a restaurant and have to order a *hambergeois* instead of a hamburger. It was shameful to be unable to post an exterior sign in English or any other language than French, or to be prohibited from having English and French on the same page if you had more than five employees.

At the entrance to the town of Sutton, where most people were bilingual anyway, someone posted a sign that read, "This is an (il)legal English sign." It was the town joke, signaling its dissent for several months, until the "language police" (what everyone called the *Regie de la langue française*) took it down. But Dr. Camille Laurin, a psychiatrist who was the Minister of Culture, explained that Quebec was like an adolescent who had to be surrounded by positive, French-language images of himself/herself in order to build a sense of identity and self-esteem. In my opinion, the reasoning of Dr. Laurin-the-psychiatrist was nuts.

The sad result of all this was that the young English-speaking people of Quebec felt they no longer had any future there. There were no jobs for them, no career paths. They might speak French, they might have been born in Quebec and their parents before them, but they weren't French-French *Québecois*. If they had any ambition, they had to leave. And they left.

University students like Janet and Shelley departed as soon as they attained their degrees. Janet graduated from McGill University in 1980 and Shelley from Concordia University with a bachelor of fine arts in 1981, the same year my book of bilingual love poems was published by a French publisher, with one page in French and the facing page in English. I sent a copy to the Minister of Culture, but the language police didn't come to get me.

Almost their entire graduating classes left the province for other places: Toronto, Calgary, Florida—but mainly Toronto, where both Janet and Shelley decided to relocate, because this city, the business engine driving Canada, had become the center for English language theater and film. This is where they would build their lives. The paths of their lives would have been different, if they had been able to remain in Montreal where their parents lived, as my generation did. They would probably have married Montreal boys; my grandchildren would be Canadian; and we would all still be freezing in Montreal in the winter instead of living in sunny California. But there were no boys. They were all leaving, too. Laura and Susan were just entering university and elected to remain in Montreal with me. I would not follow Janet and Shelley to Toronto until 1985.

This period coincided with the beginning of marital difficulties between my husband and me that would eventually culminate in divorce. There were also money troubles, as a consequence of the political turmoil. My husband's business had been established in Quebec almost one hundred years, the result of three hard-working generations of his family: Bert's grandfather, an immigrant from Russia, his father and uncles, and my husband and his siblings. Now the third generation was finding it impossible to continue because of nationalistically-inspired labor demands, which increased over several years. Eventually, there was a union war at his plant, with the politically-motivated CNTU trying to take over the long-established Catholic union. Ironically, my husband's family business paid the highest wages in the Canadian bedding industry to its workers. This didn't make any difference to the CNTU, which appeared to prefer not to have a settlement, but to do the English-language *patron* in. The union was flexing its muscles.

The CNTU called a strike, which lasted a bitter two months. During this time, some picketers carried signs sporting caricatures of the bosses, accompanied by anti-Semitic epithets (*Juifs cauchons, Juifs patrons*) upsetting enough for my husband to come home with a rifle that he placed in the front hallway. There was a chain on the door, and I had instructions not to open it to anyone I did not know. The company never recovered from this strike and, within a short time, closed its own doors. With the unrelenting labor demands, it was impossible to make a profit. Almost five hundred workers were without a job as a result, and so was my husband.

*   *   *   *

It was during this unsettling period that Janet and Shelley moved to Toronto. They stuck together through thick and thin, each other's solace, two young women who had had all the rugs pulled out from under them but were determined to make it in show biz in this big, cold, impersonal, business city. Toronto is a wonderful city for visitors to explore, but its Anglo-Saxon reserve was still apparent in the late 1970s and early 1980s, even as the city was expanding by leaps and bounds, so that twenty years later, the diverse face of the city and its inhabitants was almost unrecognizable. In 1981, if you didn't come from Tar-ahn-nah, it was still hard to make friends there.

It was also hard to rent an apartment then, because the city had an almost zero vacancy rate. Especially if you were an actor looking for work. At first, the girls shared a house with two male actors, but when they found their neighbors were mostly prostitutes and pimps, with crack houses in close proximity, and when a burglary robbed them of their jewelry and other possessions they had prized and transported to Toronto, they took an apartment on their own. "The area still isn't so hot," they rationalized, "but at least the premises are clean, our landlord is nice, and the rooms are spacious." Janet and Shelley fixed it up quite charmingly on a shoestring budget.

Ironically, these two young women fleeing from a Quebec that regarded them as Anglophones (native English-speakers) and therefore not *pur-laine* (pure wool) *Québecoises* even though they were fluently bilingual (English and French) and indistinguishable in their accents from a native French-speaker, found work in Toronto with *Le Théâtre de Petit Bonheur* (later the *Théâtre Française*), which produced plays in French! They got the jobs for three reasons: they needed jobs so desperately that they were very persuasive in both languages; they had theatrical experience in Montreal; and they would work for very little.

So Janet, who had set her sights on eventually directing, became this company's stage manager and, within a few years, had become a sought-after stage manager in Ontario, stage managing for other prestigious theatres as well, among them the Ontario Science Centre's landmark production of *Ra*. Shelley, who wanted to excel as an actress, started off doing public relations for *Le Théâtre de Petit Bonheur* but before long moved her talents to the stage, notably in *Les Fées en Soie*. She learned *joual* (a French street vernacular comparable to "Ebonics" or hip-hop slang) to play Carmen in the theatre's bilingual production (one in English, one in French) of Michel Tremblay's famous play, *Forever Yours, Marie-Lou* (*Toujours à toi, Marie-Lou*).

Stage management, while commanding a salary somewhat higher than the actors, paid poorly in comparison to the fees paid by the film industry, then burgeoning in Toronto. Janet decided to switch her talents to film, but, to her chagrin, found that she had to descend to the bottom of the ladder, all the way down to a personal assistant (known as a PA), which was a euphemism for general go-fer. Janet ran her feet off sixteen hours a day, seven days a week to earn her acceptance in the film industry. One day she was almost ready to throw in the towel. "I can't do it," she cried. "I'm not nineteen." She was then twenty-six.

Being Janet, she persevered, and just as she had done as a stage manager, started working her way to the top. She became a talent coordinator and then a third assistant director (the third AD assists the director with the background talent, among other things) for television series and feature films. The third AD also has to be able to get along with people, one of Janet's great strengths. Many top American features were being filmed in Toronto because the Canadian dollar was low, and first class crews could be found in Toronto, and so she worked with stars like Dick Van Dyke, Tom Cruise, Burt Reynolds, and Red Fox. She was an AD on television series like *T and T*, and on features such as *Police Academy* and *Switching Channels*.

Some of these films were shot repeatedly in the cold, Canadian night, and Janet wore a fur-lined parka with pockets under the arms for charcoal packets that she lit to warm her up in below zero weather. When she came home at dawn, she aligned her walkie-talkies along the apartment's floor to recharge them. She was never short of work, and one film followed another in a ceaseless procession of long days, long nights, and six-day weeks.

Soon she was promoted to the esteemed position of second assistant director, a position she was not anxious to assume but knew was necessary if she wanted to become a film director, her desired goal. The second AD is responsible for scheduling and all the operational details of the film. In film-making, every minute used means money spent, and whether a film meets or exceeds its budget can depend on the accuracy of the second AD. It is a nerve-wracking task that can make or break the film. This job demanded of Janet a discipline and accountability that was to serve her well later in her professional life.

In the film business, it is the first assistant director who actually makes the film technically, arranging the camera shots, and working hand-in-hand with the director. Some directors like to be involved technically as well, but most prefer to use their artistic energies to direct the main talent. At that point in her life, Janet had no desire to advance to first AD and remain in the technical stream; she wanted to direct films. In order to do so, she knew that she would have to find a producer who believed in her talent. The catch, of course, was this: how can a producer believe in your talent unless you demonstrate it? The other side of the coin was: how can you demonstrate it unless a producer is willing to take a chance on you? The only alternative is to become your own producer, a daunting task.

Disregarding these obstacles, Janet was concentrating on doing a great job, despite her dislike for the minutiae it entailed. It was at this point that Cameron MacDougall came into her life.

♦

2

LOVE, MARRIAGE, NO BABY CARRIAGE

The ideal of love perpetuated by our prehistoric lovers has radically changed. Or perhaps the ideal remains the same, but the practical implementation of why and how men and women come together has altered. Less than half (only 49.7 percent) of the U.S. population is currently married,[1] and married couples with children account for less than one in every four households.[2] Love and marriage no longer go together like a horse and carriage. The purpose of coupling today is not necessarily procreation, and procreation does not necessarily involve coupling.

What attracts couples to one another? Is it true that "opposites" attract? "Likes"? Throughout history, various philosophical views of love have been proposed: is love at first sight the result of two forces (love and strife) intermingling with the classical elements (earth, water, air, and fire)? Does love becomes the binding power linking all the elements together harmoniously?[3]

In the "olden" days in Western society, matchmakers tried to figure it out. Over the centuries, a variety of courtship rituals such as flowery poetry came into play, mostly rooted in medieval chivalry. Chastity and honor were prized feminine virtues. In the sixteenth and seventeenth centuries, before central heating, bundling became a courtship custom: courting couples were allowed to share a bed with a bundling board between them, so that they could get to know one another without freezing to death. By Victorian times, these courting rituals required formal introductions, calling cards, and the presence of chaperones.[4]

Now the place of these rituals, customs, and watchful eyes has largely been usurped by Internet dating sites. Sometimes, two people who are wrong for one another meet accidentally on a film set.

◆

It started innocently enough. Cameron had come from his home near Thunder Bay to visit his actor brother, Bruce, who was performing in a film currently being shot in Toronto. Since Bruce was at work all day, often into the evening hours as well, he got Cameron a job as an extra on the film for a week. In that way, at least they could have lunch and breaks together, and then go out on the town when the day's shoot was done. It just so happened that Janet was an assistant director on the film, and part of her job was directing the extras, the "background action." She and Cameron, an intelligent, personable young man, took a liking to one another. With his bright blue eyes, ruddy complexion, sandy hair, and muscular frame, Cameron looked every inch as if he were born to the cold winter air in Northern Ontario. When Cameron and Bruce went out for refreshments after the shoot, they invited Janet to come along. Sometimes other members of the crew or talent would join them as well. They all, as Canucks are wont to say, had a good old time together, eh?

Just as Cameron's stint as an extra was coming to an end, the film's director decided that it would be prudent to keep on a few extras for another couple of weeks. So, with a twinkle in her eye, Janet asked her new friend, Cameron, if he would like to do just that. "I'm having a great time being an extra, being part of the movie as it's happening," he responded happily. "Yes, sure, I'd like to do it." It went without saying that continuing to spend time with Janet was part of the incentive.

When his film role ended, he invited Janet to dinner in appreciation, and, then, when he escorted her home, he said, "Well, I have to get back to my work near Thunder Bay now, but I'd like to see you again."

"I'd like that, too," Janet smiled. "By the way, what is it you do?"

"I'm a minister," he answered.

"A minister?" she gasped, thinking he was kidding. "You mean a real church kind of minister?"

"Yes," he replied seriously. "I am."

"Oh," she said. "I'm Jewish."

He started a little in surprise. "Jewish, eh? Well, can't we have dinner again anyway? You know, just friends."

"Sure," she replied. "Just friends."

Thunder Bay is only a short flight from Toronto, so they began to enjoy friendly time together quite often. It turned out that Cameron was a highly creative, itinerant minister. He arranged educational programming for a large number of rural churches of his denomination. He wrote songs and played them on his guitar. He did sermons in mime and sign language. At first, Janet and Cameron got along together like bread and butter. Then they began to feel they were kindred spirits. Then it got romantic. They just wanted to be together; it seemed right.

They agonized over getting married. Cameron said that he did not want to be the kind of minister who took a parish; rather, he wanted to continue to use his creative gifts in the ministry in an educational way. He loved what he was doing, and he loved being a Christian working in the service of the church. Janet loved what she was doing, and her Jewish religious identity was important to her. She was clear that she would not convert, and that she would want any children they might have to be brought up as Jews.

So they began to consider alternatives that could make marriage possible if neither of them converted. They rationalized that, if Cameron went back to school to pursue a doctorate in theology, he could then *teach* religion instead of working actively in a ministry. Alternatively, he might complete a doctorate in psychology and become a psychological *counselor*. Then a marriage between them could work. The world was changing. They could make it a better world.

Yes, the world was changing. When I was a girl, intermarriage between faiths, never mind races, was still unthinkable, a scandal for the families concerned. A generation before me, an orthodox Jewish family sat *shiva* for a girl or boy who intermarried, mourned the offending person as if dead. In 1987, I still had to swallow the lump in my throat, but an interfaith marriage was entirely possible in social terms. Although statistics might have been somewhat different in the 1980s in Canada, almost half of all Jewish marriages in the United States are now "mixed."[5] While it is an oft quoted truism that marriage is hard enough even when two people are from the same background, few of my friends today don't have at least one child who is intermarried. In general, intermarriage between faiths (more than one-fifth of all U.S. households) is becoming a more frequent, almost commonplace occurrence.[6]

When Cameron and Janet confided that, despite all the apparent obstacles, they were thinking of getting married, I was of two minds: if he were to take a parish, it would be an impossible situation unless Janet converted, and I didn't want my daughter to convert. But if he didn't take a parish and considered the other routes they had outlined ... well, maybe. Apart from their mutual interest in the arts and other common interests, they seemed bound by an ethical approach to living and by deeply spiritual inner resources. They both wanted to do good things in the world, to make a difference ... two great kids.

On the other hand, there was a vast difference in backgrounds to take into account. Cameron was not only a minister, but also the son of a minister, and the grandson of a minister. He was from a part of Ontario where there was a much simpler, far less sophisticated scale of material living than in urban Toronto. Our family was very close, and we all saw a lot of one another. His family, including his half a dozen siblings, was reserved and far flung, and got together only at Christmastime. Different worlds in the same country, Canada.

"What will your family's reaction be?" I asked Cameron.

When he called his mother, she was apoplectic in the quiet way that reserved, Northern Ontarians of Anglo-Scots origin can show their displeasure. "Have you told your father?" she asked faintly. Finally, it was determined that when Cameron's father and mother visited Toronto for a ministerial convention they planned to attend, we would meet to discuss it.

So now here we were at a fine restaurant in Toronto, the six of us—Cameron's father and mother, my ex-husband and I (a traditional divorced couple!), and Cameron and Janet. For what seemed an interminable time, all of us sat there silently, looking distinctly uncomfortable and pretending to read the menu, until I decided to break the ice.

"Audrey, I imagine you and your husband are feeling very much the way my former husband and I are feeling at this moment," I ventured.

We all burst out laughing so hard that in minutes we were all wiping our eyes with a mixture of sadness and relief. From that moment on, we got along splendidly and discussed the pros and cons of Cameron and Janet's potential engagement to be married with considerable candor and apprehension. By the time we finished an excellent dinner, we were toasting their engagement over wine.

It was decided that over the summer Cameron would take Janet to meet his many relatives in Thunder Bay (when she returned with a cracked antique plate as a prized gift from Cameron's grandmother, I was less than enthusiastic), and we set a date for the engagement party, although it was not clear whether Cameron's parents would be able to return to Toronto to be present. They would attend the wedding.

We held the engagement party in my comfortable apartment in Toronto and managed to cram in seventy-five people. Although Cameron's relatives were conspicuously absent, except for his sister and her husband (who flew in from Newfoundland, where they had just purchased a farmhouse for fifteen thousand dollars), and his brother, Bruce. All of my relatives, including my "divorced" relatives from Montreal, and friends showed up. The atmosphere was festive and very supportive of the good-looking, beautifully dressed, and elegantly mannered (Cameron was at his charming best) couple about to make a brave, new world together. Being a minister seemed to give Cameron a special *élan* in the eyes of my friends—it was so distinctly un-Jewish. If they talked behind my back before and after the party and said, "Did you hear the news? Corinne's daughter is marrying a *minister*?" … I didn't care. I had made my own peace with it. Janet was happy and looked radiant, I liked Cameron very much, and that's what mattered. And their children would be Jewish. Of course.

With the engagement party behind us, the approaching marriage was a *fait accompli*, and Janet and Cameron went on to planning their new lives together as the wedding plans commenced. For a divorced couple, my ex-husband and I cooperated very well. Although Cameron didn't see why it had to be such a fancy affair ("Can't we just rent a legion hall, and everyone will bring food, like we do in Thunder Bay?"), we decided to have a brunch (rather than a very expensive dinner) at what we considered the nicest hotel in town.

The wedding had to be at a secular place, without Jewish religious associations. None of the rabbis in Toronto would marry an interfaith couple unless one of the couples would convert. My ex-husband and I didn't want the marriage to take place in a church. A civil marriage seemed too cold and didn't sit well with any of us. We explored an interdenominational chapel and various other possibilities. Finally, we located an out-of-town rabbi who agreed to perform an interfaith ceremony with participation from a minister of the other faith, in this case, Cameron's father. That's when, with immense relief, we opted for the hotel.

Every detail of the wedding was exquisite. With my urban sensibility, I was sorry, though, that, at Cameron's request, Janet chose a very simple, white wedding dress, with just a small garland of flowers in her hair. She looked lovely, modestly adorned as he wanted, but somewhat underdressed, I thought, for a wedding in an elegant hotel rather than a country setting. After all, this was Toronto, then on its way to becoming a world-class city. In retrospect, perhaps Toronto and I were both a little snobbish. In Los Angeles, you wear what you want.

The ceremony, which Cameron and Janet wrote themselves, was reverent and incorporated the major features of a Jewish ceremony. They inserted places in the text for Cameron's father to deliver a blessing, for his sister to read from the Psalms, and for me to recite a poem, "The Bond," that I wrote in their honor.

> *Amid frankincense and myrrh,*
> *spring flowers color*
> *the air with an ancient*
> *song: "I am for you and*

you are for me,"
the most fragrant lyric ever
sung.

And in the scented forest,
tall trees inhale the
resounded, spiraled notes
and release new memories.

Old roots clasp gnarled
hands more deeply in
the rich, red earth,
as butterflies dance on
green-grown leaves to celebrate
this covenant of winging
spirits.

These were the high hopes that I had for this couple, and I believed that I was happy at their union in 1989, two years after they had met, until I found myself consumed with sobs in the receiving line, with tears dripping down my cheeks as I shook the hands of our guests.

The first year of their marriage augured well. Cameron gave up his rural consultancy and took a job in Toronto as a communications director. He was still working for the Church. As part of his duties, he put out a magazine and a newsletter and created a book of songs, with one of his own acclaimed songs featured on the front cover. Janet realized that, as a married woman who intended to have children, she would have to curtail her film assignments and sixteen-hour days, and she relinquished an opportunity to go with the team she had been working with to film a documentary in Israel. Instead, she and Cameron rented a house in Toronto and furnished it, country style, adorably. They often baked brownies and other goodies and invited Shelley, Ira, and me over to taste them. To the casual observer, their home smelled not only of baked goods but of happiness.

The following summer, I had the opportunity to rent a reasonably priced apartment in the elegant *Rehavia* district of Jerusalem for a month. Excitedly, I invited all my children to visit there with me for as much time as they could manage. Susan and Laura could not take time off, and Cameron declined.

"I'd prefer to visit at Christmastime," he told me. "Can you change your reservation?"

CRYO KID

"I would gladly do it, Cameron," I replied, "but I don't have a choice that I can afford. I obtained this apartment through a friend who knows the owner—the building is a converted consulate. This lady has been teaching in Israel for more than fifty years and agreed to let me stay there this summer because she is going to London to visit her own family for a month. That's where she's from originally, England. I promised to look after her plants."

"I've never been to Israel," Cameron replied, a little ruefully. "I'd like to, but when I do visit, I want it to be at Christmas."

"It's cold in Jerusalem in the wintertime," I cajoled, but Cameron could not be persuaded. "It's alright with me if Janet goes with you," he offered generously.

"I understand," I said, giving him a hug, but the truth is, I didn't. Christmas marks the birth of Jesus Christ in Bethlehem, of course, which would obviously make a trip at that time more meaningful to Cameron, but the Holy Land is home to both Judaism and Christianity in all seasons. Many Christians visit Israel in the summertime.

I was disappointed, but, after much discussion, Janet and Shelley, who had never been to Israel before, delightedly agreed to join me there for two weeks. "I've visited Israel before, so I'd like to go there ahead of your visit to concentrate on Jerusalem," I said.

"Yes," they nodded. "And we'll take day trips together to other areas in Israel."

Actually, they almost cancelled their trip and urged me to return when a bus carrying Canadians was blown up by terrorists on the road between Tel Aviv and Jerusalem. I had traveled in the opposite direction at a similar time on the very same day. When I assured them that I was safe on my rented balcony, surrounded by cacti plants that had been nurtured there for forty years, and that it was as safe to come to Israel as it would ever be, they traveled to join me.

For Janet, who would have loved for Cameron to share this trip with her, Israel was a mind-blowing experience. She had especially moving moments at the Western Wall, where she vowed before God that her children-to-be would continue the chain of Jewish life. When she returned, she tried to communicate these deep feelings to Cameron, who seemed receptive to them.

During the following year, he seriously investigated the possibilities of entering doctoral studies in theology. Alternatively, he considered setting up a private practice in educational/psychological consulting. Then his ministerial family began exerting pressure on him from all sides. His grandfather and father told him he was letting the family and his calling down by not taking a congregation. His mother said that he could never be a true minister without a parish. His sister, who was also a minister now, got into the act.

Finally, Cameron bowed to the pressure and decided that he would take a parish. It wasn't easy. Not every congregation is prepared to accept a minister, even one with Cameron's superb qualifications and appealing *persona*, who carries the liability of a Jewish wife. But, with all those ministers, his family had connections. A Winnipeg congregation, one that considered itself to be at the liberal, cutting edge of religious practice, finally offered Cameron a job. He accepted.

And so they were off to Manitoba (a little cold air is invigorating, right?). That was the end of Janet's film career since there was no film work in Winnipeg. With Cameron's encouragement, she began considering taking a master's degree in education because that would fit into their future lifestyle, and she took a job as arts coordinator at a cultural center in Winnipeg. With the assistance of a church mortgage, they bought a little bungalow there, and at first, life proceeded happily. Cameron was installed in his new parish with an inspirational ceremony, and our family traveled to Winnipeg to hear him preach his first sermon.

When Cameron accepted the position, it was made clear to the church powers that Janet was not part of the package. She would retain her religion and would not participate in church activities or services. This was easier said than done. Once a month, she hopped on a plane to Montreal to visit her father and sisters, Susan and Laura, who still lived there, or to Toronto to visit Shelley and me.

As time went on, however, it became increasingly difficult to separate herself from Cameron, his work, and his congregation. Distressingly to her, his whole personality seemed to change. Now that he had become a minister with a congregation, more and more he took on the characteristics of his father and grandfather, who had served as ministers before him. He became intensely concerned with thrift, modesty, and appearances to the congregation, and he was increasingly moody because at heart he was not happy in his ministerial shoes. He would remain withdrawn and silent for days at a time, agonized, as he prepared the sermons that made him feel like a hypocrite. Although he loathed speaking from the pulpit, he was an excellent counselor. If he had continued with his path in that direction, Janet and Cameron might have had a chance.

Now entering her thirties, Janet wanted to have a child. Each time the subject of children came up, the issue of baptism raised its head. Although he had promised before their marriage that their children would be raised Jewish, Cameron had second thoughts. How could the children of a minister of the church be Jewish and unbaptized? How could they not go to Sunday school? How would it look to the parishioners? And he was right. How could that be?

Other problems came into the marriage. Driven by his own anger at being caught in the ministry, he began to kick the cat. The couple therapy with a church counselor, intended to make the marriage better, only made it worse. It revealed problems long festering in Cameron's family. "I have been dishonest about your Jewishness," he confessed at last to Janet. "I guess, deep down, I hoped that I would convert you to Christianity."

Eventually, they realized that it couldn't work. More in sorrow than in anger, they ended their marriage, sold the house, repaid the church mortgage, and split their possessions. Cameron resigned his position with the Winnipeg church, and Janet moved in with Laura and Susan in Montreal, where the language laws had softened somewhat now that Quebec had become a *de facto* French-speaking province. While the separatist agenda still simmered beneath the surface, the situation had at least temporarily eased.

To Janet's amazement, once Cameron was free of being a congregational minister, he was exultant. He pierced his ear, took to wearing colorful clothes along with his earring, decided to become a folk singer devoted to the service of the church, and, to Janet's great disbelief, moved in with her so-called best friend in Winnipeg, Chloe. Before long, though, Cameron moved further west to Alberta, where he lived in an artistic commune near Banff with his brother, the actor. I have always wondered if he subconsciously married a Jewish girl so that a marital disaster of this magnitude could take place—and relieve him of the great ministerial burden his family had exacted of him. I truly hope that he has done the things he wanted to do with his life, and that he is content.

Cameron and Janet never communicated again once they were divorced. She was happier without him. But the desire to have a child grew within her. It was 1991, and she was thirty-two.

*   *   *   *

In Montreal, Janet found respite in a public relations job for the Jewish community. It was as if she needed to cocoon herself in the Jewish community to heal her identity. The marriage, divorce, and separation from her community had been almost overwhelmingly traumatic. After a year or two, she found challenging work as the Montreal director of a standardized test preparatory school with an international reputation. Later, she took on the direction of the Ottawa school as well.

The possibility for a new partner in life seemed to be at a dead end, however. Given the Anglophone exodus to Toronto and elsewhere in the late 1970s and 1980s, the available Jewish men in Montreal were few. This was when she first began to seriously consider having a child on her own. She approached her good friend, Bob. He wasn't Jewish, but he was a handsome computer genius who possessed a magnetic personality, as well as being an accomplished athlete.

"Our genes would combine well," she suggested, but Bob drew away in terror, visibly shuddering at the thought of providing sperm for Janet's as yet unconceived child. "I'm sorry, Janet," he apologized, trying to soften his outright rejection. "I just can't. It's too far out, even for me."

"You are right," she told him, passing a hand over her eyes to hide sudden tears. "I can understand that you don't want to be involved in such an unorthodox enterprise. It would be better to have an unknown donor."

And with that, she started to look into what Montreal had to offer in terms of artificial insemination for a single mother. It wasn't much. The doctors she approached generally frowned on this kind of insemination unless it was for a couple. When she did persuade a doctor to inseminate her, he was cold, clinical, and unsympathetic.

Although her younger sisters, Susan and Laura, who were still living in Montreal, accompanied her to each of the several insemination procedures, all of which were unsuccessful, Janet's recollection is mainly of being told to remain lying on the table with her legs in the air for fifteen minutes after being inseminated, and of weeping because she wanted so much to get pregnant in the arms of someone she loved. In any case, none of the five or six inseminations "took," and Janet abandoned the attempt to have a child in this way when she unexpectedly met several Montreal men who seemed, for a time, to be romantic possibilities.

What she wanted in a husband had changed, however. Now she was looking at men from the standpoint of whether or not they would make a good parent, as well as a romantic partner. She considered for a time Ernie, who had a large nose and bushy eyebrows but a capacious intellect and a great sense of humor. Then there was Frank, a short, little guy who made a pleasant friend, but, despite her sincere efforts, there was just no chemistry between them. Next on the dating "dance card" was Robbie, a good-hearted man who could offer her a very prosperous lifestyle. He was loaded, in fact. He was also a former addict who had, unfortunately, fried his brains quite considerably before his recovery. Not a good prospect for fatherhood. She certainly did not want to rush into an unsuitable marriage in order to produce a child before it was too late. That would be using the man. That would not be fair to him, to herself, nor to any child that would ensue.

It was time to take her life in a new direction. She was headed for California, where her sister, Shelley, and brother-in-law, Ira, were already calling her to come and join them in the sunshine. Why? Why would she leave Montreal, the city of her birth, to which she had returned, after spurning it for Toronto when she graduated from college? It all came about because my children gave me a birthday present, but I'll tell you about that later.

*   *   *   *

In the meantime, Janet was on a plane to Los Angeles, where, transferred by the prep school company at her request, she settled down in an upscale section of the city called Brentwood (that's right, the same West LA, ritzy area where O.J. Simpson may or may not have killed his wife, and where Monica Lewinski saved the blue dress stained with a President's semen). It was a sophisticated, walk-around area (unusual for LA) and very close to her place of work.

Once again she had high hopes. Perhaps, in this new locale, she would meet the future father of her child-to-be. Once again, she met a brilliant, handsome charmer who was inappropriate to fill that role from her point of view. This time it was a cross-cultural love affair, and, once again, she met him while she was working.

The prediction is that by 2020, half of all marriages will be bicultural or biracial,[7] so the relationship between Janet and León was not much before its time. But if you want to bring up a Jewish child as you have promised God in Jerusalem, in some quarters it might be considered inadvisable to marry a Catholic from El Salvador—even if he claims ancestry from Spain, has had a superior education in both his country of origin (where his parents led a privileged life), and in the United States, even if he is very smart and employed by the government as a aerospace specialist. Other people might consider that such a union is merely the way the world is going: we will all end up as a mélange of colors, cultures, and religions, and we might as well enjoy it.

I really liked León Espinoza because his *persona*, at thirty-four, two years younger than Janet, had a lot to offer. He was unfailingly charming and respectful to me, and it was apparent that he loved Janet. Unfortunately León had baggage. The fact that he had two children by a previous marriage was not really the deterrence: the children were delightful, loving, well-mannered, and obviously being brought up well by their mother, who had custody of them most of the time. León had the children two nights a week and every other weekend. Janet, who was longing to be a mother, adored the children, and it was mutual.

Ethnicity and cultural background did come into the equation. As a Latin, León was moderately light-skinned, perhaps going back to the Spanish roots of which he was so proud. The children could "pass" in both worlds, but to landlords, the *Latino* background was obvious, and, when León moved in with Janet, before long Janet was shocked to find an eviction notice on the door of her apartment. The landlord said, via the smirking janitor, "It's because the children stay overnight in the apartment, so there are too many people in a one-bedroom apartment."

"What about the two-bedroom apartment I asked for? I've been on the waiting list a long time, and you told me it would soon be vacant," Janet gasped.

"It's taken," the janitor shrugged. This was Janet's first experience of racism in Los Angeles.

When León and the children came to visit me in Palm Springs, where I was vacationing in a rented villa, the caretaker kept hushing up the children, to the point of harassment, whenever we dipped in the swimming pool. There was no need, because the children were very well behaved, sweet children, by now very much attached to Janet.

Surprisingly, León exercised his own brand of racism. He was highly insulted if anyone mistook him for a Mexican. León had a very poor opinion of most Mexicans, who compared to a well-educated El Salvadorian from a good family, he felt, were much lower on the social scale. He was proud to be *Latino*, but not Mexican, no way. Many of his friends had political opinions that bordered on the far right, certainly not the left. As an American citizen now, who had first entered the country legally as a student, he resented comparisons with immigrants who had crossed the border illegally and even toyed with living in the northeastern United States. "There's less discrimination against *Latinos* and fewer Mexicans there. Better for me," he said, with about as much concern for societal equity as the landlord who had evicted them.

I suspected that one reason for his attraction to Janet was that he wanted to marry a Caucasian woman. He sweet-talked her into coloring her hair a blonder shade. The real fly in the ointment, though, was that León had a tendency to run up bills. That had been the trouble with his first marriage. In order to help him catch up with his debts, Janet had not asked him to pay any part of the rent for the first few months they lived together, but when he joined an expensive exercise club, she was very upset. When the eviction notice was served, he pressed her to take an expensive, two-bedroom apartment in an upscale building, one that he could certainly not pay for. The onus of supporting them would be on her. And then, the last straw, he asked if his mother could come and live with them for a little while.

Janet is no dummy. She quickly rented another one-bedroom apartment. "We can consider living together in a two-bedroom apartment once you can pay your share of the rent," she informed Léon. "In the meantime, we'll live apart."

Léon didn't take "no" for an answer easily. For a time, he called Janet day and night, but she was resolute. Her hard-to-make decision would stand. Then he got the children to call her. "We love you, Janet. We miss you so much," they pleaded in their sweet voices. Janet almost changed her mind because she loved the children, but, at the same time, she was angry with Léon for putting her—and the kids—in that position.

The situation came to an end the day my ex-husband came to visit Janet in her new apartment, and Léon called while she was out. My ex-husband is not a man to fool around with. "Don't call her again," he growled into the phone. Léon never called again.

So, at thirty-eight now, Janet had a stern talk with herself. As with so many career women of her generation, her biological clock was ticking, and she knew that even if she continued going out on a series of Internet dates that went nowhere, even if she were to find a man with marriage—and fatherhood— potential in her eyes, it would take time to develop a relationship to the point of marriage and having a family. Time was what she didn't have any more.

For most women, the chances of getting pregnant start to decline as early as the late twenties, and, with this new realization, the rush is on to have babies before fertility drops significantly in the mid-thirties and falls off a cliff in the forties.[8] According to an article in *Fortune* magazine, the number of women giving birth after age thirty-five has been increasing steadily at a rate of 1.5 percent each year.[9] The likelihood of unaided conception after the age of forty, however, is slim. "Whereas a thirty year-old woman has a 20 percent chance of getting pregnant in any given month, by age 40 those odds drop to 5 percent."[10]

Margaret Atwood's futuristic *A Handmaid's Tale*[11] was not far off the mark in predicting a society of childless career women seeking surrogates in order to have children.

♦

3

The BOOK of ADAM

At one time, a couple got married with the socially sanctioned purpose of having children. As the ideal of romantic love grew, women dreamed of having children with the man they loved, of children in his image, in their image. And men passed around cigars in pride at the products of this union. Their children were living proof that two people in love had become one. They were a family.

Even as divorce figures rise, biology and emotion remain unaffected by sociological change: most women still have both the biological urge and the emotional need to have children. In an urban environment, it's likely that they don't want to have as many children as past generations: it's so expensive to feed, house, clothe, and educate children today. Naturally they would prefer to have children with a man they care for, and many do, but, for others, as the romantic ideal fades and the ubiquitous biological clock ticks, they may consider other options.

In 1999—the year Adam donated the sperm that would turn out to be half of the genes that created the child he didn't know would be called Samantha— a Washington University anthropologist claimed that the 24,500-year-old skeleton of a Neanderthal four-year-old boy found near Lisbon, Portugal showed that both Neanderthals and early modern humans (Cro-Magnons) cohabited and produced children.[1] Also, since this little boy's skeleton showed that interbreeding between Neanderthals and humans took place, the New Stone Age couple found in close embrace could certainly have produced a child. By 1999, the world's population numbered 5.996 billion, so quite a few children had been produced after the Neanderthals, early humans, and New Stone Agers got through.

♦

Quite honestly, in 1999, I was thinking less about the 5.997 billionth kid my sperm might produce at the time I filled a little cup with it at the California Cryobank and more about the urgently needed money I would receive in return to help pay for my studies at the University of California at Los Angeles. To be truthful, it was more of a sale than a gift, although I didn't think of myself as a vendor rather than a donor then, because, despite my financial need, I did care about the child. By now you've figured out that I'm CCB donor 57590.

It's eight years later, and I'm planning to get married soon. When I examine my motives, now that I hope to have my own kids, now that I need to know—I really need to know—if that kid, if those kids, I sired are okay, I realize that I did care then, but I didn't know yet how much I would care in a few years.

In the year 1999, I was about to graduate from UCLA with a bachelor of science, a keen interest in bioethics, and a major in genetics, and I needed money desperately to continue with my studies in graduate school. On the world scene, war had erupted in Kosovo, a magnitude 7.4 earthquake had killed more than 15,600 and left 600,000 homeless in Turkey, while at home in the United States, the Senate had just acquitted President Bill Clinton after his impeachment trial and rejected a censure move. It was the year of the massacre at Columbine High School. On a more optimistic note, the Nobel Peace Prize had been awarded to Doctors without Borders.[2]

I wanted to be that kind of medical person, that kind of person at least. With the idealism of youth that I still possess, I wanted to make a difference in this world, and that's why I needed the money. I had gotten through my undergraduate years on a tight budget with the help of some academic scholarships and working at the same time. Although I'd had some partial assistance from a football scholarship as well—oh yeah, I was a quarterback—I'd still racked up some student debt. I didn't see how I could continue such a stiff work/study regimen through grad school. My family couldn't help me financially; I was on my own when it came to dollars and cents. So here I was at the California Cryobank.

I have to tell you that when I massaged myself to produce the sperm that eventually united with Janet's egg to make Samantha, I wasn't thinking noble thoughts. I was looking at a suggestive centerfold of a movie star hopeful. I hadn't yet read the late Norman Mailer's thought-provoking novel about good and evil, *The Castle in the Forest*, which was only published the year Samantha turned seven years old. I couldn't give much thought to his fascination with the way bees produce babies because he hadn't written this book yet.

As you already know, here I was about to complete four years of university, so I understood, of course, that the Queen Bee is responsible for giving birth to all the larvae. I'd also learned in grade school that the lazy male drones have only one function: to hang around the hive until the Queen is ready to be fertilized. Then only one of them, the fastest, can fertilize the Queen in mid-air.

What I didn't know is that, unfortunately, once he accomplishes this act, his sexual apparatus gets torn off inside her, and he falls to the ground and dies. The remaining drones are swept out of the hive by the Queen Bee's female attendants, who care for the larvae until they can become grown-up bees.[3]

The males are needed for only one reason. Fertilization. Not a happy thought for a guy in his early twenties, especially now that, suddenly, honey bees—the pollinators that produce our food supply—are deserting hives all around the world, and no one knows why.[4] It's a good thing I had a girlie magazine to keep me company while I was producing my sperm at the cryobank.

I did reflect for a few moments about the trio of whales that had thrilled me when my dad took me whale-watching in Hawaii one year, when our family was still intact and he had a few bucks, before he and my mom got a divorce. It was amazing to see the whales, all three of them, flip into the air and do their flying somersaults. The guide explained that the male and female whales were teaching the calf, the baby, how to emerge from the water and breathe, and they were also enjoying themselves while they were at it. I thought that the male was the father, but, no, apparently he was the escort male, which is a different whale role from siring the calf. The escort accompanies the female whale from colder waters to the warm waters of Hawaii, so that she can nurture her calf safely there. When the escort is satisfied that the calf has learned survival skills, and the mother can manage on her own, he returns to the male herd, and the mother and baby remain in Hawaii until the calf is older. No father around to help bring up baby. Just the mother.

I was truly glad to enable a mother who could not conceive a child otherwise to have one of her own. Money aside, it gave me a warm satisfaction I had not expected to feel to write a note to the mother—a note from me, the biological father, that I hoped would be meaningful to her—which the California Cryobank passed on to her when she conceived. I assumed she would be married, and I wrote one for her husband, too. It was sincere. I would not be the father in real life, the father who remained with the child, and who, in my eyes, would be the actual parent of the child. But I imagined that I was the escort, helping the mother to have a child to nurture in safe, warm waters. I guess I'll always be a romantic, kind of odd for a football player kind of guy.

In fact, when I later read David Plotz' compelling account of his "short, scary career as a sperm donor,"[5] I was really glad that I had given my sperm. Plotz wrote *The Genius Factory* (published in 2001, the year after Samantha was born) about the infamous "Nobel Prize Sperm Bank," which produced 215 live births from the sperm of "Nobel-laureate scientists, mathematical prodigies, successful businessmen and star athletes."[6] The elitist aims of the Repository for Geminal Choice (the sperm bank's real name) caused many people to be critical of sperm banks in general.

As an investigative reporter, Plotz decided to find out what happened to the babies born from the matching of donors to the recipients of this high-level sperm. Where were the babies? How did they turn out? Were they geniuses like the donors? Married and the father of two children, Plotz wanted to know what being a sperm donor was like, and, with the reluctant agreement of his wife, went through the process of donating sperm (to the Fairfax Cryobank in Washington, DC) himself.

So when I read his account, much of the process he went through was, in retrospect, similar to what I'd experienced. Unlike me, though, Plotz wasn't a donor who was providing his sperm for altruistic reasons, or because he was a student who needed the money. In consideration of his wife's feelings, he planned to ask the sperm bank—once his exploration for the sake of his book was completed—not to use his sperm.

My experience was the real thing. My name is Adam.

*   *   *   *

It's Janet here. When I got your note, Donor Number 57590, I cried. Your sincerity came through the lines of your note. I put your note in the box of treasures I've been keeping for Samantha since she was born.

It has been such a rough journey to get to the warm waters. By the time my love affair with León came to an end, I was thirty-eight years old and still childless. Emotionally, I was wrung out, not ready to date at that moment. My job was demanding and highly responsible. It would take time to meet other men and possibly have another relationship develop to the point where we could consider marriage and children. And time was running out. I didn't want to become one of the many career women I had already met who reaches fifty childless, with regrets.

In Montreal I had been inseminated artificially several times without success, but in the intervening few years, the technology had improved, especially in California. Through the medical benefits that were advantages of the job I held, I had access to the superb infertility services offered by the teaching hospital of the University of California at Los Angeles (UCLA), where I consulted with Dr. W. and his team, who encouraged me to try again.

Unlike the unsympathetic treatment I had received as a single mother from that Montreal doctor, the California team understood my position as the possessor of a rapidly aging womb and was ready to help me with all the scientific knowledge and technology at its disposal.

As part of this process, I had to choose a reputable sperm bank that could provide me with frozen sperm from one of its well-screened donors. Needless to say, in an era when the marketing of sperm (donors), eggs (in vitro), and people (surrogacy) has become a huge global import/export business, with technology and access to the Internet playing a major role, there are multiple sources around the world to obtain human sperm.[7] People can shop around! In addition, not only do different countries have different legal regulations, but people who use sperm banks are motivated by varied personal or physical reasons. In India, apparently, healthy young men with upwardly mobile career aspirations are attracted to the idea of freezing their sperm for future use.[8]

However, because of the huge monetary investment required for genetic testing, in 2007 most sperm banks are either located in countries with large populations (like the United States, Russia, Australia, or India), market to other countries around the world, or can provide sperm with specialized characteristics. Sperm from Denmark, for example, is valued for the likelihood of blue-eyed, blonde-haired genetic characteristics. In any case, for a sperm bank to survive commercially, it has to maintain a large volume of business. One Danish company that, according to the Wall Street Journal, markets to twenty-five countries has opened a branch called Cryos in the United States, and there a number of reputable American companies located across the United States to choose from as well.[9] One of them is the California Cryobank (CCB).[10]

I had already been referred to the CCB while I was under treatment in Montreal, because, at that time, it was one of the few companies that shipped donor sperm all over the world. After I telephoned CCB from Canada, they sent me a two-page catalogue of their donors. Today I would be able to select my donor from online listings.

In my opinion, the CCB is one of the best sperm banks in the world. I chose this sperm bank because it has such rigorous guidelines; they accept only two percent of all applicants. This acceptance is not based on elitism, but rather on genetic history, and the quality and size of the sperm sample. Unlike some of the earlier sperm banks that treated human sperm like the sperm of a bull, *the CCB bank strictly limits and documents the number of babies that can be born from a single donor's sperm. Another big factor, for me, was that, while the CCB guards the identity of the donor, it provides as much information as possible to the prospective mother. And while I would certainly respect my donor-to-be's privacy, I wanted to savor every detail I could obtain about the man who would hopefully father my child.*

*　　*　　*　　*

It was a weird experience for me to become a donor. I felt somewhat embarrassed and a little scared, and, although I confided what I was doing to my father, I never told my mother about it. Some men can sprinkle their seed wherever they go without a thought of the consequences to the woman if she becomes pregnant, or to the child that might result, but I am not like that. I could never be like that. So, especially with my academic and practical interest in studying the human body, I understood the care the California Cryobank took in its selection of donors. But it was quite a rigorous process, I must say, to become one of the donors.

As it states on their Web site, the CCB was established in 1977, as a "full service" sperm bank staffed with highly trained professionals. Although the idea that sperm could be frozen was first noted in 1779 by Lazaro Spallanzani, an Italian priest and physiologist, the first person to think of storing frozen sperm in a "bank" was a man called Montegazza in 1866.[11] The doctors and scientists who wanted to use human sperm for artificial insemination fought a hard battle through the decades. Declared a sin by the Pope at one time, the practice was not considered socially or legally acceptable until "the first public announcement of a successful birth from frozen sperm" was made by the 11th International Congress of Geneva in 1963, a decade after the first successful pregnancy conceived in this way was reported.[12]

When two doctors, a urologist and a pathologist, founded the CCB in California a few years later, their purpose was to alleviate the trauma of men who were expecting to be infertile—due to voluntary vasectomies or to medical conditions—by storing their frozen sperm in advance.

Thirty years later, the CCB offers an array of reproductive services to couples and individuals who cannot conceive a child naturally. It has a sterling reputation among fertility specialists around the world and uses stringent quality controls, among which are color coding donor specimens and an electronic identification system. Every month, the CCB produces "a new donor catalog with over 175 choices each month."[13] Along with the photos and other information comes an extensive medical history on each of these choices.

I was applying to be one of those choices. In 1999, I was twenty-four, well within the age qualification of nineteen to thirty-nine, the years apparently established by the American Association of Tissue Banks as years of male maximum fertility.[14] I had also graduated from an exceptional major university, UCLA, which was a preferred qualification, as it also would have been if I had graduated from University of Southern California (USC), Stanford University, Harvard, or the Massachusetts Institute of Technology (MIT).

At my first appointment, I was asked to fill out the donor application form and to leave an initial sample. Many donors, it seems, are rejected because their semen samples are insufficient. Since some of the sperm is rendered useless in the freezing process, it is important to have a large sample.

Apparently, mine were sufficiently ample, so I could proceed to the next step, providing a three-generation medical and genetic history of myself and my family to rule out various conditions such as diabetes and cancer. This is called the "long profile," and I did so, but there was to be much more. It takes two to three months to complete the process of becoming a donor.

This includes being interviewed in person by a number of CCB staff members, as well as a genetic counselor. Once they all gave me the green light as a donor, there were lab tests for a host of sexually transmitted diseases. After the tests (repeated every three months while I was a donor) showed that I was free of these diseases, I was still only a potential donor.

Before achieving that exalted status, my required initial sperm samples, all ten of them, had to be screened for cystic fibrosis (occurring most commonly in Caucasians), as well as Tay-Sachs disease, Canavan disease, Fanconi Anemia, Gaucher disease, and Niemann-Pick disease (each of which occurs most commonly in persons of Ashkenazi Jewish ancestry). If I had been of African ancestry, my sperm would have been tested for Sickle Cell Disease. Some donors also undergo a chromosome analysis to identify any problems that might cause miscarriage or birth defects.[15]

I had thought it would be a breeze to become a donor, but it took a lot of work on the part of many professionals and myself to qualify. Finally (whew!) I was accepted into the program and assigned my donor number: 57590. If I could have run around with a sign proclaiming, "My sperm is GOOD!!! And I can earn MONEY now!!!" I would have. Of course I couldn't, so I was anonymous but proud. Who wants to be a sperm donor reject?

CRYO KID

*   *   *   *

Adam wasn't the first donor I chose. When I first purchased sperm from the CCB (from afar) in Montreal, some years earlier, the donor was, quite obviously, a different man. The results, as you already know, were unsuccessful. When I resumed trying to conceive through artificial insemination again in California, some years had passed, and, of course, I selected the sperm of another donor. As a matter of fact, the year was 1998, and Adam's sperm was not even available then. I perused those catalogues for weeks on end to find just the right donor for me. The information available was not as extensive as it is in 2007. As I recall, there were no online baby photos or facial characteristic reports available yet, although I could have paid an additional sum for a genetic counseling session where I would have been given a more complete description of the donor's physical and facial characteristics. I chose not to take that option at the time, although later, I wished that I had in order to relieve some of my child's curiosity.

The anonymity of the donor was closely guarded. It was understood that, when a child born of a specific donor's sperm reached the age of eighteen, he or she could request contacting the donor, and, if he were so inclined, it could be arranged. Now there are some open donor programs, where the donor agrees ahead of time to future contact. At that time, however, only the short (published on the Internet and printable for comparison) and long profiles (written questionnaires which the donor answered prior to being accepted) were available to the purchaser of the sperm. Although audiotapes of the interviews with the prospective donor had been made, they were NOT released to the users when I was looking for the right biological father for my as yet unconceived child.

I had never forgotten the vow I made at the Western Wall in Jerusalem that I would give birth to a Jewish child to continue the chain that was broken in the Holocaust. The interfaith divide in my own marriage to Cameron was so great (and one of the major reasons for my marriage break-up), that I was determined that the donor would be of my faith. I also assumed that there would be more genetic similarities. That narrowed the selection considerably. I made a list of favorites and then streamlined it some more.

When, after consultations with my mother, my three sisters, and my friends—all of whom had plenty of opinions to offer—I finally chose a donor from the information available to me, I was ecstatic. Memory is a funny thing. Although I can barely remember anything about the characteristics of that initial CCB donor now, at that time of choosing, I felt so close to him.

There was no guarantee, of course, that I would actually become pregnant. In Montreal, six attempts at insemination had been unsuccessful. Now, with a brand new donor, I was not successful either in the first few attempts.

Buying vials of sperm is expensive. The contributor of sperm to CCB currently gets seventy-five dollars for each specimen, and if he contributes sperm the maximum of three times a week, he can make nine hundred dollars a month, but it costs the purchaser much more. In 1998, it cost the purchaser about five hundred dollars per attempt (including sperm and shipping). I bought four vials of the frozen sperm of the donor I had selected. My medical insurance did not pay for the sperm or for some of the infertility drugs. Many insurance policies consider fertility assistance to be elective. So, even with a good insurance plan, I was out-of-pocket about a thousand dollars a month. If the process had not been covered at all, I would have been spending about three thousand dollars a month. Fortunately, because my job provided the benefit of excellent medical coverage, and because I was still under forty, my visits to the fertility clinic at UCLA were covered.

After several attempts at insemination, however, I began to think that my child would forever remain unconceived. Even if I had been trying to conceive naturally and not by artificial insemination, it looks like I would have had to have some help. My periods were widely spaced and inconsistent, so it was hard to predict my times of ovulation with any certainty.

When the doctors ran their tests, I was lucky that my FSH "numbers" were still good. The Fertility Stimulation Hormone test determines how easily your ovaries can still produce eggs and assigns test scores to categorize your chances. If your numbers are low, from one to five, that's excellent. Five to seven is very good, and, at eight to eleven, you still have a good chance. If your score is over eleven, it's unlikely you will be able to produce eggs suitable for fertilization. My ovaries were still producing eggs good enough to be fertilized in the last couple of years of my thirties. Unfortunately, despite the best medical assistance—the expert fertility team at UCLA were highly knowledgeable, technologically state-of-the-art, and always provided psychological comfort and encouragement as well—something was not working.

It is hard enough for a woman who is married to conceive in this artificial way, with sperm that does or doesn't belong to her husband. It is hard for her spouse, too. These feelings are compounded for a single woman, even one who is secure emotionally and has the financial resources and support network to bring up a child on her own. Any woman I know wants to conceive a child in the arms of the man she loves. I say this as a heterosexual woman. Perhaps it is also a lonely experience for lesbians who conceive through artificial insemination.

In any case, despite the emotional roller coaster I was riding every month, working myself up to a fever pitch to find the exact time of ovulation, praying every time I was inseminated that this time it would result in conception, checking the strips of the pregnancy test the moment it was the date to find out if I was pregnant or not. Each time, the colored stripe on the test strip showed that I was not, I would test again in a couple of days anyway, hoping against hope to find a different result.

After the second unsuccessful attempt, my doctors advised me to significantly increase the fertility drugs I was taking. I don't know if anyone reading this has ever used fertility drugs, but if you have, you know that they blow you up like a walking balloon. Your cheeks look as if they are stuffed with two hamburgers each and, to be kind, your body resembles a soft sculpture. And while this walking balloon-soft sculpture combination called Janet was undergoing repeated fertility treatments, she was also going for job interviews.

Although I loved my job in the education sector and the good feeling it gave me to know that I was helping people move up the ladder, I realized that I needed more lucrative employment. I was determined to succeed in having a child, but my repeated attempts were draining my savings. Once a child was born, I would need more money than I was currently earning to give that child every advantage I could manage.

In the meantime, I bought a third vial from the cryobank. And a fourth. Another two thousand dollars down the drain. When the fourth vial didn't work, the chief doctor, Dr. W., who was highly efficient but normally offered little in the way of speech, suggested that I change donors.

"You've been inseminated with this donor's sperm four times now, Janet, and it didn't work," he said, offering some plain and honest talk. "From experience, we set a limit of seven attempts at insemination, and if it doesn't work, we will have to discuss another method of conception: in vitro.*"*

When I gasped, he continued kindly, "We can try three more times with a new *donor, but there is no point continuing with this donor or beyond seven tries. The odds would be too small." Despite my best effort, I could not prevent a tear from escaping down my cheek as he explained further, "In natural circumstances, women have about a 25 percent chance of insemination. With donor insemination, you're down to about 10 percent, and the odds decrease, rather than increase with each insemination. We're not sure why, but that's what we understand."*

It was heart-breaking to hear this news. I was bonded to the donor profile, but now I was getting really scared that I wouldn't even get pregnant. Sadly, I

*had to say goodbye to my first anonymous donor, my chosen man through four
vials of his sperm.*

This is what he would look like forever after in my dreams: a blank page:

Anonymous Donor Number One[i]

---

i   After four unsuccessful inseminations with Janet at 1,000 dollars per shot, this
     sperm donor, despite his superb physical characteristics, keen intellect, excellent
     medical history, and dynamic personality, has been permanently retired. So sorry
     it didn't work out.

And that's when I found Adam. Donor Number 57590. He was the fifth vial. His short profile had attracted me, and, yes, he was Jewish. As a matter of fact, he was one of two Jewish donors who were currently listed, apart from the one I had just retired from any chance of biological fatherhood of my child. So that made the choice easier. Of the two, I liked him better.

When I requested his "long profile," written in his own left-slanted hand-writing that my yet unborn daughter Samantha cherished and hugged to her chest when I showed it to her a few years later, things started looking up. Physically he seemed very appealing: six feet, two inches tall, with a medium to large build, green eyes and light brown, wavy hair. His complexion was fair; racially he was Caucasian; and his religion was Jewish. His mother's forebears were Germanic, his father's Polish, and his maternal grandmother was living in Montreal.

Canada! Donor Number 57590 seemed to be a predestined choice.

Wow! He loved music. He played the guitar. He excelled in math and computer science. He played football. He liked other sports. He was voted the most likely to succeed in high school. He had a great GPA score.

Could you ask for anything more?

To get pregnant, that's all. The year 1998 had long since rolled into the New Year. Spring was in the air. It was May, 1999, and I would be forty in July. Throughout my multiple attempts to conceive, I was trying so hard to contain my emotions, to contain my disappointment, to focus on my new job. My safety valve was a diary that I kept throughout this process to record my private thoughts. So, for the most part, my emotions were contained in a ribbon-tied book that I was keeping for the child that might be born to treasure. "I'm thirty-nine, turning forty on July 5th, "I wrote in my diary." Pre-happy birthday. If I stay pregnant and have a healthy baby, I'll love being forty."

*   *   *   *

Excerpts from Janet's Diary
May 25, 1999

Took a pregnancy test yesterday morning and shocked, disbelieving, and ecstatic, discovered I was pregnant. This comes after five attempts using a donor—I conceived on May 7th with my new donor [Adam] ... I was starting to lose hope with the process. Now I have to go to the doctor tomorrow for a blood test to confim (please, please!) the pregnancy. And then three months to know if it will "take." I pray it does. If you are in there, my unborn child, I love you already.

The process has been difficult. Five months of fertility drugs, doctors' appointments, ultrasounds, donor selection. The last two months have been the most difficult ... waiting to see if I would get my period, getting my hopes up ... and trying not to, only to see them dashed as my period would set in.

But this morning: the line showed up in the square window within ten seconds. I couldn't believe it. Of course, I called Shelley right away and then started crying. I've held in a lot of emotion these last five months in order to curb my disappointments. But after tomorrow, even though my body will be deciding if the fetus is good or not, once I have confirmation on the blood test ... all I can do is wait and let nature take her course.

Deep breath (can't sleep between 3:00 and 5:00 AM, so it means stress is stopping my REM). Take deep breaths, go back to sleep.

Wednesday, May 26, 1999

It's official. I'm pregnant. Took the blood test at the hospital yesterday, and YUP!! I am preggos!! My very next appointment is June 9th for an ultrasound and to see if I might be having twins.

It hasn't sunk in yet.... I "know" that I'm pregnant, but I don't really get it yet. Mummy and Daddy are very excited, and so are Laura and Sue. Shelley, Ira, and my nephew, Joshua, came over last night to congratulate me. Shelley brought maternity clothes and the Expecting book ... so I'm off to a good start. I called Jacqueline but no one else. I know I am in a danger zone for three months, so I still need to keep my emotions somewhat in check for now.

Wednesday, June 9, 1999

Today I saw my little baby! I went to see Dr. W. and Dr. H. for a seven-week ultrasound, and, WOW, saw a little, little baby with a heartbeat. So very exciting.

I've now been referred to Dr. B., a specialist in "high risk" pregnancy, who Dr. W. thinks is terrific. First appointment with her is June 24th.

Saturday, June 12, 1999

The physical and emotional changes you go through are interesting, incredible, and uncontrollable.... I was so overexcited by having seen my baby that I ended up having a reaction of total exhaustion with a kind of internal shaking. I felt really ill. Thursday it happened again at lunchtime and then again, just before falling asleep tonight. I guess it is all just part of the hormonal changes. But over and under it all, is the joy and disbelief that I'm pregnant and that my baby's heart is beating away inside me....

I remember when I saw [my colleague] George in Toronto, he "warned" me (as if I hadn't thought of it before) that I'd be undesirable as a mate, being a single mother. I just laugh now. I'll give up ten years of freedom, of dating, for the privilege of having this child. There is nothing more important to me. Nothing. I'm already totally in love with my little baby. He/she is about three-quarters of an inch long by now.

Saturday, June 25, 5:10 AM

I'm excited, so I can't sleep. My brain is running in a thousand directions. I saw my baby again yesterday. I had my first meeting with Dr. B., my new oby/gyn. She is going to be great. She has a very open, nurturing approach and is very calm. She is very crunchy granola, with long blond hair tied back in a low ponytail, wire-rimmed glasses, and Roots/Birkenstock type shoes. Her nurse, Goldie (they've been together 18 years!), is very maternal. So I'm very pleased with where my care is coming from.

So ... I had my consultation with her—we spoke for about half an hour to forty-five minutes, and then did the internal exam with ultrasound. I saw my baby. His/her head is big, with a little, teeny body, and I saw his/her little, tiny feet and arms moving about, saw the read-out of the heartbeat and heard his/her heartbeat too. They use a Doppler machine, so

*the sound is very electronic and tinny. It sounded like BAM-
BAM ...
BAMBAM ... BAMBAM ...*

The sound of Samantha.

* * * *

*The sound of Adam. Although I didn't hear it until 2006, an audiotape was
recorded in May, 1999 with Donor Number 57590. That was you, Adam. After
all the initial secrecy about your identity, what a shock it was when, in 2006—
doing research for my career woman sister, Susan (then childless at forty-two
and following in my footsteps)—I discovered an available audio CD of your
voice, just as you were interviewed ... for only ten dollars! I bought it online
that minute. I had been completely unaware that such a tape existed. It was a
weird, unsettling experience for me to listen to the cadences and timbre of
your speech, to try and reconcile the reality of what you were articulating to
the interviewer with the mental image I had previously formed of you. I almost
wished that I hadn't listened. I wished that I could have the opportunity to
interact with you instead of the interviewer, who was obviously impressed by
your physical self. Maybe I was envious of him because I would have liked to
ask you the things I wanted to know. This isn't the way it happened, but let's
pretend that I'm the interviewer, and that I'm the one sitting in a chair across
from you with the tape recorder switched on. The substance, though, is real.
It's May, 1999.*

Adam:
Well, I had already given a lot of the information you heard on the tape in the
written questionnaire that the Cryobank gave you. I guess you just about
memorized that. I would have.

Janet:
*And so did my mother—and Samantha when we shared it with her as she grew
older. Yes, much of what you had to say in the audiotape about your physical
characteristics we already knew. What I didn't know was that you weren't
quite big enough to compete in college football with the big bruisers weighing
several hundred pounds unless you took steroids, and you chose not to do that.
I respect your integrity for that. Actually, my sister Laura, who, believe it or*

not, played rugby across Canada and the United States, didn't want to move into professional sports for the same reason.

Adam:

That's right. I didn't want to take steroids, but at the college level, it gets very competitive, and, at that time, you were getting pushed in that direction.

Janet:

And yet you were offered four full football scholarships at other universities and turned them down. That was another thing I didn't know.

Adam:

I was recruited, it's true, but the academics were far more important to me, and football was secondary. You know, I played football throughout high school— I'd been playing for twelve years because I started when I was five!—but the universities that offered me football scholarships didn't have the quality of academic education that UCLA offered, so I decided to forgo the full scholarships, even if it meant more financial stress for me, and attend UCLA. I did go to a football school there, but I didn't play. I had another consideration, too. I like my knees!

Janet:

You like your knees?

Adam:

Yes. I'd like to have them intact to play with my kids someday. I'd like to teach them to snowboard, which is my favorite sport, and to play basketball, not just watch it on TV, and to have a lifestyle that will allow me to interact with them.

Janet:

I almost cried when I heard you say that you were looking forward to having your own family someday, as soon as you were physically and mentally able, and when you said that a tight family bond is very important to you.

Adam:

It is. My Dad and I are very close. We're best friends and talk all the time. He's a great father who has taken a vested interest in my life, and he instilled in me that love and family, the two of them connected together, are the most important things in life. I respect him for that and for many other things.

Janet:
You did a lot of projects together. You rebuilt a house?

Adam:
I guess that's when we really bonded. He bought this fixer-upper. I helped him rebuild it, and we've been close ever since. We tinker with old cars. One of the things that draw us together is that we're both very passionate about the things we do. Once we get an idea in our heads, we're totally focused. If there are problems, we're great at working out how to get around any obstacles or how to alleviate the problems. I get these qualities from my Dad. He worries a lot, though. It probably comes from his ancestors in the *shtetl*, and it gave him an ulcer. Otherwise, we're a pretty healthy family.

Janet:
Is it because of the way you feel about your Dad that you wrote a note, not just for me, but also for the father of the child who would be born from your sperm?

Adam:
Of course, I had no way of knowing that the sperm would be going to a single mother, which is alright with me. It's the values that my Dad imparted to me that are so important to me, so I think I was putting myself in the place of the father of the unborn child. I really put a lot of thought into it. I can understand that it might be tough for him to think that this baby is not his child, but the truth is, I want to say to him, "This is *your* child. You bring it up; you instill its values; everything it believes in; what it stands for; everything it will be."

Janet:
If I ever marry again, it would be nice to tell that to Samantha's new father.

Adam:
Step-families are tricky things. When my Mom re-married, I was seven, and my two-stepbrothers were getting out of high school. There were ten years or so difference between us, so we were never close. But I am very close with my sister, who is just a couple of years older than me. We have a great relationship.

As a matter of fact, we just had a late breakfast together. She lives quite far way, though, so we have to make opportunities to get together.

Janet:

Is she a sister or a step-sister?

Adam:

A step-sister, actually, but I think of her as my sister.

Janet:

Is she a lot like you?

Adam:

She's quite different, really. I'm more interested in medical stuff, in science and research and computers. I spend a lot of time with computers, and I've designed some computer programs. My sister's more like my Mom. Both of them are in the fashion industry and socially oriented. I'm a social animal, too, in that I like most people, but I tend to be more intellectual in my interests.

Janet:

You seem to have a lot of affection for your mom, too.

Adam:

My Mom and I are really tight. She lives on the east coast, so there are time zone differences that keep us from talking together on the phone as much as we'd like. And with me working full time and studying part time, and her working as well, there just isn't a lot of free time for much else. But we do manage to talk at least three times a month, and when we get together in person, we have a good time. She worked for a big company in the fashion industry for a long time. Then she started her own business. She is a very enterprising person. She's of German-Jewish descent, you know. Intent on achieving her goals.

Janet:

I was surprised when you mentioned that you'd like to have your own business one day, too. Like your mom. Your answers on the questionnaire made me think that you'd probably become a doctor.

Adam:

I seriously considered going into medicine. As you know, I graduated from UCLA with a BA majoring in genetics. For a time I considered becoming a medical doctor. I worked for a doctor for a year, so I had a good opportunity to observe his practice and the various afflictions of the patients who came to his office. I enjoyed it but decided that the way health care is going, it is becoming less and less attractive to become a doctor, and, because of my financial constraints, I didn't want to wind up with huge student loans to repay.

Janet:
So is that when you thought of becoming a medical researcher in genetics?

Adam:

I was thinking of both future quality of life and my current finances, and also I had spent a year and a half doing research in genetics, and I liked it a lot. The field is fairly lucrative, and you don't have to wear a pager. I gave it a lot of thought and decided to get an MA in genetics, which will allow me to become a senior medical researcher more quickly than I can become a doctor. I'm taking a few courses at UCLA now, on a part-time basis, to keep myself refreshed and current, and to show that I can compete in the upper graduate levels. At the same time, I just took a new job with an oncologist, doing research in ovarian tumors, and I'm anticipating that this new job will eventually allow me to get into the computer field. I think it may lead me in a new direction, and I might change fields a bit.

Janet:
Into the computer field?

Adam:

You know the old adage: you should have three careers in a lifetime. I think that will be me. I'll be a medical researcher for a while to earn money, and it's something I'll enjoy. And then I'd like to start my own business. There are a lot of links between medicine and computers today. I have some ideas about it.

Janet:
What kind of friend do you value, Adam?

Adam:

First and foremost, a friend who is honest. I can tell when a person is honest and genuine. Someone who has some humility when he or she has done something wrong. Humor is a big thing with me. I like people who can have some fun, someone you can have a good time with. Intellect is very important to me. I think when intellectual qualities and humor go hand-in-hand, they feed off one another.

Janet:

I hope you meet someday, Adam, when Samantha is grown up, and that you find my little daughter has those qualities you value.

◆

4

THE BOOK of SAMANTHA

Sadly for our Neolithic lovers, biological interpretations reduce love to interpersonal sexual chemistry, categorizing it as an animal drive like hunger or thirst.[1] That's the thinking of anthropologist Helen Fisher, who divides love into three categories, lust, attraction (related to a specific person), and attachment (bonding), each of which overlap. The first two have time limits (a few weeks or months for Stage One and up to three years for Stage Two).

Contemporary neuroscience tells us that these stages involve the release of chemicals (including testosterone, estrogen, dopamine, norepinephrine, and serotonin) that promote mating, stimulate the pleasure centers of the brain like amphetamines, and create the side effects that poets write about: increased heart rate, loss of appetite and sleep, and an intense feeling of excitement.[2] Long term commitment (attachment) is usually based on marriage and children and mutual friendship and interests. This stage involves the increased release of chemicals like oxytocin and vasopressin.[3]

There must have been plenty of chemicals flowing in the first recorded instance of romantic love in the Bible, the attraction of Jacob to Rachel at the well. He loved her so much that he worked fourteen years (seven for Leah, the wife he was duped into taking, and seven more for Rachel[4]) for his father-in-law, Laban, in order to wed her. If we believe the scientists, Jacob's chemicals had to keep flowing for a long time in order for him to progress from Stage One to Stage Three. In the biblical view of love, though, there is no mention of chemicals: emotional attitudes and actions stem from a set of clear moral values.[5]

♦

CRYO KID

Excerpt from Janet's Diary
Tuesday, December 28, 1999

Boy, oh boy, oh boy. What a day! I went for my ultrasound this afternoon. I saw Samantha's face. I was totally unprepared—I never realized that I'd see her face so clearly. I was so shocked that I burst into tears of absolute joy. Literally couldn't control my emotions for several minutes. What a beautiful little face. My little baby girl.

She is facing the right side of my body, and Dr. B. says her head will engage this week, which means she'll be in the right position. Later, when I give birth, she'll turn to the left and corkscrew down the canal.

Now I can't wait to see her face for real. She looks like a Samantha. She has very long legs (like me!), and she weighs seven pounds already. She'll weigh between eight and nine pounds. when she is born, so I'm a little worried about labor. I'll just do my best.

Goodnight, my beautiful little baby. I'm going to look at the ultrasound image of your face again. I love you already. Three to four weeks to go until I hold you in my arms, instead of inside me. I'm so proud of you and so in awe of the miracle that is you. Beautiful, beautiful Samantha.

*   *   *   *

My Grandma showed me the pictures of when my Mom was pregnant. When she stood sideways the month before I was born, there was a big bump where I was growing inside. A really big bump because I was born big and healthy: eight pounds, six ounces and twenty-one inches long at 1:34 AM. I'm a lucky child because I was born in the millennial year, which is supposed to be special because people can always tell how old you are. So in 2007, I am seven years old. In 2008, I will be eight years old.

My Grandma is very old; she is seventy-one, and I take care of her and help her get our groceries from the car and things like that because I don't want her to die. She takes care of me, too. She takes me to school and picks me up after school because my Mom has to drive two hours to get home from work, so my Grandma makes dinner for me. Usually I like pasta with my Mom's famous cream cheese sauce, or a grilled cheese sandwich on *challah* bread, and lots of cocoa. But never give me vegetables. I like blueberries and strawberries and green apples, so that's okay for vitamins and minerals. I eat four-minute egg whites but not the yolks. And fish sticks, and I started to like hamburgers. That's protein, like nuts, and I like nuts. But I don't think people should kill animals for food. They should let nature grow and not hurt it.

*   *   *   *

Excerpt from Janet's Diary

Saturday, June 5, 1999

    Started getting nauseous two days ago, with some serious food aversions—broccoli, green stuff! Cottage cheese is good, salmon on toast okay, eggs ...

*   *   *   *

My Grandma says she will try to live to be a hundred, so at least she can come to my *bat-mitzvah* (when she will give me gold charms from her charm bracelet) and with all the new things they are discovering for health today, she might even get to be a hundred and twenty and come to my wedding. If I marry in my early twenties like she did, that would help a lot, and then she might have great-grand-children.

*   *   *   *

This is Samantha's MOTHER, Janet, who hopes she will survive these two-hour commutes through traffic so that one day when she is eighty years old, SHE can be a grandmother. The same month that I found Adam as my new donor, I got the job I'd been looking for. Lots of scope for growth, lots of challenge, an increased salary, a huge daily commute if I did conceive, but, based on previous attempts, it didn't look then as if I were about to get pregnant in a hurry.

Life has its surprises. I did. First try with Adam's sperm. When I checked the pregnancy test strips that month, I had expected to find that it hadn't happened. When Dr. W. had opened the vial and tested it, despite his normal restraint, he made a face.

"I don't think it will work, Janet. It is not a good sample ... the sperm are motile, but there is just not sufficient quantity." Some of the little swimmers did not survive the freezing, and they were dead.

· 59 ·

"We might as well go ahead anyway. Maybe we'll be lucky," he said, but his disappointment showed.

I cried bitterly. "Should we even do the insemination, Dr. W.?"

He paused for a moment, his brow furrowing, considering, as I tried to wipe away my tears. "Well ... let's try anyway," he urged.

"Okay," I whispered, as if resigned to the outcome. Although outwardly I seemed back in control of myself, I wondered if I could bear to wait another two weeks to see if I were pregnant or not. After being inseminated, I couldn't stop crying miserably for days. The thrown out money didn't bother me ... another thousand dollars wasted, so what? But this was my fifth attempt, and I just didn't know if I had the emotional strength to even try a sixth, or, heaven forbid, a last, seventh time.

So when the pregnancy test was positive, I couldn't believe it at first. (Please look at the footnote. Important.[i]) And then, when it turned out to be true ... I was really going to have a child, I was overjoyed. Then at the three week mark, I started to bleed. The doctor had me stay in bed a couple of days, and, miraculously, the pregnancy held.

*   *   *   *

Excerpt from Janet's Diary

Saturday, June 5, 1999

Had a scare last week. I started spotting. I spotted Thursday and Friday, went in to the doctor's office. It was too early to determine if I was miscarrying or not, but they saw the sac, and it was in a good place.

Dr. W. suggested I take it easy over the weekend and said that I might miscarry while in Vegas, so I cancelled my planned trip for Memorial Day and basically lay in bed with my feet up most of the whole, long weekend. Monday I felt a little better, so I bought some groceries, did some laundry, walked a little, and had very red spotting Tuesday morning. It disappeared by Tuesday night, and I haven't spotted since, so that's good for now.

I'm excited about being pregnant, but also trying to contain my enthusiasm in case the baby doesn't "take." It's out of

i   This is Adam here. I promise not to keep butting in, but I told you my samples were awesome. They were mighty swimmers, so a few ruined ones didn't matter.

my hands now. Nature will make the decisions. I'm entering my seventh week (technically—it's dated from two weeks before ovulation).

* * * *

I waited to release my emotions beyond my diary until the ultrasound some months later revealed that it would be a little girl. I would have taken anything, boy, girl, as long as the child was healthy, but a little girl who could grow up and be my friend like Mummy and me ... I was overjoyed, and I wanted the world to know it. I was living in a one-bedroom apartment in upscale Brentwood. Great for a single lady, but not right for a single mother. I wanted a house for my little girl.

So I braved the house market in Los Angeles, which was just starting to rise but still affordable. It was quite a search, wedged in between my working hours, the constant, overwhelming fatigue engendered by my new pregnancy, my inability to sleep at night, and my struggle to keep food down. It seemed logical, at first, to endeavor to find a house close to where I was working, but the down side was that I would be far from Shelley, who lived in the San Fernando Valley. Mummy had not yet permanently arrived, and I was counting on my sister as a major support once the baby was born.

* * * *

Excerpts from Janet's Diary
Tuesday, June 15, 1999

I thought I was going to put an offer in on a house last night, but when Shelley came to see it, I realized (with her help!) that the area really wasn't a good one. It's off Robertson and surrounded by two bad [crime] areas, not where I want my baby to grow up. Anyway, the search continues.

Wednesday, June 16, 1999

I'm going to start looking for a house in Redondo [close to work]. I want to be in a good area for my child to go to school. I think there are better schools out there ... and even if I have to send my child to a private school, the overall neighborhood is a good one. So Sunday afternoon, I'll head out *there with my agent—who, after meeting me, is going to see Dr. W. and Dr. H. for a consultation.*

Sunday, August 8, 1999
    The house search in areas close to work is proving fruit-less in terms of affordability. My job is still new, and, with a baby in my tummy, I'm afraid to take a chance on over-extending myself. As my baby grows, it seems more and more important to be close to Shelley.

Sunday, August 29, 1999
    In the nick of time, Grand'mère *appeared in my dreams to take charge of the situation. Yes,* Grand'mère *has been send-ing messages again—as she promised (so I think!). Here are the coincidences. Two days ago I had a very vivid dream about her, and I haven't for a while. Yesterday I saw a house that I liked [in the San Fernando Valley, not far from Shelley]. The lady living there was dressed in* PURPLE—Grand'mère's *color—and she was kind of wacky, just like* Grand'mère.... *So today, the day of* Grand'mère's *unveiling [in Montreal], I put an offer in on that house,* AND *I felt my baby move (still mov-ing!!). So HELLO,* Grand'mere. *We're thinking of you, and thanks for helping me find a house. Light a candle [wherever you are] so that my offer gets accepted!*

Friday, November 5, 1999
    The house is mine*! Closed everything on Wednesday. The floors are getting started tomorrow. Shelley is orchestrating all* the floor work. *I'm so grateful.... And she added my fridge yesterday (gift from Dad).*

*   *   *   *

    And that's how I bought that house in Encino, a pretty suburb in the San Fernando Valley for my little girl—with so much gratitude for my family, including the one residing in the spiritual world. It had a garden in back with mature fruit trees and a front lawn where we could plant roses to greet Mummy, who had promised to come and help me for four months when the baby was born.

Still living in Toronto, Canada, Mummy had been taking care of Grand'mere *for a long time. In fact,* Grand'mère *lived with my mother for eight years (and* Grand'mère *could be difficult!!!), and then, totally blind after a massive stroke, she spent the last two years of her life in a nursing home near Mummy, who visited her daily until she passed away a few months after Joshua was born, and just before Samantha came into this world. The unveiling of her headstone, which in Jewish custom marks the finality of death, took place eleven months after her funeral. (The unveiling must take place before a full year has passed, because, just as it is appropriate to mourn, there is a time for mourning to end, so that, in this instance,* Grand'mère's *family should return to living a joyful life.)*

Mummy came to visit me for a few weeks—instantly—as soon as she heard my happy news that I was pregnant. She searched the racks of department stores for clothes that would cover my girth but not look too much like maternity clothes, because I had just started my new job. Then she went back to Canada to sell her house so she would be free to come to Los Angeles to help me when the baby was born. My whole family, who had supported me emotionally through all my efforts to have a child, continued to behave like cheerleaders. They were so happy for me. Happy but worried.

They had good reason. My work situation posed somewhat of a problem. The job was so new, required quite a bit of traveling, and there was a three month probation period before it became permanent. After trying fruitlessly to conceive for so long, how was I to know that I would get pregnant the very month I started a new job? Since pregnancy hadn't been part of my hiring arrangement, I was afraid of losing my employment if it were discovered that I was carrying a child before I proved my worth. The fact that I still looked like a balloon came in handy. Fertility drugs take a while to get out of your system.

Every time I left my office, I became expert at walking very quickly through the corridors half bent over, with my hair falling over my face, and one hand covering my body as I pushed my hair behind my ear. I affected loose clothes to cover my emerging profile. My stomach had popped out alarmingly before the three months had passed, but I guess my boss and co-workers assumed that the company had hired a very talented but very fat director of educational services, with a puffy, round face.

Apparently, despite my worries, my boss was able to overlook my surprise pregnancy when I finally confessed—I promised that I would return as soon after maternity leave as possible—and I continued to work every day right into the first week of my ninth month.

CRYO KID

*   *   *   *

Excerpts from Janet's Diary
July 22, 1999, 3:00 AM

   Can't sleep. Yesterday I told my boss that I was pregnant. I couldn't wait until my introductory period was over. I felt too dishonest, and I didn't want her to think I'd been duplicitous. I BURST into tears as I was telling her, and I couldn't stop crying!!! I was embarrassed, relieved, scared, you name it. But she seemed very happy for me, and I affirmed my commitment to the position. It was the right decision, and I feel very relieved. I'm not going to tell my staff until next week, and my boss thought I can wait as long as I want to tell them—I need to start wearing my maternity clothes! I don't have anything that fits!!!

   I'm falling in love with my baby, and I pray she is healthy, and everything will be okay. I told my boss a white lie. I told her that the baby's father was a dear friend from Canada who wouldn't be involved. I didn't want to disclose something as personal as the sperm bank and fertility treatment.

   Goodnight, my baby. I love you. (P.S. Look how little my fortieth birthday meant to me with you inside me!)

August 4, 1999

   I wore a maternity shirt to work for the first time yesterday and also told my staff. Everyone is pretty happy for me.

   Had some stress this past week but trying to stay unaffected, so it doesn't hurt my baby.

Sunday, August 15, 1999

   Going to Bangkok in two days. I am excited, but also nervous about the flight. Have my amnio scheduled for September 1st. Shelley is going with me. I'm feeling pretty good. I am enjoying being pregnant and NOT holding my stomach in!!! Got a manicure/pedicure today. Feel pretty.

Friday, August 24, 1999

   Got back from Bangkok yesterday, but I would never go back there again, unless I had to. In terms of my growing baby, everything seems fine. The flight there, though, was so long, eighteen hours flying and stopover (in Osaka) time— plus getting to and from the airport was close to two hours in travel time.[ii]

The hotel was very nice, and I had a lovely room, but the city is hot and humid, polluted and filthy. Even the hotel smelled so moldy and bad (in August, at any rate), I was gagging every morning and night in my room. I'm so happy to be home. The last hour of the flight, I was getting nauseous and claustrophobic. All my instincts were screaming to get home. (The support hose were fantastic—Dad's idea.)

Notes of interest: the canal cruise through Bangkok, billed as "The Venice of the East." Such poverty! We don't realize how absolutely privileged we are to live in the United States and Canada. The "homes" along the canal were mostly wood shanties, with no sewage, plumbing, or water—nothing. So all raw sewage gets tossed directly into the Chao Praya river. The river is brown and smells like excrement and sewage. The children swim and play in the same water—also used for drinking, baking, washing clothes. Garbage is left hanging over the river in plastic bags—on decks—for pickup by boat, but a lot simply ends up in the river. There are thousands of stray dogs (and stray cats) all over Bangkok. They are sickly, with mangy coats, open sores (especially around the anus). People are so very poor. Little kids sell drugs, prostitute themselves, as young as three or four for what is the equivalent here of fifty cents a day. The maximum wage is five dollars a week. Oftentimes, the parents have gambling and drug debts, and send their children to work selling drugs or to a pimp to pay off their debts.

*   *   *   *

---

ii   This is Samantha's footnote. Even at seven years old, I know that this was not a wise thing to do, Mom. When a baby is growing in your tummy, you have to take very good care of yourself and what you eat, and you have to keep very good health rules, like washing your hands and brushing your teeth. If I had been born, I would have told you not to go. You are more important than your job. Right, Mom?

CRYO KID

I had a great deal of trepidation about making a trip to Bangkok when I was five months pregnant, but the convention scheduled to take place there was an international educational gathering that was part of my job to oversee. If I had to do it again, with the knowledge I have now of the late August filth, and the stench to which I would be exposed as a pregnant woman, I wouldn't have made the trip. At the time, despite my mother's anxiety about it, I was afraid to jeopardize the job I needed to keep to support the baby still in my womb. Whenever I left the hotel, I covered my mouth and nose with a scarf.

When I returned from Bangkok to Encino, I was so grateful that the child I would bring into the world would grow up in America, in beautiful California, with privileges and advantages those children a world away would never have. My long commute to work seemed a small price to pay. Although I enjoyed delightful restaurants in Thailand, graceful Thai dance, and tours to opulent temple complexes with gold inlaid everywhere, and although the night market was inexpensive, and I had two silk (purple and burgundy) maternity suits made (that didn't fit properly when I got home), I found the contrast to the poverty of the Thai people sad and disappointing. Overall, my memory of Bangkok will be the steamy heat, the pervading putrid smell, and the plight of the exploited little children. And I was so relieved that the amniocentesis in September showed that Samantha was fine.

As I entered my ninth month, my belly was so large that I could barely fit behind the wheel to drive to work and back. I would get off the highway at intervals to go to the bathroom because baby was pressing on my bladder. I carried packets of antacids for the upward movements. My mother, who had again traveled from Canada to stay with me through my last month of pregnancy—she would have to apply to U.S. Immigration for a green card, a lengthy process, in order to remain permanently in the United States—begged me to stop work, and finally I felt secure enough in my job to do so.

I'm not sure if my boss believed that I would return, but I had given my word. I would do so. Besides, I needed the money. It was not true, as the whispers that circulated around my gossipy work environment, consisting mainly of women, would have it, that I had a trust fund to support me. No way! I was going to need that salary, especially as a now proud home owner.

Meanwhile my Dad also visited from Canada and played a major and deeply appreciated role in getting my new home up to scratch. It wasn't exactly a fixer-upper, but it sure needed a lot of fixing up. I was thirty-three weeks pregnant when I moved into my beautiful new home on November 13, 1999, just three days after my Dad flew in, on November 10th, and two days before his birthday, which Shelley spent with him on the beach (his only time on the beach on this visit), to help me with the move and with getting settled in. He did a whole lot more than that!

* * * *

Excerpts from Janet's Diary
Saturday, December 11, 1999

A lot of stress was immediately alleviated by Dad's being here. Not only was he a huge help, but he worked non-stop to fix up my home for four weeks. He bought me a fridge, washer, and dryer, installed my dishwasher (gift from Shelley), renovated my kitchen, and did SO much, it is impossible to list everything. Anyway, during the four weeks of his "visit," he sat in the sun for two hours. That's it!

Meanwhile, Mummy finally sold her house in Toronto on November 24th, and my sister Sue flew from Montreal to Toronto to help Mummy put all HER things in storage, and then Mummy flew to LA with her gorgeous, big, black poodle, Singa (who thought he was a person, not a dog, and was so mad at Mummy for flying him out caged in the belly of the plane that he wouldn't "talk" to her for three days after he arrived!), to help me a week earlier than she had planned.

So here were Mummy[iii] and Dad (who had been divorced for sixteen years) helping me at the same time. Then Laura and Sue flew here from Canada for my baby shower. I was so totally surprised and caught off guard that I didn't even really care if anyone else was there!

Sunday, December 12, 1999

My friend, Darlene, helped with the shower, but Shelley, Mummy, and Dad did a great prep job, AND Laura and Susan cleaned up my entire house.

It was a lot of fun, and I got some beautiful clothes and presents for the baby. My boss didn't attend, but she lent me a

---

iii This is Corinne, your Mummy, otherwise known as Grandma once Samantha was born. The timing did get a little messed up. Fortunately, as your parents, we were both united in the "cause"—YOU—and remained on good behavior. Even though Singa wouldn't "talk" to me, your Dad and I got along fine.

whole bunch of stuff—from a baby bassinet, to a baby bouncer, to TONS of clothes.

Anyway, my pregnancy is going very well. I'm starting to feel BIG and tired now at thirty-three weeks, though. My baby is kicking up a storm (not all the time, but fairly frequently), and I think that overnight, the baby kind of went into position—head down in my pelvis, because it feels very different than before (kind of hurts, actually!). It's 4:41 AM, so I'm going to watch a movie for a while and try to sleep soon.

*   *   *   *

It was time for Samantha to be born.

My mother says that she'll never forget walking up and down the streets of Encino with me in the last stages of my pregnancy. I had continual contractions, and, although Samantha was over a week past her due date, she seemed in no hurry to arrive.

Since Mummy was new to Los Angeles, doesn't really like to drive, although she does because she has to, we practiced over and over again a route to the hospital that would circumvent traffic in an emergency. I drew a map for her, and we practiced going to the hospital several times. We even practiced going in the right entrance and rode the elevator up to the obstetrical floor. We were a team.

The contractions continued, but still no baby. Four times we went to the hospital thinking I was in real labor, and four times we returned when the contractions and the degree of my dilation—four—remained static. No way was I going to open up yet.

I tried to plant a tree in the garden in honor of my little daughter's imminent birth, shoveling and sweating in the fervent hope that real labor would start, and she would arrive. No such luck.

Finally the contractions were so continuous that my mother said, "That's it. We're going to the hospital, and we're not coming back until the baby is born." And that's what we did.

*   *   *   *

This is Grandma speaking, and please don't reduce me to a footnote. I will never forget the night Samantha came into the world because I thought we might lose both the baby and my daughter. It was a terrible labor, the kind you hope that you, and certainly not your daughter, will ever have.

After Janet's contractions went on and on at home, we set out on our pre-planned route for the hospital. As on three previous "false alarms," she was dilated only to number four. She still had six "numbers" to go before reaching the full "ten" that meant the cervix was fully open and ready to produce a child.

"We're not going home this time," I asserted through clenched teeth. "You're going to stay here till you have your baby."

Fortunately the nurses agreed with me, and we began settling in for what would turn out to be a long night. This was still early afternoon, and Samantha would be born well after midnight, at 1:34 AM actually. The contractions continued at the quick pace that had propelled us to the hospital, but Janet was opening very slowly.

When her obstetrician, a lanky woman with her blonde hair pulled back in a ponytail and wearing the traditional white lab coat, looked in to check on Janet's progress, she looked a little concerned. Part of the high risk pregnancy team that treated Janet, this doctor had offered excellent emotional support, along with her medical expertise, throughout Janet's pregnancy, and Janet trusted her.

Janet wanted to have a natural childbirth, a desire that this doctor endorsed as preferable. After all, they were both products of a feminist generation. Now, however, it was beginning to look as if the baby might need more assistance to enter this world. The doctor regretfully uttered the "C" word for the first time. "Well, we'll only opt for a Caesarian as a last resort."

"As a last resort," Janet agreed.

As the hours went by, it looked to me as if the last resort had arrived. "Never mind last resort. I've had four children," I growled, "and this isn't normal. You need a Caesarian."

"Mummy, I'd like to have the baby naturally, if it's at all possible."

"She needs a Caesarian," I snapped to the obstetrical nurse who was at that moment checking Janet's vitals and the progress of her contractions on a computer screen. "This isn't a normal labor."

My daughter Shelley had arrived at the hospital some time before and was presently coaching her sister through her contractions. She had been helping her with the breathing exercises and the counting. Now her worried, brown eyes met my equally troubled, green ones. Shelley is physically built like me, with womanly hips, and her babies arrive the way mine did. They practically fall out of the womb when it is time for them to be born. Both of us have experienced very short, very intense labors.

Janet is built differently, more like the slim-hipped women in her father's family. All of them have narrow pelvises inside and had difficult labors requiring surgical intervention. "Janet needs a Caesarian," I insisted again, my voice rising each time I repeated this refrain.

"Please don't make a scene, Mummy," Janet begged between contractions.[iv] (After all, I have dramatic talent.) She had just been given a drug to induce labor, and the contractions were very frequent, intense, and painful. "Please. I don't want you to upset the staff."

"I'm more concerned about you than the nurses," I retorted.

At this point, a senior obstetrical nurse poked her head in the door and took in the scene. She was a small woman with wizened, dark skin, graying hair, and a wise smile. Her hands were small, too. "I have a lot of experience with cases like this," she said, exuding confidence and settling herself comfortably beside Janet. "Your baby is not in the right position, but I think I can turn her head around."

Amid Janet's increasingly intense contractions, she began to manipulate my daughter internally. At about this time the doctor looked in again. "Shall we get the operating room ready?" she asked.

"I think I can turn the baby around," the nurse responded, smiling. "I can do it. I don't think we'll need the operating room."

"Okay," the doctor said, popping out again. "Let me know immediately if that changes." She came running back in again in a few minutes when Janet's contractions increased to a non-stop pace. My daughter was writhing and screaming with pain, and the bed shook. The obstetrical nurse was crestfallen, her stethoscope on Janet's belly. She had assumed too much.

"The baby is in distress," she advised the doctor, and in seconds a bevy of staff members swooped down upon Janet, carting her off to an operating room that was not yet ready to receive her. The anesthetist fumed at the lost minutes so important to the safe delivery of the stressed baby … and my daughter.

The obstetrician's face was grimly set. She looked at Shelley and me standing anxiously by and ordered, "Only one of you in the operating room with Janet." As she was being wheeled away, Janet couldn't decide between us. She had asked me long ago if I would cut the umbilical cord when her baby was born, but she wanted her sister at her side, too. Gasping between contractions,

---

iv   Hi. This is Janet. Have to make a quick comment here. What an idiot I was! Had I but known what lay ahead, I would have scheduled a C-section well in advance. Natural, schmatural. What a bunch of hooey! Always listen to your mother.

she found the strength to call out, "Shelley, I want Shelley. She can help me with my breathing."

In seconds, Shelley donned the operating room clothes, cap, and shoes required for sanitation reasons and literally tossed to her by a nurse, and away she went running after Janet's wheeled bed right into the operating room. I stood there with my heart in my mouth, praying that I would be only temporarily bereft of my daughter. I was so afraid she was going to die.

Within moments, a nurse came running out of the operating room. "The doctor says that you can come in to cut the umbilical cord once the baby is born. I'll tell you when." She tossed me another set of surgical clothes, and I donned them and waited, willing my emotions to freeze like a deer in the headlights.

When the surgical nurse finally emerged to usher me back with her into the operating room, I continued struggling to contain my emotions for my daughter's sake. There she was lying on an operating table with a curtain shielding her eyes from the sight of the lower half of her body. The skin had been cut away so that it looked like the side of a skinned cow rather than a human being that was lying there. The doctors were in the process of putting her back together again. My daughter.

The nurse quickly averted my attention from this scene and directed me to a table where the newly born baby—not yet cleaned up from the birth process—was lying. Another nurse was already examining her fingers and toes, stethoscope at the ready. The umbilical cord that I was to cut was still attached to the placenta, lying on a table beside the baby. The nurse placed two clamps on either side of the place where I was to cut the cord and handed me a scissors. It was an eerie feeling to cut the cord that I had expected to find still attached to my daughter's body. Emotionally it was difficult, but physically it was easy. It was like cutting into butter. I had never cut an umbilical cord before.[v]

"Hello, little baby," I whispered to Samantha, this little girl child, lying red-faced and battered from the tremendous effort she had made to be born, this eight-pound, six-ounce baby who would come to mean so much to me, this infant whose head had been wedged in a corner of her mother's pelvic bone, so that it could not pass through the birth canal. She had been liberated from her intense efforts over many hours by the skillful strokes of a surgeon's knife. "Welcome to this world," I whispered, gently touching her little hand with the tip of my finger encased in a surgical glove. "Welcome to this beautiful world."

---

v   Janet again. This was not reflective of the symbolic, significant moment I had envisioned for my mother. Who'd have thunk the placenta would be on the table?

CRYO KID

Excerpt from Janet's Diary

April 16, 2000

Have been intending to write for the past three months, but my beautiful Samantha keeps me very busy. I gave birth after twenty-six hours of labor followed by a C-section. Sam was unable to navigate the birth canal, and her head was smashing into my pelvis and bladder, so they had to operate. It was a horrendous experience with a very long recovery, but for this little angel, I would go through it all over again if I had to. It's amazing how your mind blocks out the memory ... I'm still recuperating from the C-section—takes a long time for the muscles to remember how to function.

"Let us get her cleaned up," the nurse offered kindly. "And then you can bring her to your daughter."

She led me to Janet's side. The doctors were nearly finished stitching her up, but my daughter was still in shock, shaking uncontrollably and retching into a metal basin that Shelley was holding to the side of her mouth. "Your daughter is lovely," I told her, trying to put a smile on my worried face. I was still fearful that I might lose Janet. Her eyes searched mine for assurance. "She is lovely," I repeated. "She is perfect."

"She is twenty-one inches long," the nurse informed me, bringing a clean, sweet-smelling baby wrapped up in a blanket to my side. "She is going to be tall."

I placed my grandchild carefully in Janet's arms. "Here is Samantha Isabel," I said, voicing reverently the name Janet had already chosen for her daughter.

As she held her daughter close to her for the first time, Janet gradually stopped shaking. She was a mother now. Samantha was her first concern.

"Flesh of my flesh," she would croon to Samantha when she regained some of her strength. "Heart of my heart." It would be Samantha's favorite lullaby, the one her mother wrote to welcome her.

> *Flesh of my flesh,*
> *Heart of my heart,*
> *Breath of my breath,*
> *A part of every part.*
>
> *Oh my little girl,*
> *How I love you so,*

Flesh of my flesh,
Heart of my heart.

When my daughter Janet brought her daughter—my grandchild—home from the hospital, she placed the tiny hat that covered her head on top of the diary in the ribbon-tied keepsake box. For Samantha to treasure when she grew up.

♦

5

I NEVER MET MY DADDY

Women who are unmarried, by "a certain age," as the French put it, may have invested too many years, not only in their careers, but in "living" with a male "partner," who does not want to get married (after all, marriage is only a piece of paper), does not want to have children, or, at any rate, not marriage or children with them. All of these women in different circumstances do, however, have one thing in common. The biological urge for children may become an all-consuming desire. So, in the final analysis, it comes down to this question: is biology, is the mammalian urge to reproduce oneself, really stronger than romance? And, if so, what do you do about it?

From the Neolithic couple discovered lying in one another's arms, we have "progressed" over the millennia to the awesome possibilities of the donor sperm bank. A new "ism, *spermeticism* we might call it, has come into being in this post-post modern era: the twenty-first century has spawned a generation of young women—perhaps some of the best and brightest—that procreates alone. "Go forth and multiply," the Book of Genesis tells us.[1] That imperative does not stipulate *how*.

♦

I am seven years old now, not grown up yet, but I'm getting older every year. My Grandma says that in two or three years, my breasts will start to fill out a little, and my body will start developing into a woman's body. Sometimes I put tennis balls or socks in my T-shirt and look in the mirror to see what I'll look like when that happens.

I love to wear pretty dresses. My Grandma buys them on sale at a fancy kid's store, where they have really beautiful but very expensive clothes that she can only afford when they are half-price. She says she is developing my tastes. My mother buys my clothes at a big department store, because they have nice knock-off fashions in pretty colors, and I grow out of them quickly, but she buys me the best quality shoes at a small store near our house, because they take the trouble to fit me well.

My Mom works very hard and doesn't come home until seven o'clock at night, because she has a two-hour commute each way to get to her job.

She would quit and stay home with me, but she earns a lot of money there, because her job is important, and this money pays for our comfy house, and our food and clothes from the big department store, and the good times we have, and our travels. It pays for my cocoa, my DVDS, including Sponge Bob, and my dog, Daisy Mae, who is a rescue dog and is very loving, because we rescued her. My Mummy doesn't have to buy me many toys because my Aunt Sue is in the toy business, and she gives me enough toys for an army of kids. I have so many toys we don't know where to put them anymore. I like to do magic tricks now, and my best friend, Sally, and I did four magic tricks at school in the Talent Show.

Today I played with my other best friend, Rowena, and, just for fun, we dressed up like boys with our baseball caps (my Auntie Sue gave me mine with the words "Pooh" on it) on backward, and we smudged dirt on our faces, and practiced a boy attitude, and went for a jog for a couple of blocks and then walked the rest of the way to the park, where we played on the swings and slides. Rowena is very athletic. We only want to be boys for a day, though, because we like pretty dresses, and my favorite color is pink (sometimes it's blue or purple), and my whole bedroom is pink and white. Rowena likes pink, too, even though she takes gymnastics and might be on a National Team next year.

Rowena has been my best friend since we started Pre-school together. It is a very good school, and I loved all my teachers, and the arts and crafts we did there, and the music, and learning about all the Jewish holidays, and how to say the blessings. I went to Pre-school for three years—Nursery School, Pre-school, and a special class that my teacher says is like a bridge that helps you get ready for Kindergarten in real school. My Mom wants me to have the best education she can afford, and that's how come I went to Pre-school, which is a private school and cost her ten thousand dollars a year. It was in Sherman Oaks, not Encino, so my Grandma had to drive for half an hour in the traffic every morning and every afternoon to take me there and back.

For two years, I took Hebrew immersion classes there, so that I would learn my language that's in the Bible and Israel. It will help a lot when I'm ready to study for my *Bat Mitzvah*, which Jewish girls usually have today when they are thirteen. A long time ago, only boys had *Bar Mitzvahs*, but now girls can do things that boys do in places like California, but not so much everywhere else.

Before I went to Pre-school, I went to day care in a big, big white house with a very, very big garden, and a tall fence all around that my Mom calls wrought iron. My Grandma said that it was a mansion, but the lady who owned it had a husband who got sick with cancer, so she opened a daycare in her house for a few little children too young to go to school, and that's how she made some money to pay the mortgage. Her name was Ronit, and she had long, blonde hair and very blue eyes, and her helper was called Maria, and she had long, black hair and toasty brown eyes, and they took very good care of me and loved me a lot, and I loved them. Ronit taught everyone to eat with a fork, and have good manners, and go to the potty, and not hit each other. We learned to share our toys, and hug each other to make up, and sing the Teddy Bear song. And we played on the swings and tricycles and ran around outside in the very big garden. My Grandma says that not every little girl is lucky enough to have a daycare in the White House.

Excerpt from Janet's Diary

April 26, 2000

> *Today was Samantha's first day at daycare. I only brought her for four and a half hours, but when I left her, I wept all morning. It felt like my heart was being ripped apart. I am so in love with her. At birth she weighed eight pounds, six ounces. Today she is probably twelve and a half pounds, and I love, love every pore, every cell, every finger, every toe— even the strawberry patch at the back of her head. She is my life, my reason—when they say that no one but a mother can understand "mother love"—it is because this precious child is your heart, out on your sleeve for the world to see. It is painfully tender, achingly wonderful.*

Ronit speaks English with an Israeli accent, and Maria speaks English with a Spanish accent. I used to call water *agua*, which is Spanish, and to call my Mom

Ema in Hebrew, but I am American and speak English with an American accent. My Grandma comes from Canada, and she has a very big vocabulary and speaks English very well, and she and my Mom read me lots of stories, so I have a big vocabulary too and even help my Grandma when she's stuck in a crossword puzzle. Now that I'm in Grade One, I can read at Grade Four Level. I am very good in math, too, like my biological father, but I'll tell you more about that later. And I'm an artist, like my great-grandmother who died before I was born. I like to draw everything, and I took a cartooning enrichment class, so now I make up my own characters.

*   *   *   *

As long as my little daughter, Samantha, has a pencil or paintbrush in her hand, she is happy. She seems to have inherited Grand'mère's *visually expressed talent (and, thankfully, Mummy's sunny disposition). I've always felt that* Grand'mère *was watching over Samantha. Throughout my attempts to become pregnant, I carried on a conversation in my head with* Grand'mère, *who died on March 5, 1999, two months before I conceived Samantha, and then, when I did conceive, I truly believed she was continuing to watch over my unborn child from an unknown realm. I connected* Grand'mère's *creativity to the creation of a child, and to the Creator of life. Not rational, I know, but I was comforted that, through the medium of my grandmother, a supernatural force would stay by my side, by the side of the child in my womb, until that child was born. Intuitively, I sensed when* Grand'mère's *creative spirit was close by.*

Excerpt from Janet's Diary
Saturday, January 12, 2000, 5:10 AM
   I know that no one really believes me—well, maybe Mummy—but I know. And part of the reason I know is because Grand'mère *and I made an agreement that if there was any way to contact me after her death, she would, and she would make it obvious—every time it has been two days before a significant date or event that concerns her, like just before Mummy's birthday, when she came to me in a dream. [By that time, my plucky Mummy had come from Canada to live with me while I waited for Samantha to be born.] So I just know.* Grand'mère *was beginning to lose her physicality in the dream, so I know that she's almost ready to go from my*

dream world, but she is sticking around a little longer to see Samantha.

Well, Grand'mère, *thanks for watching over me. If you can, will you please visit Shelley? She wants to know that you have experienced Joshua. It would make her feel really good to say hello to you in a dream....*

Time for me to go back to sleep.

*　　*　　*　　*

Now that I'm in Grade One, I am not at Pre-school anymore, and my Mom doesn't have to pay so much money a year for private school any more, because I go to the elementary school right here in Encino. It only takes ten minutes for my Grandma to drive me back and forth to school. It is a very good school, my Mom says, because there's lots of parent involvement. That means that the parents raise a lot of money to have things that the school wouldn't have otherwise, like Phys. Ed., after school sports, and computer, art, and drama classes. The parents take turns volunteering as street crossing guards in the morning, and some of them volunteer to help the teachers in the classroom. My Grandma goes to a lot of school things that my Mom can't get to because she works. But my Mom makes a big effort to get to as many things at the school as she can, and she runs the Parents Association Web site. Our school is getting very good scores now. For "Reading Rocks!" week, our whole school was supposed to read six thousand books as our goal, and we read ten thousand books.

Do you know that I own one hundred and twenty-seven books that we keep on bookshelves in my room? (Sometimes, a lot of times, I forget to put them back and leave them around the house or on the floor with some of my other toys, but I am trying, most of the time, to be neater, like my Grandma, and put things in place. My Mom doesn't have time to be neat, because she is always rushing to work, so she leaves things on the floor, too. Also, we gave my cousin Rachel a lot of books that are too young for me now, so I have more room on my shelves.)

Do you know that I print very nicely and am learning how to write in cursive? Also, to put question marks at the end of sentences that are questions. I usually write my name, Samantha, at the top or bottom of the page, but sometimes I sign my artwork "Samee," because my Mom likes to call me Samee. Grandma always calls me Samantha, because she thinks it is a musical name. I have a middle name, too, Isabel. Some kids don't like their names, but I like mine. My Mom did a good job when she chose my name. It wasn't easy, and she says that a name is important, because you have it for your whole life, and so she gave it a lot of thought when I was in her tummy. She says that when she went to Joshua's birthday party almost four months before I was born, she realized it was time to choose a name for me.

Excerpts from Janet's Diary
Sunday, October 3, 1999
I like Isabel, but it may not be the best name. I want to choose something that she will love—nicknames and all. With every name, I try to think of what kids may call her. (I was always Janet-From-Another-Planet.) Shelley is going to help me look at names, and so is Mummy.

Thursday, October 14, 1999, 4:50 AM
I'm thinking Samantha Isabel. Samantha, Sam, Sammy, Samee. It sits better with me. Still a beautiful name but cleaner than Isabel. And Sam is a VERY cool nickname for a girl. Plus, if my little angel prefers Isabel, she can always call herself that later on!

I know that education is very, very important because it gives you knowledge, so that I can grow up to do good things in the world, and I like science and math a lot, too, like my father. I am taking an enrichment course called "Insectology." We examine little bugs and learn all about them. When I was in Pre-school, my teacher, Ilona, often gave me a magnifying glass, and we would walk around outside and see what kind of insects we could find. I liked to hold round little lady bugs in my hand. They don't hurt you. I also took an enrichment course called "Math Magic," where we did magic with numbers.

Besides Math and Science, I have a lot of other good things that come from my Dad. They come from my genes that are his. I get other things from my Mom's genes, and even from my Grandma and Grampie and *Grand'mère* who died, like her art. The things genes give can also be the way you look, like green eyes, or wavy brown hair, or if you're going to be tall. I get the eyes from my Mom and the hair and tallness from my Dad.

You know, people are surprised when I talk about my Dad, because he is not the kind of Dad that lives in your house. He is a biological father that is the kind you get when your mother is inseminated by a donor. When I was at Pre-school, the teachers always made sure that I could draw a picture or make a present for my Grampie or my Uncle Ira on Father's Day, so that I wouldn't feel bad that I didn't have a Dad who lives with us. Some other kids, you know, don't have Dads that live with them, because their Mom and Dad got a divorce, so they only see their Dads every second weekend or on holidays. There was a boy in my class who had two Dads but no Mom.

There are all kinds of families, you know. Not every family has a Mom and Dad. In our family, we have a Mom and a Grandma and Me. That's our family. We are also lucky to have an extended family. That means you have aunts and uncles and cousins that you see a lot, and they help you, and you help them.

We have Friday night dinners every week and birthday parties with Aunt Shelley and Uncle Ira, who whooshes me up to the ceiling in his arms and holds me in his lap just like my cousins, Joshua and Rachel. If he buys ice cream for his kids, he buys ice cream for me, too. My Mom says he is a wonderful role model.

When I was little, two or three years old, I would call him "Daddy" because that's what Rachel and Joshua called him. But each time, either my Mom or Uncle Ira would say, "No, Uncle Ira is not your Daddy. He is Rachel's Daddy. He is Joshua's Daddy. And he is your Uncle." I am seven years old now, and, of course, I know that an uncle is different from a daddy. I knew that even when I was three and a half or four years old, because my cousin, Joshua, who was a year older than me, asked my Mom, "Where's Samantha's Daddy?" And right there in my Aunt Shelley's living room, my Mom said, "Samantha has a Daddy who doesn't live with us."

Joshua said, "Oh."

I said, "Oh." Then we both went back to his room to play with his Lego blocks.

That's when my Mom started to tell me more about my big-word father. The big word is *biological*. She taught me how to pronounce it and explained that I was a wonderful gift from a kind man, who helped her to have a baby because she wanted one so badly. My Mom didn't have a husband, and she was afraid she was getting too old to have a baby, and so she went to a place called a *sperm bank* where the doctor took sperm from the kind man who is called a *donor*, and the doctor put it inside my Mom with a special tube. You see, my Mom has eggs inside her body, and the sperm has to swim inside her body to join together with the egg. This is called *fertilization*. Like apple trees but a little different. More like cats and kittens. And that's how I was born. From the sperm and the egg together. Everyone is born from a sperm and an egg that join together.

Since I really like books, my Grandma went to the library to see if she could find some books for little kids about sperm banks, and donors, and eggs, and fertilization, but she couldn't find very much about it. Not even at the book stores or on Amazon.com. She could find books about kids that were adopted, or about families that didn't have any daddies, but she couldn't find one that was exactly right for me. Did you know that my Grandma is a writer? She wrote some books for grown-ups, but she never tried to write one for kids, but she loves me, so she wrote one specially for me about kids like me. It is called "Cindy's Daddy," not "Samantha's Daddy," to keep my name private—between my Mom, my Grandma, and me—just in case someone else like me wants to read it to find out how they were born. When my Grandma wrote the book, I couldn't read much yet, so it's a book for a Mom or Grandma to read to their kids out loud, and it has lots of pictures to make it fun. That's why it's called a picture book. Now I can read, of course, so I can read it myself and look at the pictures also.[i]

When it's Father's Day at school, I don't draw a picture or make a gift for Uncle Ira or Grampie any more. I have a biological father who doesn't live with us. So I make something nice for my Mom instead. Some schools just have Parents' Day instead of Mothers' or Fathers' Days now. That's because so many kids live in different kinds of families. Plus my Mom likes having two Mother's Days in one year.[ii]

Mrs. K., my kindergarten teacher at the public school in Encino, which is part of the Los Angeles Unified School Education (LAUSD) system, taught us what concepts are and how to see patterns, because that is the beginning of learning. I was in the gifted stream, so everyone in my class had learned about the alphabet and the numbers on a calendar a long time ago. She taught us how to make graphs to measure things with the wrappers of little Hershey Bars and Snickers and Crackles. Our classroom was full of animals and plants that we learned to take care of, because they are living things and part of nature. We are part of nature, too. Mrs. K. buys *fertilized* eggs so we can watch them hatch into chicks, so I know that how we are born is a natural thing, but sometimes both animals and people need some help to have babies. My Mom said Mrs. K. is a gifted teacher.

My first grade teacher, Mrs. P., likes us to read chapter stories without many pictures by ourselves, but she also reads out loud to us every day in a voice with lots of expression. She shows us that books teach us about so many wonderful things. There is so much to find out in books. She breaks down our class time into little sections, so that we never get bored, and she doesn't need too much help from the parents, thank you very much. I think learning to be organized like Mrs. P. is a very good thing to know. My Mom has to be very organized to walk our dog in the morning, take care of me with Grandma, drive two hours to work, work like a horse all day, do Yoga, fly once or twice a month to different places to

---

i   If you want to look at the pictures, you have to buy the book!
ii   This is Mom. Yes. I LOVE having two Mother's Days in one year! Especially the gifts. I love when you bring me breakfast in bed, Samee.

supervise some of the people who work for her company, and still show up for Parents' Association meetings and run the Web site for our school. She is on our school's council, too, which is a lot of work she doesn't get paid for. I want to be organized, too, because it helps you get a lot done.

Sometimes when my Mom travels, my Grandma and I go with her to keep her company. So I have been to a lot of places in the United States: New York, Chicago, San Francisco, San Diego, Phoenix, Scottsdale, and Disneyworld in Florida (we already went to Disneyland in Anaheim, California), where my Mom had to go to a convention. These are all places where the company she works for has schools, and my Mom is in charge of nineteen schools in the United States of America. While my Mom is working during the day, my Grandma looks on the Internet and in newspapers and magazines to see what's happening, and she takes me to museums, and zoos, and aquariums, and all sorts of interesting places. At the aquarium in Chicago, I was picked to stand with the trainers on an island overlooking the dolphin pool and feed the dolphins fish! My Mom could hardly believe it when we told her later. My Grandma could hardly believe she let me do it. I had to say my name, age, and where I came from (Encino, California, of course) into the microphone, and everybody clapped. At night, my Mom, my Grandma, and I went to the theater. We love going to the theater to see things that are okay for kids to see, especially in New York, where I have been a few times now. We love going to the theater in Los Angeles, too.

My Mom says I am an experienced traveler now: taking a plane is like taking a bus. I have my own pink (I used to like everything pink, now I like blue and purple better) suitcase that I pull along on wheels, and I pack lightly with just the things I need. Sometimes we travel on vacation, not work—places like Hawaii, where we went with Uncle Ira, and Auntie Shelley, and Joshua, and Rachel, just for fun. Or Carmel, where we rented a house with our whole family—even Auntie Laura came from Vancouver. On holiday, my Mom can be with me all day, not just after work. So we go to Lake Arrowhead for a week in the winter, and Santa Barbara for a week with the people who went to school at the University of California. My Mom graduated from McGill University in Montreal, but they let her come with the University of California people anyway. The University of California is so beautiful, and, when I am old enough, I will go to university there, or maybe McGill, because it is much cheaper.

It costs so much to go to college that we are saving already. I have money in my piggy bank saved up, almost two hundred dollars, and my Mom puts money every month into a special account for me. I also have a Coogan account (so the money has to be saved for me, not used up by anyone else) because we live near Hollywood, and my Aunt Sue, who is in the toy business, put me in a few commercials. I was really good on the camera and followed directions well, so some agents wanted to sign me up, but my Mom said no, she didn't want me to take time from school, now that I'll soon be in Grade Two, to run around to auditions, and also she didn't think it was good for kids if people chose other kids instead of them. When I was chosen, and Joshua wasn't, he felt bad. So if Auntie Sue or someone who knows me wants ME for a commercial once in a while, that's okay, but I can't go to auditions just so that people can make up their minds whether they want me or not.

So you see, I have a very busy life. Next year I may even go to a Magnet school for very smart kids. I was accepted as qualified, but you can only get in through a lottery because so many people want to go, and there are not enough places. So we don't know yet. My Grandma says it's easier to drive me to the school I'm going to now because it's near our house, so she'll be happier if I don't get in, but if I do get in, she'll drive me there anyway.

My Mom is dating a bit now since it's seven years since I was born, and she didn't date anyone for a couple of years before that, and ten years would be too long to wait to find me a Daddy who could live in our house. We have *very strict* qualifications, though. First of all, he can't be just a nice date who is fun to be with; he has to be someone who likes kids and would make a good father. Secondly, he has to be responsible with money, because my Mom works very hard, and he has to earn money and pitch in. Not a lazy loafer looking for a nice woman with a nice house to support him.

"Right, Mom?" I say. Seven is older than you think.

"Right, Samantha!" She says this, tossing her California-blondy-brown hair in agreement. Her hair has extra blonde streaks that come from the sun.

Thirdly, he has to like our dog. Did you know that Mrs. P. teaches us to make logical speeches with points?

Fourthly, I have to like him.

"Right, Mom?"

"That goes without saying. Otherwise he's out," she says, winking one of the blue-green eyes I get from *her* genes. Everyone says they are beautiful.

I made up the fifth point myself. He has to really, really love my Mom.

So when people ask me—some nosy people do, you know—where my Dad is, or how come I don't have a Daddy, or if I mind not knowing who my Dad is, I toss the wavy brown hair I get from *his* genes. "I never met him, so I don't miss him."

Who can feel the touch of God?
Is it our sleeping child

CRYO KID

caressing once more
the wounded world
with wakened wonder?[2]

◆

PART II

MY TRANSFORMATIONAL FAMILY

"Of course if you like your kids, if you love them from the moment they begin, you yourself begin all over again, in them, with them, and so there is something more to the world again."

—William Saroyen
American Writer (1908-1981)

6

A FAMILY in PROGRESS

The idea of courtly love was introduced by the troubadours in the twelfth century C.E. Then, as intimacy (what we call "personal relationships") gradually replaced obedience, "love conquered marriage" and weakened it as a social institution, according to feminist Stephanie Coontz. "Marriage has changed more in the last thirty years than in the last 3,000," she observes.[1] Also, as life expectancy increases, it seems to be getting harder for some people to contemplate living with one mate for the rest of their lives. "Prior to antibiotics," Barbara Kingsolvers asserts, "no marriage was expected to last many decades—in Colonial days the average couple lived to be married less than twelve years."[2] In more recent centuries, with or without antibiotics, lots of couples have lived to celebrate twenty-fifth and fiftieth anniversaries together.

So many "experts" have written about the family in crisis in Western society, about the decline of family values, perhaps aggravated by changes in the labor market, by the ascendancy of feminists in the work force and in politics, by the wild 1960s, by the availability of the pill and the sexual revolution, by no-fault divorce, and by "our growing sense of entitlement to happiness and safety from abuse,"[3] that it's hard to know which expert to believe. Most of us have some common sense, and as individuals and as families, we learn to adapt.

In tracing family life back to the Stone Age, Coontz writes that "many of the things people now see as unprecedented in family life are not actually new. Stepfamilies, out of wedlock births, even same sex relationships existed throughout human history."[4] Even the Romans complained about their children's outrageous behavior. In modern technological terms, I suppose that one could even argue that the biblical Eve, created from Adam's rib—from a mature cell—was the world's first clone. And that's how the adaptable family life of our species got started.

♦

I've just read over the preceding chapters and realize how well they reflect my family, with everybody butting in and giving their opinion all the time. We're opinionated but informed, full of vim and vigor, and generally happy. When most people meet us for the first time, we do tend to seem a little overwhelming at first and somewhat intrusive in each other's lives. We like it that way, and, after the initial immersion period, most people grow to like us a lot, maybe even love us, because our strongest point is that, as a well-welded unit, we have a lot of love to go around and usually share. I suppose you could call us an alternative family, although people usually use that term to describe homosexual relationships, and that is not the sense of the word that I am using here. My definition of an alternative family is one that differs from the societal norm. It's adaptable.

By now you've understood that this is Grandma speaking. I came of age in the fifties in a middle class family and a middle class neighborhood that was certainly more upper than lower. Most of the breadwinners who lived in the Montreal area called Notre Dame de Grace (usually abbreviated as NDG and referred to affectionately as "No Damn Good") were established professionals or businessmen. As the children of immigrants, they had already attained considerable upward mobility in their generation. Participating in the rituals of an extended family and continuing the upward rise was the expectation. These were our parents, and as the children of these parents, we NDGers anticipated that we would emerge even better educated than our parents from the prestigious universities available to us in the same city, fall in love and marry partners in the same social strata, and live close to our parents when we did. I wonder if any of us anticipated the changes that were to take place in one generation.

I do not belong to the angry boomer generation who believed that every value their parents had taught them was swept away when Jack Kennedy was assassinated, who agonized that Camelot was over, and boasted that a new morality would prevail. In 1963, I was already married with two small children and twins in my belly at the age of twenty-seven before the advent of "the pill" in Canada, and so I was not part of: the sexual revolution, Woodstock, pot and LSD, refusing to attend university graduation ceremonies because degrees no longer meant anything, jeans *uber alles*, civil rights demonstrations, and backpacking to Europe and India. Indeed, I wept when these kids, only a few years older than me, asserted that anyone over thirty could not be trusted.

But still, I was involved to a large degree in the generational transformation that occurred then (the Baby Boomers, with my own kids at the tail end, pronouncing themselves the majority that counts through every decade). It continued into the next generation (the disillusioned Gen Xers, unemployable in a decade without jobs, as the Broadway play, *Rent*, evidenced), and the next (the Gen Y kids, my grandchildren, already tagged the ADHD—Attention Deficit Disorder—generation). The sweeping changes that take place within a generation are now closer to a decade than the quarter of a century a generation traditionally represented.

*   *   *   *

Species that don't adapt die out, like the dinosaurs. I still remember my amazement when I discovered, some thirty-five years ago, that the province of Alberta had badlands similar to the badlands in the United States.

"I didn't know that there was a semi-desert in Canada," I remember exclaiming at the time. It was 1972. I bought a fragment of ancient dinosaur bone, sold as a pendant at the lone small gift shop for an incredible dollar and a half. Once, so long ago, these lands were swamps frequented by dinosaurs. Now archeologists search the dry bed sites for their remains and exchange information about them with China, which apparently has a similar regional geography to explore. Even geography changes over geologic time. You adapt, you change, or you die. That is the lesson of life.

In our century, in an era of accelerating innovation that we already take for granted, mere change—even discovery—has become ubiquitous. Take the realm of biology. When we turn on the news over morning coffee, National Public Radio (NPR) informs us that one hundred and eighty million years ago, a genetic divergence occurred between placental mammals (animals that carry and nourish their young for a long gestational period inside their bodies, as humans do, and bear live babies) and marsupials (animals like kangaroos and opossums whose tiny live babies complete the gestational process in pouches outside their body). Apparently, scientists have newly discovered that the vast majority of evolutionary innovations occur not in the invention of new genes (regulated by the DNA, the musical notes of the body) but through regulations (like on and off switches) in the genes by "transposons" (similar to composers who orchestrate the notes).[5]

It took a long, long time for this divergence that occurred in the age of dinosaurs to develop. Today we expect change to occur non-stop, like clicking the remote to instant images on multiple channels. Do you remember when smart cards to unlock hotel room doors were amazing innovations? Now, in the realm of medicine, there are smart drugs that know what to do when they get into your system, and we're not even surprised to hear about them.

In his astonishing book, *The Singularity Is Near,* Ray Kurzweil explains that in this twenty-first century, change is occurring exponentially, at a much faster rate than in previous centuries.[6] He envisions a time in the not too distant future when biological intelligence will be far out-stripped by artificial intelligence (nanotechnology), and when the distinctions between humans and computers will become blurred. As what was once science fiction becomes fact, human beings will be able to transcend their biology to accomplish things we have not yet imagined, although Kurzweil does an amazing job of predicting what was formerly thought impossible.

My friend, Jeremy—a former mathematics professor and an avid chess player—who first worked with computers when mainframes occupied a whole room, is a skeptic. While the great strengths of computers are calculation, speed, and the fact that they never forget, he says, they lack judgment, and in 2007 at any rate, they still need humans to program them.[i] "Does a computer that wins at chess know that it is playing chess?" Jeremy asks.[ii]

I have more faith in humanity—and in Kurzweil's predictions—than Jeremy, and I am prepared to let my computer's capabilities astound me. There are always those who will subvert the new technologies to evil intent— pornography, criminal actions, hate, terror—but I truly believe that brilliant men and women globally will fulfill their potential to use technologies as yet undiscovered to benefit our world. Who believed that so many of the far-out predictions of visionaries like H.G. Wells, Orwell, or Evelyn Waugh would come to be? Or that the still televised, fictional voyages of *Star Trek* contained in them the glimmer of possibility? In the comic books I devoured as a kid, Flash Gordon sported a lazar gun and Dick Tracy a two-way wrist radio. Comic book heroes traveled in space—marvelous, unattainable fantasies born in the minds of artists!

Recently I attended a Los Angeles art exhibition where one of the artists had created an avian alphabet (the characters appeared to be Asian) with collected, fragile bird bones. Each letter of the alphabet had a musical equivalent, so that the bones could be transformed into a computerized musical scale that played a song. Another artist had meticulously built thousands of miniscule

---

i   Just a minute, Jeremy. It's Grandma's computer here. Why are you dissing my technological species? Don't you realize that I can beat you at chess anytime, anywhere?

ii   Duh! You're underestimating me because I'm a computer, not a human. It's not about how you play the game; it's about winning or losing. I'm a winner, Jeremy. I'll never forget you.

mice bones (gathered from dead mice and boiled to prevent infection!) into the shape of a tornado captured in an hour glass. It sounds gruesome, yet her visual portrayal of the connectedness of all living things was incredibly moving.[7] This was transformation, alright—was it art? Science? They are exponentially blending, too.

Societally, we are not just changing; we are transforming into something else, and, like the bird bones, transcending what we were, and whether it is "better" than what we have been remains to be seen. I think that something similar is happening with families. It seems to me that "alternative" or "nontraditional" have ceased to be terms precise enough to describe families outside what used to be the social "norm," because a transformational factor is in progress, and we don't know yet where it will lead. So when I think of my family and the changes we have undergone together, I don't think of it as alternative or nontraditional any more, but rather as transformational. We are a transformational family that has left the nuclear age of families behind, but the way we once thought of extended families ties has also changed. We are a family in progress, in the process of transcending what we were before.

*   *   *   *

My friend, Jeremy, who is also a widower, doesn't know what I'm talking about. "I was married for forty years and never divorced. My two daughters are married and were never divorced. Your facts are correct, but your interpretation of them is different than mine." Did I mention that Jeremy is very conservative? His family group definitely falls in the traditional "forty-nine percent married" category, and one of his daughters prefers to be a stay-at-home mother with a part-time job. However, for the life of these traditional marriages, as their jobs took them to various places, both generations— Jeremy, his late wife, and his daughters—have lived as nuclear families in cities far removed from their extended families. They have seen one another rarely. So, even though he doesn't recognize that his family has already departed from the patterns of his grandparents, and that the other half (fifty-one percent) of people in the United States live in non-traditional patterns, his family has also started the process of transformation, in this case, because of the distances that separate them.

Increasing inter-religious/inter-cultural blending is a major factor to take into account in the transformational process overtaking families today. The homogeneous religious backgrounds that traditional American families (whether Catholic, Protestant, Greek Orthodox, Mormon, Muslim, or Buddhist) used to embrace not so long ago are rapidly fading into the past.[8]

When I was growing up, "nice" Jewish girls were admonished by their parents not to date gentile boys, although, with the usual double standard, a blind eye was turned to Jewish boys who sowed their wild oats with blond and blue-eyed *shikses* (the *Yiddish* word means "outsider") with up-turned noses—as long as they didn't marry them. This was understood and deeply resented by the brothers of these *shikses* who knew what was going on in the back of the car. Today approximately two-thirds of Jewish people who get married in the United States, Europe, and South America choose a non-Jewish spouse.[9] Increasingly, families are blending.

So what is traditional, what is nontraditional? Who can tell anymore? We are in a transformative period. Who knows where this transformation will take us? It is uncharted territory, and the possibilities can be challenging, exciting, and potentially positive. Unlike my friend, Jeremy, who believes that societal change is usually for the worse, I am an optimist. I stand with those who refused to believe the earth is flat and instead discovered the New World.

Surprisingly, Europeans are ahead of Americans when it comes to familial transformation. Criticizing people who don't get married because they prefer the single life, conservative former Massachusetts governor Mitt Romney (a presidential candidate for the 2008 U.S. elections) was quoted by the *Washington Post*: "In France, for instance, I'm told that marriage is more frequently contracted in seven-year terms where either party may move on when their term is up. How shallow and how different from Europe of the past."[10] Ah, to be "ahead," or not to be "ahead": that is the question.

But the past is the past. I think that my friend, Jeremy, like many others, is in a state of denial. Transformation is occurring at many levels in the Western world. As Barbara Kingsolver puts it so cogently, "Divorce, remarriage, single parenthood, gay parents, and blended families simply are. They're facts of our time."[11] For better or worse, concepts of family are in the process of being reshaped. It's an ongoing process, just like geology or biology or technology.

◆

7

THE LAND of REFUGE

Concepts of love and marriage have evolved for centuries and over civilizations. For the ancient Greeks, marriage had to do with social organization and procreation. Love was a bond that largely existed between men. Unlike the father seahorse, though, Greek men did not get pregnant. That was left to the women.

The Greeks divided love into four abstract categories that included a very wide range of feelings. Each of these categories had a special name.[1]

Eros was the name for passionate love, what we would call romantic love today. The accompanying carnal desire was hopefully so intense that it would evolve into an appreciation of the inner beauty of the loved one. The second name for love, *Philia*, is interpreted as friendship in contemporary times, but, for Aristotle, it was a dispassionate love that included loyalty to family, friends, and community. *Agape* (which still means "love" in modern Greek) involves the element of self-sacrifice. It refers to a spiritual kind of love.

What about the love we feel for our families? That's what *Storge* is all about, the natural affection parents feel for children and family relationships.

All four of these elements of love are mixed into the history of my family's relationships—and most likely yours. Romantic love brought my grandparents together in another land. As friends committed loyally to one another, they had the courage to leave their persecuted communities behind. It was hope for their children-to-be that propelled them to emigrate to this continent. Here, with considerable self-sacrifice, they built a better life in a land of refuge.

◆

Even though life is longer than it used to be, it's still too short, and there's so much I want to share with you while I'm here. You guessed it! It's still Grandma telling her tale. Like many other families, my family *is* what it is. A nontraditional family. A fact of life. How did it get that way? I guess it was a process, but it certainly wasn't intentional. You wouldn't have guessed it from my grandparents on both sides of the family, although, like countless immigrants to North America, all four of them had the courage to "get up and go" in response to persecution in their homelands. In this case, the land of refuge was Canada.

My maternal grandfather, Joseph (*Yossel*) Freedman, a Jewish Pole born in Warsaw, was always proud to say that he had survived being pressed into service in the army of the Russian Czar, and a photograph of him wearing bristling mustachios and a sword always adorned my grandparents' living room. When he was stationed near Odessa, he chanced upon my angelic-looking grandmother, Rachel—one of my grandchildren is named after her—blond and blue-eyed, with a song ever on her lips, waiting on customers in her father's store and immediately fell in love. He married her and swept her away to Canada as soon as they could, where she arrived with one babe already in her arms at the age of seventeen. It was 1903, when continuing pogroms in Poland and Russia brought ever-increasing waves of immigrants from Eastern Europe to Canada and the United States.

My grandfather always considered himself extremely fortunate to have been brought to Montreal by his half-brother, Philip, an entrepreneurial spirit who had already made a lot of money in the New World. Whenever Uncle Philip, with his patrician demeanor and well-tailored clothes, entered my grandparents' home, they greeted him like royalty. Nothing was too good for Philip; they would be forever grateful. Together the half-brothers managed to get the rest of the family—parents, sisters—out of harm's way in the old country and settled in the new land.

Like Philip, my grandfather was highly intelligent and very well read in *Yiddish* and secular literature, although he prided himself on being both an atheist and a socialist and denied his sons *bar-mitzvahs*. As an urban Warsaw Jew, he considered himself way above the Russian "peasants" who were his fellow immigrants, but nevertheless was very active in the Russian-Polish Society and a founder of the Russian-Polish cemetery, in which all the members of my family were subsequently buried. At work, where his superb tailoring and, later, designing skills were highly prized, he was a labor organizer to contend with, and very well respected in both the Jewish and gentile communities. Often, he would be playing cards with a priest who reached into the dark folds of his robe to produce an apple for me whenever I visited my grandfather.

My grandfather's passion was education, and he worked eighteen-hour days and scrimped and saved for years to send four, first-generation children to college. The family lived for years in a run-down neighborhood to save on rent money and use it for education instead. In order to prevent his children from contact with the low life elements that inhabited the near-by dwellings, my grandfather did not allow his children to play outside—my mother would tell me stories of hearing detectives run over the roofs at night and the sound of gunshots. The four children went to school and came home. No one ever circumvented my grandfather's orders because his temper was legendary. "It's because he's Polish," the Russian Jews would explain. (Later, he could be cantankerous with his grandchildren, too, kicking my cousin, Alan, but for some reason he liked me. "Here, *Corele*," he would say, using the *Yiddish* diminutive, "here's two cents. Buy an ice cream cone." It was then, indeed, two cents.)

My sweet-tempered grandmother always supported my grandfather in his educational aims. When one of my uncles came home from university to announce that he was quitting, she hit him with a broom until he went back. She insisted on having few things her way, but, despite my grandfather's atheistic dictums, she always maintained a traditionally religious home, keeping kosher laws, and making sure that the children had instruction in the Jewish religion and Hebrew language. In her first years in Canada, she had no one to help her with her quickly growing brood of children and would tie the younger ones to chairs while she ran downstairs to buy milk and other necessities at a neighborhood store.

Sometimes her sister, Dora (*Dobbe*) and her children visited, or her sister Annie, who was much pitied as an *aguna* (a woman whose husband leaves her but does not grant her a Jewish divorce—a *get*—so that, under Jewish law, she cannot remarry). My gentle great-grandmother, *Chaya*, for whom I was named but never met, as she died before I was born, was often at my grandmother's home as well. Although my grandmother was very quiet when my grandfather was home, during his hours at work, she filled the house with her melodious singing. She knew hundreds of songs but never had the chance to fulfill her musical talent. There was only one thing that she ardently desired: for her children to have a good life in the new land. And they did. The immigrant Freedman family produced a doctor, a lawyer, a teacher, and an accountant, all of whom took very good care of their parents throughout their lives.

The other dominant force of my grandparents' home life was culture. All the children inherited my grandmother's musical talent and learned to play a musical instrument extraordinarily well. My Aunt Sylvia's singing voice was magnificent enough for the concert stage (my grandfather tore up the contract, her prize when she secretly won a singing contest; my aunt lost her hair the next day, and it didn't grow back for a year), and my mother inherited my grandfather's artistic talent. My grandfather always made beautifully tailored clothes for his children, gorgeous dresses for the two girls, often pieced skillfully together from fine materials he salvaged from the creations he sewed at work. He taught them to love fabrics, to love good things, but he did not allow my mother to exhibit her paintings (she used a pseudonym throughout her life) and tried to persuade her to become a fashion designer in the needle trade (actually it would have been a happy choice for my mother), but, as he had taught her, she aspired to finer things and became a teacher instead. One of my mother's driving forces was to elevate her life, and she continually practiced the refinements she later taught me.

My parents and I lived with my grandparents for a short time during the Great Depression (by that time my grandparents lived in an upgraded district on St. Joseph Boulevard, but the apartment was still above a series of stores). I played downstairs with the kind of wooden soldier sign that is a collectable today but was then standing in front of the cigar store. He was my only friend.

During that time, my grandmother would take a shot glass of whiskey after dinner each night, her *hartz* (heart) medicine, she called it, and then she would wax loquacious, put her finger to her lips, and show me the little purse she kept hidden in her bosom. "A woman has to have a *bombe* (a nest egg)," she would instruct me. At other times, she would give me a hard candy and say, "It's good to have something in *der moil* (the mouth)." Other dictums were, "If you're *foil* (lazy), you have nothing to eat." There was always something cooking in my grandmother's house. Although she would often converse with my mother in *Yiddish*, she was firm on one thing: "it's the new country; we must speak to *Corele* only in *Anglish*." (Years later, she was still surprised when the waiter brought her pizza pie instead of what she thought she was ordering: a piece of pie.) Her inspired concept of God as a benign deity—God will understand"—influenced me all my life.[2] I loved my beautiful, serene grandmother. Her hair was always pulled back neatly into a bun, and Samantha, who never knew her, inherited her dramatic widow's peak. When I married, my grandmother was at my Friday night table every week.

My paternal grandparents were a different kettle of fish. I never got to know them or my father's brothers and sisters very well because my mother thought they were all "common," and, by the time I was born, refused to visit them. Although my Dad visited his parents regularly, I accompanied him only from time to time. Like my mother's parents, Isaac (*Yitzhak*) and Celia (*Tzipporah*) Copnick, had emigrated from Eastern Europe. They came from a rural area of the (at that time) Russian Ukraine near Kiev, and perhaps that's why my father always had a touch of farmer in his soul and loved to plant and tend a vegetable garden.

When his parents immigrated—my grandmother was fifteen when they married—they were first sent, but never knew why, to Carleton Place, Ontario, where my Dad was born. Their arrival was chiefly memorable for my grandfather's renaming: when the Irish immigration inspector asked my grandfather's name, he replied with the Russian pronunciation, *Hacupnik*, and the inspector transliterated it as O'Copnick. There is still a Toronto branch of the family that calls itself Ocopnick, but my father changed his name from Issie (short for Israel) O'Copnick to Irving Copnick at the request of the Dean when my father graduated from McGill University in Dentistry. The Dean thought it a more appropriate name for a McGill graduate, and so Irving Copnick, D.D.S., is the name that appears on his graduation certificate.

Since all the *landzman* that my grandparents knew from the old country had been allocated to Montreal, they managed to move to the *Papineau* area of Montreal some three years after my father's birth. Here my grandfather started a small farm to meet the family's needs and established a junk business. Today it would be referred to as a scrap metal or recycling business, and indeed it is, because a friend of my father's purchased it after World War II for next to nothing and made a fortune with it. At any rate, in my father's youth, my grandfather had a horse and wagon—later it would become a truck proudly marked "I. Copnick Reg'd"—and with it, he managed to support his large family of eight children. My father often joined him on the truck, and, from my grandfather, developed the people skills and genuine interest in everyone he met that marked his life.

Isaac and Celia's home never lacked for food, and there were always big bowls of fruit and cake set out when we visited. Two of their children died in infancy, as did many babies at that time, so my father ended up with two older brothers, Dan and Joe, and three sisters, Rose, Annie, and Mary, all of whom made it through high school. Only my father had the motivation to go to university. Except for Mary, who had a sad life, the sisters married men who made good money and produced children who were educated and upwardly mobile.

My second daughter Shelley is named after Celia (*Tzipporah* means little bird, and, indeed, she was a dainty little bird of a woman). Although my paternal grandmother was already blinded by diabetes (insulin had not yet been discovered, so the treatment consisted of eating as little as possible), what I chiefly recall about her was her cleanliness and her dignity—even when she was dying, she managed to tie up her silvery hair with bright little ribbons—and the way she and my grandfather walked hand-in-hand like two lovers who had never lost their romantic feeling for one another.

Like my father, my grandfather was an extremely handsome man with a thick shock of very white hair and bright blue eyes under bushy eyebrows. Well over six feet, he towered over my Dad, who was short, like his mother's family. Although *Zaideh* Isaac wasn't educated, he revered knowledge, and the fact that I could read books beyond my years. I still treasure a fine, leather-bound but incomplete, set of Shakespeare's works that he salvaged from the junk he purchased and gave to me. In his inarticulate way, he tried to show that he understood how difficult were my father's efforts to rise, unaided by any-one, above the educational level of his family. Rather than supporting his efforts, my father's brothers mocked him for going to school instead of mak-ing decent money, and his sisters unconcernedly drew with crayons on his term papers.

My grandfather was an amazing physical specimen, but soon after he was hit by a truck one snowy day, he suffered pains in his chest. I watched my father bending over him with concern as *Zaideh* motioned to his chest and kept repeating in *Yiddish*, "It hurts me here." He lingered for a while but then suffered a massive heart attack. When he passed away, *Tzippe* lost her will to live. "*Der longe nacht, der longe nacht*," she murmured over and over on the night she died. She believed fervently that Elijah would come on a chariot to carry her to her beloved *Yitzhak*, and she could not wait to join him.

As a matter of fact, my father probably inherited the mystical aspect of his personality from his mother. Part of his *Papineau* experience was his immer-sion, encouraged by his mother, in the life of the orthodox synagogues there. The white (*weisse*) *shul* (or so it was popularly called) served the immigrant White Russians (elitists) and the red (*roite*) *shul* served the immigrant Red Russians (the workers). My Dad had a natural poetic affinity for languages (he ended up speaking eight of them, several with fluency, including conversa-tional Latin), something he acquired from the beauty of the Hebrew language and letters and the imagery of the Bible. After his *bar mitzvah*, he served as a Torah reader at both the opposing *shuls*, running from one to the other.

These were the families in which both my parents grew up, the families that shaped them. In a sense, like all immigrants, they were transformational families, too. They were parented by people who had the courage of youth to leave a situation they could not accept behind them, and to strive with all their might to make a better world for the children they would bring into it.

*   *   *   *

Drawing on the legacy of the White and Red *shuls*, the wholesome farm in *Papineau*, the instinctive love of people that his own father imparted to him, the mystical beliefs of his mother, and the formal education he acquired by "pulling himself up by the bootstraps," my father grew up to be an extraordinarily kind man, so filled with goodness that when I mention his name to anyone who knew him, they draw in a quick breath and sigh reverently, "O-h-h, Irving. I loved him. He was such a good man." He imparted to me his belief in a chain of goodness: "if you do something kind for someone," he would tell me, "one day they will do something kind for someone else, and that's how the chain grows." He also taught me about the ancient Jewish legend of the *'lamed vavs*, that if there are only thirty-six just men in the corners of the world (the pillars of society that hold it up, I suppose), the world will always be all right.

My Dad was a man who acted upon his beliefs. He was extraordinarily caring to his patients, often making a house call to an elderly patient, even though he was a dentist, not a doctor. During the depression, my father's office was in our home, and, after my Dad passed away, I wrote a story (excerpted here) about an incident I witnessed as a little girl.[3]

> *Although he was very proud of his surgical skills, what I remember most about my father was his compassion. Quite simply, he cared about his patients. He was the kind of dentist who brought morning tea and toast to a disabled patient he was worried about. Once I saw him give back money to a black woman who paid him in handkerchief-wrapped dimes and quarters.*
>
> *"You'll pay me when you have a little more money," he said softly. And when his patients didn't have any in those depression days, they could bring some bread or home-baked cake or garden peas—or a chicken.*
>
> *I was just a little girl in 1939, but I remember playing with toys in my father's waiting room. I remember watching the stream of dental patients come with food and go out with fillings. I remember the incredulous screams of joy that, even to*

a child who didn't understand about miracles yet, signaled something momentous was taking place in my father's office.

As I peeked in the doorway, I could see that an elderly woman who had come with a chicken was sitting in the dental chair. Tears were streaming down her cheeks ... My father stood beside her, transfixed....

"You can see?" he asked in a hushed tone.

"I can see, I can see," the woman smiled through her tears. "Oh, dear God, I can see!"

... To go to a dentist cost money she couldn't afford, and she had waited and waited until she couldn't bear the pain [of the agonizing toothache] any more. How could one little tooth hurt so much? ... The tooth had been pressing on an optic nerve—for all of the several years the woman had been unable to see. In my father's dental chair, as the tooth was removed, as the pressure on the nerve was taken away, she began to see ... that the world was a wondrous place where miracles can happen. And that there were people like my father in it.

It was not long after this incident that my father began to feed his family (now there was my sister) with a monthly check from the army. And in the newsletter printed by the Canadian army in Canada, and also in England where my father was stationed during World War II, a poem that he wrote appeared. The poem was called, "Why hurt, little tooth?" It didn't mention the elderly lady. It didn't mention the miracle. I was only a little girl, but even I knew that the little tooth didn't hurt any more.

*　　*　　*　　*

When my father met my mother, for him it was not only the depths of the Great Depression, it was also love at first sight. My mother wasn't sure. It was 1932. She had just returned from a summer "grand" tour of Europe with the graduating class of Macdonald College, a teacher's college affiliated with McGill University, and where she was one of two or three Jewish girls in the class. At Macdonald College, she had worn a plaid kilt and green blazer and acquired the niceties that would stay with her for the rest of her life. She longed for culture, finesse, gentility. Her teacher's trip to Europe (in Germany, where Hitler's star was rising, the Jewish girls on the tour were not permitted to attend several parties but did not understand why, and my mother continued to happily sketch castles on the Rhine) remained one of the peak experiences of her life.

When she met my Dad, my ambitious mother had already rejected several suitors, one of whom made her heart beat fast, and she regretted it when he married her best friend, but now, with her trip to Europe behind her, she was twenty-three, getting late for a girl of that era to be unwed. And my father was a professional, good looking, kind-hearted, full of fun. Although he was poor, the potential was good, so they began to "see" one another. I don't believe she was ever "in love" with him, but it was impossible not to love my father, and she did grow fond of him as they got to know one another. For him, she was the passion of his life. As a young girl, I would watch him gaze at her. "Mother is so beautiful," he would say. "She has such pearly teeth."

At any rate, in the fall of 1932, with certification from teacher's college, my mother was looking for a job with the Protestant School Board (unless they went to costly parochial school, Jewish children were accepted by the Protestant School Board as "others;" the Catholic schools would not let them in). There were none to be had for inexperienced teachers and less than none for Jewish teachers. So my spunky mother, realizing she wouldn't get a job without teaching experience, opted to accept a job as the sole teacher in a rural school in Sault Ste. Marie, considerably north of Montreal. Here, for a whole year, she taught eight grades in one room—no small task for a first time teacher—lived with one of the rural families who offered her adequate country style accommodation, and put up with the miserable winter. And she thought about accepting my father's marriage proposal.

In 1933, she accepted with alacrity the job that now opened for her in the city, and she also agreed to marry my Dad. There was, however, a hitch. Married female teachers were not permitted to teach at the Protestant School Board. In a time of severe unemployment, it was thought that they would be taking a job away from a man who needed to support his family. My mother, however, needed the job to support my father who was entering his last year of dentistry with insufficient funds to complete it. So they married secretly on May 27, 1933, and she continued to teach at Mount Royal School, a poor, mainly Jewish, immigrant area in Montreal, with fifty-eight students in her class and without anyone knowing that she had a husband, until my presence in her tummy became apparent, and she had to quit teaching. I was born on a wintry day in 1936.

With her abundant creative gifts and love of learning, my mother was a born teacher. She reveled in her teaching and bought the children milk with her own pocket money. Many years later in her early nineties, when she had dementia, she would relive the scenes of her classroom aloud over and over again.

"I was *little* Miss Freedman," she would say, her face radiant with the memory. "Not *big* Miss Freedman because they didn't like *her*. *I* was the one they loved."

She found motherhood less satisfying, but she tried very hard. In some ways, she was born two generations before her time. In other ways, though, she was still very much a woman of her generation, especially in regard to the relationships between men and women. When my father, driven both by the ideological goal of fighting against Hitler and by his inability to support his family with hard cash in the heart of the depression, enlisted in the army, my mother reacted with terror to the news that he would be sent overseas. She literally swooned at the thought of being left alone with two little children. My father carried her into the living room and closed the door, so, of course, I don't know what was said between them.

I do remember standing with my father at the window in his office. He lifted the Venetian blind and held me in his arms to watch the troops marching in the street below. "I'll be wearing a uniform like that," he said.

Nevertheless, during the years my father was stationed in England, my mother felt deeply shamed. She worried as much that "people" would think he had run away from her as she did about his safety, and instilled in me the mantras: "people don't treat you well when you're a woman alone;" or, "men try to take advantage of you when you're a woman alone;" or, "a woman is nothing without a man."

At night and on the weekends, she played the piano to assuage her loneliness, and my mother, my baby sister, and I would sing the lyrics of the day from sheet music: "I'll walk alone, because to tell you the truth I'll be lonely. I don't mind being lonely, if only you are lonely, too."[4] After my sister and I went to bed, she was beset by the terror of being alone, and would wake me with a plea: "sit with me a while, Corinne. Let's have a cup of tea." At five, six, seven years old, I would sit up long hours with my mother at night, make her a cup of tea to allay her fears until, at last, both of us could go to sleep.

Sometimes my Uncle Fritz (so nicknamed in childhood after the mischievous boy in the comic strip, *The Katzenjammer Kids*, would come over and talk to her, calm her down. "Goitee (Gertie) is noivous (nervous)," my *Bubbe* Rachel would explain to me.

Her son, Uncle Fritz (his real name was Hyman Michael), was a doctor. On some weekends, he would take me for nature walks, turn over caterpillars, and show me their myriad legs. Despite his own family and busy schedule, he tried to be a substitute father as much as he could. I loved him dearly as long as he lived. Sometimes he would take me for a drive in the rumble seat—an extra seat where the trunks of cars are today—of his car or take me along with him on his round of house calls. I waited in the car while he went in briefly to see his patients.

"Don't touch me," he would caution when he emerged from one run-down house after another. "They didn't have any running water." That's how I learned that, although we certainly didn't have any money to spare, some people were really poor.

Weekends were the best. My mother would count her pennies, and I would return glass bottles for two cents each to the grocery store. Then we would figure out if we had enough money to get across town to my Aunt Sylvia and Uncle Moe's home in Outremont for Saturday afternoon.

"Hmm," my mother would calculate. "We have enough to take the streetcar, or we have enough to walk and buy a chocolate milkshake at Woolworth's halfway. We'll still have enough to ride home. What do you think?"

Of course my sister and I would opt for the milkshake, and we sang songs lustily as we rhythmically marched all the way to our aunt and uncle's home. "Left (marching step), left (marching step), left, right, left, my father got drunk and packed his trunk and left...."

Once we got to my aunt and uncle's home, where my grandparents lived in an adjacent apartment, we had a great time. We would have lunch and busy conversation over the dining room table and then adjourn to the living room around the grand piano. My aunt sang, my uncle accompanied (he was an accomplished musician, all by ear since he had never learned to read music), and my four cousins played their various instruments superbly—Nathan on piano, Terry on accordion, Lenny on oboe, and David on clarinet. They gave youthful, award-winning concerts as "The Four Rosens." And we all sang, especially the canary. On such occasions, my aunt's canary, released from its cage, would perch on the grand piano beside her and warble in accompaniment while she sang. My mother painted the canary. It was a grand occasion indeed. Meanwhile, in England the bombs fell.

The army dentists helped the doctors with reconstructive surgery (facial, jaws) and with identification of victims (teeth), and, in the midst of the blitz in London, my father did much of his work in a mobile van. Although the van's top was marked with a red cross, the Germans shot at it from the air despite the Geneva Conventions. The driver jumped out to save himself, and the van rolled over into a ditch with my father locked in the dental unit inside. He suffered a back injury that plagued him for the rest of his life. My Dad spent his last six months in England as a patient in an army hospital.

He returned, though, to find that my mother had not only scrimped and saved from his army salary to pay off their debts but had also beautifully—within their limited means—furnished a four-room apartment to receive him. (Our rent at the apartment building on *boulevard Décarie*, two short blocks from Snowdon Junction, where the streetcar lines met and were demolished when the *Décarie* freeway was built, was fifty-two dollars per month). In the morning, my Dad would rest on the sofa in the living room, which was separated from the rest of the apartment by double glass doors, and my mother would whisper to my sister and me, "Don't disturb Daddy. He is not feeling well."

As he reestablished his dental practice in Canada (we scorned the manufacturers who had grown rich with "war" money, while my father and others like him had gone overseas to protect them), my father remained deeply concerned about the Jewish children—and their mothers, if they had any—who had survived the Holocaust but still languished in displaced persons camps. Israel had not yet declared independence. The Arabs—and the appeasing British (who then held the mandate over Palestine)—were preventing the Jewish survivors from entering that land. Nor did other countries open their arms to receive them.[5]

In 1946, my Dad became active in a clandestine movement, mostly made up of men who had served patriotically in World War II, to help these survivors get to Palestine. My father would listen to the short wave radio he kept in his bedroom to find out through a coded message when a boat would arrive. Young volunteers from across Canada passed through our home for dinner—I always knew when a young man was coming because my mother made coconut-dipped, baked apples for dessert. My father would inform them and place the young men on the ship. Although their role was strictly defensive—to protect the women and children on their way to the Holy Land, they were each given a weapon for that purpose. Many of the ships were diverted to Cyprus by the British authorities, but some of them made it to their destination.

Once the Royal Canadian Mounted Police came to search our house. They were looking for weapons. Quickly my mother whispered to my sister and me to sit on the toy chest. "Play cards," she instructed, and, while the police searched our recreation room in the basement, we happily played cards. My little sister did not know, of course, that guns had been placed overnight in the toy chest, but I knew—I had long known that some things cannot be spoken—and while the police were searching, my heart beat so hard in my chest that I was sure they could hear it. My parents never permitted guns to be stored in our house again, but, to this day, I dislike playing cards.

A number of war orphans were allowed into Canada through the intervention of various Jewish agencies. For a couple of years, we temporarily "adopted" four sisters who refused to be separated, and had indeed promised their parents, who were sent to the death camps, that they would never be separated. It proved impossible to place all four of them together, so, in the interim, the girls spent every weekend with our family. We showed them the sights and helped them adjust to Canadian life. Finally, when Naomi, the eldest sister, turned eighteen, she accepted an offer of marriage from an elderly Jewish man who was willing to take in all four sisters. She sacrificed her youth to keep her promise to her parents. In return, he treated them all very well and provided them with a fine education. One of the sisters, Rebecca, became a well known Canadian ballerina. Another became a lawyer. All of them became mothers.

In those initial years after the war, most North Americans did not really understand the traumatic events Holocaust survivors had gone through, could not comprehend why the sisters insisted on staying together, when each of them could have been adopted into a good home separately. When, at my mother's behest, I showed Naomi how to use a lipstick, how to shave her underarms, how shallow she must have thought we all were! My father replaced all her silver front teeth with natural-looking, North American substitutes. He, along with other Jewish men who had been "overseas," did understand what Naomi had experienced, and many of them became heavily involved in supporting Israel's struggle for independence.

As soon as they could, my parents had, by the skin of their teeth, purchased their very first home, a stone cottage on Hingston Avenue in a lovely area next to the tennis courts (and adjacent to the upscale area called Hampstead, because, even after the war, a gentleman's agreement in Hampstead prevented Jewish children from attending their schools) that I thought was paradise. It was 1948, and I was twelve years old when we moved in. My sister and I ran up and down the stairs all day long in blissful freedom. Mrs. Smith-the-terrifying-neighbor-downstairs was no longer there to bang on the ceiling with her broom or harangue us on the stairs if we made too much noise in our apartment. The war was over, and like the rest of the world we were *free* and *together*. I had my *own room*. The house was so large in my memory that when I revisited it years later, I could not believe that it was so much smaller.

Nevertheless, in the little living room and dining room of that charming house, for all the teenage years of my growing up, dedicated Zionists gathered often, loudly debating the pros and cons for *Eretz Yisroel*, the National Home for the Jews, and artists sipped coffee while they outlined passionately their artistic points of view. Everywhere there were idealists of one kind or another happily arguing at the tops of their voices. The musicians in our family played the piano with *brio*, and soon we were belting out happier songs than the wartime songs we sang when my father was away, and my mother was alone: "Cruising down the river on a Sunday afternoon. With one you love, the sun above, waiting for the moon. The two of us together ..."[6]

◆

8

THE MOMMY TRACK

It took a long time for religious views of love to move from pre-biblical, pagan attachment to natural objects to the devotion to an abstract God that was the monotheistic basis of Judaism and later Christianity.[1]

The Bible suggests that God is the ultimate love, and that love between man and a woman is the re-creation of that love, so that marriage becomes a sacred covenant rather than merely a contract between a man and a woman. "Place me like a seal over your heart, like a seal on your arm," exults the Song of Songs, praising the ideal of marriage in the Old Testament; "for love is as strong as death, its jealousy unyielding as the grave. Many waters cannot quench love; rivers cannot wash it away." [2]

Do we choose our own routes to love, or do our paths choose us?

♦

CRYO KID

My daughter Janet tells me that the family in which I grew up was definitely different from other families in our neighborhood, a little kooky perhaps. I suppose that is true, but it wasn't the kind of difference, say, that makes your family different when you reply, "Yes, I'd like some grapes," and your parents offer you a burstingly ripe bunch that is probably a quarter of a pound, while your friend Martha's Anglo parents up the street give you four drying grapes as an act of generosity.

On Sundays, I avoided the home of my friend, Lorna, because her strict Baptist father wouldn't let us go to the movies, play music, or do almost anything we wanted to do. Instead he would inveigle his daughters' friends to pose for his "art" photography since, apparently, his beliefs did not prevent him from taking pictures on Sundays of adolescent girls in the buff from the waist up, thinly shrouded in transparent veils. "The human body is beautiful," he would assure us. I sensed that there was something out of synch about it, something sneakily different from the creative atmosphere that freely prevailed in my parents' home. So what is the difference that makes a family so different they are beyond the norm?

In my family, I proudly, if reluctantly (I'd rather read a book), posed nude for my mother's canvases because that was *art*, and our bathroom's magazine rack held art books filled with representations of magnificent paintings, including nudes. (It also held a volume called *The Wisdom of Israel*.) That's where I learned about painters and sculptors from Michaelangelo to Renoir to Chagall to Picasso, as well as by osmosis from all the artists that frequented my parental home, who grabbed me to pose whenever they could, and from the museums and art galleries my mother routinely took me to where I absorbed the paintings—memorized them, in fact—and realized at a tender age that all life is art.

At my childhood home, you were likely to find linseed oil lined up with the food in the refrigerator, turpentine in the sugar bowl, and paint brushes in the bread box (remember bread boxes, to keep the bread fresh?). I did, however, resent my mother's artistic temperament because you never knew when her high-strung emotional balance was likely to explode. When it did, I hid in my room, losing myself in books until the storm passed. As I grew older, I simply stayed away when she was tempered, absorbed by that time in my own theatrical activities and university studies. When I was eleven years old, I wrote a poem about my mother, "The Mad Artist." Of course, it was a child's exaggeration, but she was a good sport about it and drew a sketch of herself to illustrate my poem.

She doesn't wear a beret,
She doesn't wear a tam,
But when she does a piece of work
Expects you to salaam.

She wears a canvas for a hat,
Drinks turpentine for tea,
And when she goes to bed at night,
All she can say is ME!

That she is one real egoist,
You will and can forgive,
For though she is the mad artist,
Her works will always live.

Everybody, including me, adored my mother, though, because the joy and childlike wonderment with which she approached life—and which was her gift to me—was contagious. My mother was a beauty, with milk-white skin, magnificent blue/grey eyes, and jet black hair that I wish she had imparted to me, instead of the frizzy hair that I hated all my life until I moved to California, where, miraculously, the dry climate turned it into attractively clinging curls. With her delicate, heart-shaped face and luscious figure, she commanded attention everywhere she went, and she loved being the center of attention, a trait she also imparted to me. It stood me in good stead as an actor.

* * * *

As a child, the world of fantasy was closer to me than the real world. It was the fantasy world I longed to live in when I walked every day after school to the NDG Children's Library to return yesterday's book and get a new one (When I had chickenpox, my mother took the bus on a snowy day to purchase thirteen, used "Bobbsey Twin" books, popular for children at that time. She thought they would keep me from scratching throughout my illness. I remember her dismay when I finished them all in two days.) I devoured books and quickly plowed through almost every biography in the library. It was the lives of the truly great that fascinated me, the ones the Stephen Spender poem that I have loved all my life tells us "signed the air with their honor."[3]

I loved the theater passionately from the first time my mother took me to hear "The Singing Lady" when I was three years old and came home repeating every song word for word. When she took me to see a play performed by *children*, I pointed to the stage in excitement and cried, "I want to do that!" That's how the locally famous Children's Theatre, devotedly taught for years by Dorothy Davis and Violet Walters, became an integral part of my life from the age of seven. Twice a week I took lessons in elocution, deportment (walking tall with books on my head), eurhythmics (hand movements), speech (speaking with a pencil between my teeth to get rid of my lisp), mime—and *acting*. I learned how to curtsey and make a straight bow. Soon I was *on stage* at Victoria Hall in the same kind of play that had enticed me into the world of make-believe. I took lessons in radio performance as well, and by age ten was appearing every week on "Calling All Children," a Saturday morning drama for kids on CFCF, a local Montreal radio station. We pasted our onion paper scripts on cardboard, so they wouldn't make any noise when we dropped them on the floor, one by one, during the broadcast.

Dorothy Davis and Violet Walters were like second mothers to me, and I loved them both with all my heart. After school, I took the bus myself to my drama classes and often was invited to stay for a light dinner (her maid made it) at Dorothy Davis' studio on *Girouard* and stayed even later for the evening rehearsals for the radio shows. Rehearsals for the plays took place on Saturdays and Sundays, so for several years, I was spending as much time at the Children's Theatre as I did at home and fitting in my homework in between. Although I still managed to be an "A" student, sporting a merit badge on my school uniform, I lived for the after school moments when Miss Davis, a squat little woman who had been a character actress, or Miss Walters, elegant and graceful (she choreographed the shows) would look at me approvingly and pronounce, "Clever girl!" in their cultivated Oxfordian accents. I knew I was born to be a great actress.

My mother got into the backstage act. She used her artistic skills with the costuming, made arm bands for the ushers, and generally helped out. She believed I was born to be a great actress, too, and encouraged me in every way. I have never considered her to be a "stage mother," because she involved her own talent in the productions.

At age ten, I also made my first professional appearance on the *Lambert Cough Syrup Hour*, and by age twelve was appearing quite regularly on shows produced by Montreal radio producer, Rupert Caplan, one of the greats in the annals of the Golden Age of Canadian radio. When I first auditioned for him on my own initiative, he looked over his spectacles at me—I had already reached my full height, augmented by high heels and make-up that I thought made me look much older—from the control room and asked, "How old are you, little girl?"

By the time I was sixteen, I was on CBC (Canadian Broadcasting Corporation) radio almost every day, appearing as a regular character on a radio serial, *Laura Limited,* and on a host of other programs (*Montreal Playhouse, Summer Stage, In His Spirit*—popularly called "the Bible Show"—the *Canada Bond Series, Tess of the D'Urbervilles,* and occasionally on *My Uncle Louis,* and *CBC Wednesday Night,* when it was produced in Montreal rather than in Toronto). I also performed in plays for CBC International, which at that time broadcast live, as did most shows at CBC before the age of taped programs arrived. Even then, sponsors didn't like it at first because the quality of tape was not as good as the live show at that time. Also, as an actor in a day before e-mail or the Internet, it was such a thrill to be "on air," knowing that words emanating from your mouth could be heard "from coast to coast," let alone, in the case of CBC International, another country.[i] The electricity between the live actors almost palpated in the air and certainly transmitted dynamically to the listeners. We had live musicians and, for the big shows, even orchestras in the studio, providing the musical effects.

During my years at high school, I was so bored by the repetitiveness of the lessons that radio and the theater comprised my "other life." Fortunately, my mother alleviated my academic boredom by taking me out of school every Wednesday afternoon to go to the theater or a concert or a museum. She considered it part of my education, and she was right. Today's kids take "enrichment" classes. Every Thursday morning, I gave the teacher a note of excuse from my mother, with regrets that I had suffered a cold on Wednesday. Yes, I guess we were a little different from some other families. I probably irritated the hell out of some of my teachers by graduating with the Sir William Birks' Medal for Academic Achievement.

From the time I was twelve years old, I was playing roles that I had auditioned for against adults in summertime Shakespearean performances sponsored by the Mayor of Montreal at Beaver Lake. Today Shakespeare performed in a park is commonplace in North America, but then it was a first in Canada. It preceded the renowned Stratford Festival in Ontario, and many

---

i   This is Grandma's computer. Grandma says that she acted in some cowboy-style stories for CBC International—the producer was Gunnar Rugheimer—that were aired live in Sweden to teach the school children English. She had to emote lines like, "Don't s-h-o-o-o-t!" very slowly. We had to cut this story out though, because it is starting to sound like bragging.

of the actors who played with the Canadian Open Air Playhouse later became famous there and elsewhere, among them Christopher Plummer (who played the piano so beautifully he could have been a concert pianist as well), William Shatner (a charmingly handsome lad and a Children's Theatre and CBC alumnus, whose family were trying to dissuade him from becoming an actor who would never make a living instead of going into the family business), John Colicos, Eric Donkin, Eleanor Stewart, Leo Ciceri, Mary Douglas, the Silvano brothers, and Stanley Mann—and, of course, Corinne Copnick. Malcolm Morley was brought over to direct from England. For me, it was a wonderland. As Audrey in *As You Like It*, I tended real sheep in a real rural setting in a make-believe play. How I loved the world of make-believe!

During the summers, I also performed, served as prop girl, and whatever else was needed at the Mountain Playhouse (atop Mount Royal) established by Joy Thomson and later continued with distinction by Montreal theatrical legend, Norma Springford.

It was during these summer experiences that I began to realize that some people were sexually different from others, something I accepted as a fact of life of show biz. When I sewed costumes with Beverly, the lover of an actress called Carla, I understood that Beverly had both a husband and a lesbian lover, and I also instinctively knew that she was committed to Carla and would never make a pass at me. I was safe. John and Bill shared the same bed, and I didn't wonder why. It just was. Another homosexual actor—the only one who danced with me at cast parties—usually walked me down the mountain after rehearsals or performances safely to my father's car, so that my devoted Dad wouldn't have to climb up the hill to get me. Safeguarding me from the wild, wild world of theater, my dear father came to pick me up every single night of rehearsals or performances, even if it was two o'clock in the morning!

My mother was in the background much of the time as well, usually helping with costuming—she designed and crocheted all the snoods for the performances of *Much Ado About Nothing*—or with other production tasks. She not only kept an eye on me, she encouraged all my efforts and, to some extent, was living out her own artistic ambitions through me. She didn't have to. She was an inspired if unpromoted visual artist herself.

Often she brought her sketch pad, and some of her paintings of that time—sketches of the actors in the make-up tent, on the open air stage—that I still have in my possession are both artistically and historically intriguing. Other artists, Jack Der and Bruce McLean, who became well known, exhibited their paintings at a little kiosk they erected near the Mountain Playhouse, but my mother never had the courage to do so.

One summer, there was a tragic occurrence that remained etched in my memory. A famous actor was recruited from New York to play a specific part at the Mountain Playhouse. Although I watched him pluck his eyebrows daintily in the make-up mirror, it did not occur to me that he was homosexual. When he departed at the end of the play's run, a young and very handsome actor—Harris—newly graduated from university studies in theater, took his own life. He had invested much more in his first love affair than the more experienced, older actor who had toyed with him. In 1952, homosexuality was very much a closet affair and considered a stain on a family's standing in the community. When I later played in the Red and White Revue at McGill University, I met a talented, introverted pianist, Randy, who gave me a brilliant, private concert on the gold-leafed grand piano in his family's vast, Sherbrooke Street apartment. Randy would periodically leave town for New York so that his homosexual practices would not shame his family in Montreal. Yes, this is how I came to understand about sexual differences, and that not all families are alike.

*   *   *   *

By the time I was a freshman at university at the age of sixteen, I was taxiing back and forth on a daily basis between my classes at McGill University and the CBC studios, which then were on the corner of Bishop, a fifteen-minute ride away from McGill. If I left my classes five minutes early, I could make it. I loved those years. Until the bitter CBC strike in 1962, French and English actors shared the building with a glorious camaraderie. After our respective French- and English-language shows, we filled the lounges with laughter and repartee. Then it ended, and after the unions had negotiated their deals, it became difficult for French- and English-language actors to appear on the same shows. The CBC (the French counterpart is called *Radio-Canada*) eventually moved its headquarters to Dorchester Street, and the era of radio ended. Television had taken over, and for English-language actors, the center of activity was now Toronto.

Meanwhile, I was having the time of my life. As much as I had hated high school, that's how much and more that I loved McGill. My whole world opened up with an explosion of learning. It was as if I were absorbing every aspect of that vital university, that old world campus, through my pores. In addition to my courses and my almost daily work at the CBC, I wrote for the *McGill Daily*, I acted with the McGill Players' Club, I took leading roles acting, singing, and dancing with the Red and White Revue (some of its luminaries like Bernie Rothman and Tim Rice achieved theatrical and musical fame in the United States and elsewhere; Don Johnson became a cabinet minister).

I loved being a "star," reveled in my first fifteen minutes of fame. My picture was often in the newspapers. (I still relish: a cartoon of myself with British actor Barry Morse that was published in the *Montreal Star* when we appeared in a play at the Mountain Playhouse; an attractive photo of myself standing in a barrel in a toga and pulling the ear of journalist Peter Desbarats; but I hated the arty profile shot that highlighted my somewhat prominent nose and was published over and over again.) I performed monologues with the McGill Variety Show at the Veteran's Hospital and other venues, as shy Leonard Cohen with his hair cut short and dressed conservatively like a Westmount boy in white shirt and tie, navy blue blazer, and grey flannels, sang the lyrics of his poems and accompanied them on the guitar.

I contributed two dollars (a fortune for me when streetcar tickets cost seven cents each, so two dollars meant almost three weeks worth of streetcar tickets) to the publication of Leonard's first book. His friend Ruth Wisse, now a distinguished Professor in her own right, collected the money from 500 students, and *Let Us Compare Mythologies* was published in London, England because no Canadian publisher would run the risk of Canadian poetry in those days. Poets simply circulated mimeographed copies of their poems, which they cranked out in purple multiples and shared with a tight circle of literary lights.

McGill was very formal in those days. Professors wore black robes and mortar board hats to give their lectures, and I was addressed formally as Miss Copnick. Professor Louis Dudek, a highly respected Canadian poet who supported Leonard Cohen's genius, created a sensation when he took off his mortar board and instituted a long oval table around which his students participated in the lectures by giving their *own* presentations. The atmosphere in his classroom was electric.

McGill was also elitist; there was no downgrading of standards here. This is how the Dean of Arts and Science welcomed the freshman class in 1952: "Ladies and gentleman, look to the right of you, look to the left of you. Two of you won't be here next year." We knew we were expected to work hard, and, apart from a group of incorrigibles who played cards for money all day in the Students' Union building, we did so with pride. This was McGill University. *We* were McGill University. (Most of the incorrigibles graduated with "Cs" but later made fortunes in their business pursuits.)

At the end of my first and second year, I was the recipient of two faculty scholarships. It was fortunate because my father had suffered a financial setback, and my family had a hard time with money issues for a couple of years.

In fact, I almost didn't get to university because, in the autumn of 1952, when I was slated to enter McGill, I'd had to contribute all the money I'd saved that summer to my parents. We urgently needed to pay the mortgage on the house and other pressing bills. I started university without knowing whether I would be able to pay the first installment on my semester, due without fail at the end of the first six weeks. Meanwhile, in order to pull us through this crisis, my mother returned to teaching, and, somehow, between all of us, we didn't lose the sweet house on Hingston Avenue; no one repossessed our stove and fridge or cut off the electricity and heat; and my first semester was paid in the nick of time.

However, there wasn't enough money left for text books, not if we wanted to have food, so for that entire first semester, I did all my reading at the library, and, later in the year, with more radio money accumulated, I was able to purchase used texts from other students. In the end, I was grateful for this experience because studying at the library taught me deep habits of concentration (so deep, in fact, that sometimes they can be annoying to other people, who think I am spaced out. But I'm not simply gazing out the window, or into the distance, and ignoring them; I'm thinking. That's a very useful activity.) There were no photocopiers in those days, so I learned to take concise notes on index cards and to increase my powers of memory and retention, already well-honed from my theatrical experience. My memory is photographic in nature, so that even in my seventies, I can scan a page quickly and later visualize where the words I'm seeking are located on the page.

In order to do well academically, perform on the radio, and participate in college activities to the extent I did, I had to be well organized. I would rise at five-thirty in the morning, take the long walk past the tennis courts and still empty fields on Hingston Avenue to the bus at Somerled and Grand, open a book on my lap during the long ride to the McGill Students' Union, which opened at 6:00 AM, and study in the lounge uninterruptedly until breakfast was available in the cafeteria at 7:00 AM. After a quick breakfast, I would study again until my 9:00 AM lecture. At 9:50 AM, I would sprint from the classroom to catch the taxi on Sherbrooke Street that would transport me to my 10:15 AM rehearsal at the CBC. (It paid eighteen dollars each morning, so, if I were on for five episodes in one week, I could earn ninety dollars, a lot of money when a man doing well might be bringing home fifty dollars a week.)

When the morning show ended at noon hour, I would walk back to McGill to get a little exercise before the first of my afternoon lectures. My dinner would be taken at the Students' Union as well, so that I could attend the evening's extracurricular activities. By 10:00 PM. or so, I would be catching the Number 3 bus that, with one transfer, would take me back home to Hingston Avenue. My parents didn't see much of me during the academic year, but the rigorous work/study discipline that I imposed on myself has served me well all my life.

*   *   *   *

I was trying to live two scripts at the same time, however, a practice that caused me grief throughout my early life. On the one hand, my mother wanted me to become a famous actress and seemed to live vicariously through my triumphs. On the other hand, she wanted me to marry, as a "nice Jewish girl" was expected to do, and to follow a path that would lead to securing a suitable husband. Although boys were attracted to me, and I had plenty of dates, she was smart enough to see that I was an oddball—an arty theater person was frowned upon in the finding-a-husband department in Jewish circles ("Danny likes you, and he's a 'catch,'" urged one of my friends. "Tell him acting is only a hobby." "No," I snapped, "It is my life."). Finally, my mother persuaded me to join a sorority, which apparently girls-in-the-know were doing in the second year of college. I took a good look at these girls, purchased a couple of tweedy wool skirts (worn over stiff crinolines!) in brown and heather tones, two matching, oh-so-soft cashmere sweaters (until then I owned one bottle green, scratchy, wool cardigan, which I also wore back to front to turn it into a pullover), a string of cultured pearls, and became a *soror* by accepting the offer extended by Sigma Delta Tau (SDT).

By the age of seventeen, I was not only attending sorority socials intended to introduce us to pre-selected young men, but I had also been appointed to the international SDT Hall of Fame for my theatrical and academic accomplishments. Although I was never really a comfortable fit with sorority life, some of the young women who were my friends then have remained lifetime friends. At the end of one academic year, I was awarded a scholarship funded by Delta Phi Epsilon (a competitive sorority composed of girls who came mainly from richer, snootier families than my SDT sisters). Ironically, DPhiE had not extended a bid to me when I was a rushee. Since I had never liked feeling that I had been invited to join the second best sorority, the scholarship was deeply satisfying to me.

Dating was interwoven with my theatrical activities, and I seemed to attract either introverted men who were mesmerized by my outgoing personality, or extroverted men who wanted a celebrity of sorts as a trophy date. I fell in love briefly a couple of times, but a match was not what I had on my mind. In 1956, the year I would be graduating, it was apparent that television would soon overtake radio entertainment in Canada, and the television center for English-language productions would be Toronto. The Montreal actors were urging me to go. So right after graduation, I made a trip to Toronto to meet with producers there. My plan was to live for a couple of years with my Aunt Sylvia and Uncle Moe, that musically gifted duo, who were then living in Toronto (a "nice Jewish girl" did not, horrors!, live on her own before she was married, and, anyway, I would have been afraid to do so) while I made my way as an actress in Toronto. I told all the producers I would be coming in the autumn.

My Aunt Sylvia, who had always considered herself my second mother—she had helped my mother a lot when I was born—was thrilled because she had four sons and no daughter. My own parents, however, were considerably less thrilled. Many of my girlfriends were already engaged and getting married during the summer I traveled to Toronto. By the last year of university, a college girl was expected to have made her match. Here I was, twenty years old, a university graduate, and *not engaged*. My parents persuaded me to enter graduate studies, take my master's degree in literature in Montreal, and thus remain in a university *milieu*, where I could yet meet a suitable husband. My mother had no trouble synthesizing the double script she intended for me: she wanted me to be a famous actress, with a husband educated at McGill and from a nice, preferably rich, Montreal family. God forbid that I should marry a Toronto actor who couldn't make a living!

Giving in to parental pressure, I remained in Montreal for another year and completed all the graduate courses required for the master of arts degree; and I met the man who was to become my husband, Bert. He was fun-loving, adventurous (my mother was leery and called him a playboy who belonged to the rich, fast Outremont set that everyone knew drank and gambled), and I was attracted to him. Let's face it, I was a virgin who wanted to get married, just like my engaged sorority friends, who were also mostly virgins. How much necking can you do in the back of a car and still consider yourself a nice girl? At twenty-one, the unrequited sex drive—you did *not* have sex before you were married, unthinkable—called me just as strongly as the theater. He was twenty-eight, and he was not a virgin, but it was time to move out, albeit reluctantly, of his parents' comfortable home, get married, and have children. That was the expectation. So we decided that we were in love.

His family was so different from my family, we might have come from different worlds. In some ways, however, there were similarities. Like my grandparents, both his paternal and maternal grandparents had emigrated from central Europe in 1903, when pogroms were rampant.

Bert's paternal grandparents, John (*Isaie*) and Etta (*Nadia*) were born respectively in Russia on Dec. 4, 1868 and 1862.[4] They gave birth to my father-in-law, Harry (*Gershon/Grisha*) in Ekaterinoslav, Russia on Aug. 15, 1898. He married my mother-in-law, Mary (*Masha Raisa*) who was born in Riga, Latvia on Mar. 5, 1898, and emigrated to the United States with her parents as a young child), soon after they met in New York. He named his mattress-producing business St. Louis Bedding after the song that was "theirs" when they fell in love: "Meet me in St. Louis, Louis, meet me at the fair ..."[5]

Harry started the business in Montreal, along with his five brothers and the guidance of his father. At the beginning, they had neither truck nor horse and wagon, and the brothers transported mattresses to customers on their strong backs. From this small beginning, Harry and his brother Colin—the other brothers quarreled and moved away—built up a business that grew to have almost four hundred employees and a fleet of trucks. During World War II, it grew to be the second largest bedding company in Canada. Meanwhile Mary reveled in her role as housewife, although when she felt depressed she would confide to her daughters-in-law (over and over again; we knew the story by heart) that she had done well in school and aspired to be a doctor. But she had given it all up for Harry. It was, indeed, at least when I entered the family, a marriage of mutual adoration. The world was together, and their marriage was a model of *shalom bayit*, peace in the home. Since temperamentally my father-in-law was a one-man hurricane, it was rumored that their marriage had been stormy in their early years, but in her fifties, my mother-in-law had learned to keep calm by taking tranquilizers, and to get whatever she wanted from her husband by manipulating her sons, especially my husband-to-be, Bert.

On Saturday afternoons, instead of the music, art, and idealistic conversations that dominated my parental home, their home resonated with conversations about business. Any arguments that occurred were always about business. While, in my parents' home, we got up to sing and dance and gestured wildly to the accompaniment of our arguments, my parents-in-law and their children sat quietly on chairs and sipped tea and cake after a delicious lunch in their large dining room, which was prepared by my mother-in-law every week, with the help of her faithful maid, Madeleine. It was the highlight of her week. On other days or nights of the week, they played cards with their friends or had dinner at the club. As in my grandfather's home, bowls of delectable fruit, selected carefully at a fine fruit store, were everywhere and usually emptied by the end of the afternoon.

However, the children—the number of cousins kept growing with subsequent births—ate in the breakfast nook and played in the recreation room in the basement. It wasn't exactly an expectation that children should be seen and not heard, but the children were rarely seen and heard upstairs after lunch until it was time to depart.

Like my parental home, the premises were well populated, but the atmosphere was much more restrained. Much more traditional, I suppose, in retrospect. My entrance into this family, though, was very restrained indeed. I felt as if I were living under a bleak cloud, like Joe Bfstplk in Al Capp's popular comic strip *L'il Abner*, a feeling that did not dispel for a long time.

The enduring cloud was the result of a tragic, and scandalous, incident that occurred only a day or two after my husband presented me with a gorgeous engagement ring, and I accepted his offer of marriage. My little sister, Rifka, almost lost her life, and the reason why was in all the newspapers and broadcast on radio and television. She was a celebrity, albeit a negative one, too.

*   *   *   *

I have thought of my sister as my "little" sister all my life, but she is only four years younger than I am. As I write this story, she is sixty-seven, and I am seventy-one. At the time I became engaged, however, she had already been married for a year—she got married at the age of seventeen to a newly graduated doctor, eight years her senior. At twenty-one, I smiled sweetly when one of my aunts called me the "old maid of honor" at my sister's teenage wedding. The newlyweds moved to Chicago, where Rifka's husband, Marvin, was interning.

Rifka was the sister who did not excel at school. Although my parents gave her the same opportunities that I had—Brownies, drama, dance, music, art, the NDG Children's Festival—my sister did not respond to them with enthusiasm. She had a beautiful face and a short, stocky, O'Copnick body with thick legs. I grew to have a lovely figure. She covered herself up at the beach. She wet her bed. My parents took her to various doctors to find out why she was so sluggish. Knowledge about diabetes was not what it is today, so they did not diagnose what doctors years later said was juvenile diabetes. As she entered teen age, an endocrinologist pronounced that she had "glandular problems" and put her on some pills that seemed to help, but she still did poorly at school, had few friends, no dates, and low self-esteem.

That is why, at my mother's urging, I took my sister along with me to a McGill dance, where she met her future husband, who fell in love with both her angelic face and her insecurities. He was her first boyfriend, a genius on scholarship, who nervously talked non-stop, came from the proverbial wrong side of the tracks, and whose mother had been in and out of mental hospitals much of her life, although we didn't know that at the time. My father, who had also climbed the societal ladder through academic prowess, responded to him with his customary kindness. He took Marvin under his wing like a newly found son.

My mother, on the other hand, was openly and vocally skeptical: Marvin was so much older than Rifka; there was something wrong. But, although she expressed vigorous objections to the marriage, her timing was off; she was most heated about it the night before the wedding. I think, at heart, she didn't know what to do about my sister and was glad that she had found a husband.

So my parents consented to the marriage, but in Chicago things didn't go well. Marvin was subject to sudden rages, and, with the pressure and fatigue of the internship, his outbursts grew violent. My sister wanted to leave him, but she was frightened—he threatened to kill her first. "I'll make headlines for you," he said. She called my parents and asked them to come and get her.

When they arrived in Chicago, Marvin locked the apartment door and refused to let them in. My parents went to the police, who responded, "We can't do anything about it, Sir, because no crime has been committed." By the time they returned to the apartment with a detective in tow, Marvin had stabbed my sister several times, and my sister was screaming. When the detective burst into the apartment, Marvin was already remorseful, trying to staunch the blood flow with bath towels. "Baby, baby, I love you, I love you," he cried.

My mother collapsed in hysterics as my sister was ambulanced to the hospital on a stretcher. Although Rifka's life was on the line for the next several days—the blade had barely missed her heart—she eventually survived the stabbings physically, if not psychologically.

Meanwhile, the already alerted media had snapped photos of Marvin being led away in handcuffs, and the morning after what the police alleged was attempted murder, Marvin had fulfilled his promise to make headlines. "Canadian MD Stabs Teenage Wife in Chicago" was on the front page of newspapers across the United States and Canada, and it spiced up radio and television news for a couple of days. My father tried to cope with the aftermath of this nightmare. There were legalities to be dealt with. My parents remained, of course, in Chicago while Rifka was in the hospital, and until she could be moved safely to Montreal.

I had not read the newspapers or listened to the radio when I set out for the CBC the morning after Marvin's evening attack on my sister's life. Since I routinely left home very early in the morning, I had not yet heard from my parents, who were barely coping in Chicago, and so I was puzzled when my fellow actors gave me little hugs when I arrived at the studio, or said things like, "There, there, don't worry." Our producer, Rupert Caplan, patted me on the head and said, "You're a wonderful girl. We're all behind you."

I had a difficult scene to play, and so I thought they were kindly offering their artistic support. (I played the screaming victim of a rape scene, and, to accede to listener demand, I would re-enact the scene live more than a dozen times, as various characters on the show had flashbacks of the event). I simply finished the broadcast, went to my classes, and continued my day. No one else mentioned anything to me. Cell phones did not exist, so I had no contact with my parents until I returned home that evening. As I entered the house, the phone was off the hook. Our house had been robbed. Criminals who read or listened to the news reports had taken advantage of my parents' absence in Chicago to compound our misery. I had been violated twice that day, once in make-believe on the radio, and a second time in reality by burglars who ransacked our home.

When I replaced the phone in its cradle, it rang immediately. It was my parents conveying to me the sad news. They were still praying that my sister, who was in intensive care, would survive. I was in shock, but sufficiently in command of myself that I did not tell them about the robbery. They had enough to contend with. Instead I called my mother's brother, my affable Uncle Louis, who was a lawyer, and he came over immediately to take charge of the situation. Together we phoned the insurance company, and then, passing his hand agitatedly over his balding pate, he said, "Just leave everything the way it is. You're coming home with me."

My uncle and aunt lived only a short distance away, and I stayed with them for a week or so until my parents returned, but as soon as Uncle Louis and I arrived at his home, I called Bert, my brand new fiancé, whose engagement ring I had been wearing for only two days. Before the tragedy, we were planning to formally announce our engagement on the weekend. (The social custom in Montreal was to place captioned photographs of the happy couple in the local newspapers.) Now as I called my fiancé from my uncle's home, my heart was in my mouth. In the face of this scandal, would he still want to marry me?

"I've been trying to contact you all day," he said in relief when he took my call. "I was so worried about you. I'm coming to get you right away." That he did, but as we entered his parents' home, they were sitting on the sofa, newspapers with the sordid headlines about the stabbing piled around them. To their credit, they put them away and, although they were not demonstrative people, they put their arms around me. "We're so sorry," my future father-in-law said. "Are you all right?"

I held back my tears as my mother-in-law asked, "Have you had dinner?" As I shook my head, she said, "You'll have dinner with us," and she hurried away to set the table.

They were good people, my in-laws. What they discussed in private I don't know, but once Bert put that engagement ring on my finger, in public I was their future daughter-in-law, and they would take care of me. Nevertheless, even though I had no part in those headlines, I felt deeply ashamed. My sister was the unfortunate victim, but her subsequent divorce—let alone a stabbing, let alone those newspaper headlines—was a stigma[6] in that togetherness era. If she had died, people would have sympathized. Since she didn't, they whispered. With all my accomplishments, I felt demeaned. All of us—my mother, my father, my sister, and I—felt as if our whole family had been stained with the blood that Marvin had shed. Many years later, I wrote, in a different context, a poem expressing these feelings. It was called "Icicle."

> *The day I froze inside*
> *the knife in your*
> *hand*
> *was pointed*
> *straight*
> *at me.*
>
> *How could a lover? How could my lover?*
>
> *I knew if I stayed*
> *very quiet, just*
> *let the liquid*
> *fill my eyes,*
> *the moment soon*
> *would pass and*
> *I would be*
> *congealed.[7]*

Although it was my sister's body that the point of that knife entered repeatedly, it had the effect of wounding all the members of my family collectively. Although each of us eventually went on with our lives and busied ourselves with other people, other goals, although we worked hard, played hard, laughed hard, and loved hard, at some deeper level, the emotional wound had not congealed. For my sister, the moment has never passed.

When my future mother-in-law invited me to dinner that dreadful night, it was crystal clear to me what I most valued. It was important to have a loving family, a husband, and children. It was important, thank God, that my sister had survived. The theater was a fantasy world. Sitting at a dinner table with people who loved you and supported you in the midst of your grief was real. In that moment, I determined to be a perfect wife, a perfect housewife, a perfect mother. I would be a stay-at-home mother with a togetherness family and cook my mother-in-law's recipes. In 1957, it did not occur to me that I could have both a demanding career and children. Some women did, but they were rare. In the later parlance of the power-suited 1980s, that night I chose the Mommy track.

◆

9

MY FOUR KIDS

From biblical times, one of the main reasons for people to get married was very practical: to produce a legitimate heir to property, and usually women had no property rights. They were the property of their husbands. Some cultures expected the bride's family to provide a dowry (and still do). In other cultures, the groom was required to pay a bride's price (and still is). Some marriages even took place by proxy.

For centuries, economic factors, political alliances, social organization, and procreation were the usual reasons for matrimony. Marriage was essentially a legal framework for organizing all levels of society. The wealthy, aristocratic, and powerful usually took care to marry the wealthy, aristocratic, and powerful to ensure that their families remained so. While people knew their "places" in society, it was better to marry "up" than "down."

Whether contract or covenant, whether romantic, practical, or spiritual, and no matter which side puts up the money, all cultures seem to agree that marriage is a formalized bond between two people. It involves responsibilities— legal, financial, and moral—that may differ in accordance with the culture, and it requires continued commitment. And therein lies the rub.

♦

It's hard to put my finger on the pulse of my seniority. When I reached half a century a few years before the media proclaimed loudly that the baby boomers were approaching fifty—no generation preceding them had ever aged, it seemed—my hairdresser began talking obliquely about other clients who were "over the hill" and thus needed additional upscale services like facials, massage, and electrolysis. Some of my maturing friends were already getting "eye tucks," not to mention chin lifts for their turkey necks. My cab driver confided that women like me in his country of origin were either old hags or dead. My would-be lover murmured with minted breath that I was *still* a hot number, and that I must *have been* a dish.

After producing four kids, twins included, in my early twenties, I had believed that I was almost middle-aged when I returned to McGill University to undertake a master's degree in developmental drama (Department of English) at the age of thirty-seven. It was 1974. My kids were teenagers. Seventeen years had passed since I had attended undergraduate classes, and I was mortified to find that the library systems had totally altered. Computer classifications were the new thing, not simple index cards like in the 1950s. I nearly had a mid-life crisis learning to figure it all out. Actually, in the 1970s, you were supposed to have a mid-life crisis at the age of forty anyway in order to re-evaluate what life was all about. Achievements already attained (like raising a delightful family) were supposed to seem curiously empty, courtesy of Betty Friedan *et al.*, and failures (to reach your *optimal human potential*) could be shelved for new dreams.

Nowadays, you don't get to be *really* middle-aged until you are fifty-five, and your employers shove you off the work force under the euphemism of "early retirement." Either you rediscover hedonism because you're "the demographic with the money," or you worry about how long your funds will hold out (Elderhostel, maybe? Free outdoor concerts in the summer? Earlybird suppers?) if you don't continue to work at *something*. Still, you are bugged by that worrisome thought that you are in the process of leaving middle-age and are entering—horrors!—the third age. That's the 'hood, baby.

My daughters reason that exactly when you get older has changed, at least in North America. Our life span has undeniably expanded. If people enjoy an extended adolescence, have children in their thirties or later, and are going to live into their nineties or more, then it's natural to be middle-aged in your fifties. It's popular now to say that fifty is the new forty; sixty is the new fifty, and so on.

There is little doubt that earlier established categories of aging have to be rethought: an elongated variation on Shakespeare's seven stages perhaps. If being fifty plus—fifty-five, say—is middle-aged, when does young-old begin? At sixty? What is old-old in an age of future centenarians? Seventy-five? Or from ninety to the biblical one hundred and twenty? If so, logically speaking, at seventy-one, I am authentically middle-old, middle-aged by extension, you might say. Not everyone gets the chance to be middle-aged twice.

These were some of the thoughts running through my mind as I relaxed in the California sunshine with my children and grandchildren, brunching in our garden on Mother's Day this year. Not only do I love my four smart kids and my three exuberant grandkids, and my solo son-in-law with the smile that lights up a room, I really like them. They are everything I hope they could be. Only my daughter Laura is not with us today, but she telephoned last night and twice today so that she could get to talk to everyone.

My four kids don't have to tell you that they had an idyllic childhood. When we prepared an audio-visual presentation of the different stages in my life for my seventieth birthday party last year, you could see them all in living color—the many birthday parties, peopled by friends and extended family, that we had for *them* in the various gardens of our family life: the one behind our first home, the split-level on *rue Capitaine Bernier* that Bert and I bought in a new development north of the Town of Mount Royal just before our wedding for under twenty thousand dollars. (The down payment of seven thousand dollars was a gift from his parents, and the carpeting, curtaining, and appliances were a gift from my parents, who borrowed the money.) We incurred the parental wrath of his father when we decided to landscape the garden (grass, hedges, and fruit trees because they take time to grow) before we bought furniture. In time, it became a beautiful, bountiful garden that included a willow tree, from which lollipop strips magically streamed when the kids had a birthday party, and it featured a travertine marble ramp and patio, lovingly built with my husband's own hands, and framed by a fairy story, white, wrought iron railing with pretty loopy bows. A colorful rock garden bordered the ramp, which uncoiled from sliding doors at the back of the house and made it easy to transport all kinds of delicacies to the tables set out on the lawn. A stone barbecue, also my husband's handiwork, could grill twenty-four aromatic hamburgers at the same time.

On these festive occasions, there would be an above-ground swimming pool (even Grandpa Irving, who couldn't swim, took a splashy dip) and a sturdy swing/slide set, on which four- and five-year old Janet and Shelley could scream with delight. There would be the two-year old twins in their gingham dresses and bonnets giggling in the playpen. There were also the neighborhood kids that lived next door or around the corner, so that you could walk back and forth with them to school or just play outside. Then the "Super 8" camera would pan around, and you would see Grandma Gertie, *Bubbe* Rachel, Grandpa Harry and Grandma Mary, Uncle Morris and Auntie Evelyn (who might have baked a birthday cake in the shape of a Teddy Bear, unless I had emulated her culinary prowess and baked a cake in the shape of a castle), and their kids (Dickie, Helaine, and Bobby), and Uncle Eddie and glamorous Auntie Pola (who never forgave me for having four girls), and their five boys (Danny, Tommy—who died in his twenties of a brain tumor—Johnny, Andy, and Jimmy). Uncle Kenny and Auntie Sheila, and their two kids (Donna and Karen) would be there (until Bert and Kenny quarreled and didn't speak to one another anymore). Cousins Miriam and Abe, and their five kids (Carolyn, Lenny, Brian, Anne, and Tina) might be there, too. Everyone was wearing sunglasses and smiling. We were so close and spent so much time together that it is hard to believe we rarely see that extended family now. Time. Distance. Death. Divorce, that dissolver of family networks.

But at the time our camera was creating records of a happy, traditional family, we really did have a splendid family life. We had a ski chalet and traversed the slopes together on winter weekends. In the summer, we went to Ogunquit, Maine (MacDougal's motel, the only one right on the beach, had no television) on weekends (on one of them, I fell off my bicycle and wound up in the hospital with a concussion). The sand was so white and fine in Ogunquit that you could pour it through a salt shaker, and the ocean was as cold as the sand was fine, even in August, which was when we vacationed there for a longer period. We loved browsing through the *avant garde* artist's "shacks" at the cove and picking up little treasures—I was the only member of our family who ate lobster at the pier, with my husband clacking the lobster's claws at me to make me lose my appetite.

We traveled up the Maine coast to Massachusetts, and, at a time when Cape Cod was in the limelight because the Kennedys had a compound in Hyannisport, we fell in love with West Dennis Beach and rented a summer cottage there for several years. Here the sand was a little coarser than Ogunquit's, but the big, cresting waves were warm and welcoming when we jumped in them. So many pictures of those misty Cape Cod summers fill our family photo albums. Every summer we would take the kids to Tanglewood for the music festival and to Jacob's Pillow to experience modern dance. As they grew older, we took our four children to the Stratford Shakespearean Festival in Ontario every year, as well as to Niagara-on-the-Lake for the Shaw Festival.

One summer, we flew from Montreal to Calgary for the annual big rodeo show, visited the emerald green lakes of Jasper and Lake Louise and the majestic mountain peaks of Banff, and then drove through the magnificent splendor of the Canadian Rocky Mountains, following the Fraser River from its tiny source in the ice-fields of Alberta to the raging rapids that expanded torrent manifested in British Columbia. We marveled at the heroism of the early settlers, who somehow floated down that death-defying river in rafts to settle the Canadian West. When we reached Vancouver, I gasped at the captivating beauty of the city's harbor, framed by snowy mountain peaks and tall trees in the pleasant summer air. "Let's not go back east," I said and meant it.

Practicality intervened, however. Our house was in Montreal, along with our livelihood, and eventually we regretfully went back home, but not until we drove over log roads on Vancouver Island—huge logs stretching side by side over yawning canyons. ("Look at that!" my husband would say, taking his hand from the wheel to point out a scenic wonder, and I would squeal in fright, "You drive, I'll take care of the scenery!") But when we got there, and the white beach serenely unrolled an undisturbed maritime tapestry for many miles, I believed that I had seen the most beautiful place in the world.

We stayed at a nearby inn, aptly named Paradise Cove. I think we would have succumbed to buying land there (which would have been a great real estate purchase, because property values in Tofino are out-of-sight today) had not Shelley accidentally sat on Janet's wrist at a bad angle, bruising it badly. I was afraid it was broken, but there was no way to get to the mainland quickly for a doctor's services. The ferry only ran a couple of times a week then, and planes were occasional. The only way out was by car (back over the log roads) to Port Alberni, a paper mill town, where we decided to take the ferry back to Vancouver to seek a doctor. When we finally located a medical man at the nearest hospital, he turned out to be an intern and consulted a medical book before examining Janet's wrist. Only a sprain.

Undaunted, the next summer we traveled by car and ferry to the farthest limits of the east coast of Canada, exploring Nova Scotia's lush, winding Cabot trail, the fascinating tides and underwater caves of New Brunswick's Bay of Fundy, and the red sand cliffs of pastoral Prince Edward Island. After breakfasting in the Captain's cabin, we dumped the contents of our stomachs in the rough waters that led to Newfoundland, so unpopulated for the most part then, and so unexpectedly beautiful with its mountains and fresh water lakes complementing ocean-side beaches everywhere we turned.

A few summers later, we traveled, again by car, through as many American states as we could to get to California and back. By this time, my four children were all teenagers, and there were tensions between my older girls and their father. They all loved their Dad, but he tended to be too controlling as they grew into their teens. While the kids were young and our marriage was child-centered, my husband and I had a great marriage, at least most of the time, although from the outset he had a tendency to retreat into silent mode for long periods, if he did not get his own way. In those early years, I was an artistic girl who was grateful to have a husband who knew how to do so many practical things well, and who was always glad to lend a hand with the children, whom he adored. He was an excellent provider. We had a good life. But there was another side to the coin. As with his father, with whom he constantly quarreled because they were so alike, there was only one opinion. So early on, I learned to bite my tongue and walk on eggshells. Still, in those years, if I had made a pro and con list, the pros would have predominated. Slowly, slowly, the balance changed.

This book is not the venue for an outpouring of the mid-life reasons for the break-up of our marriage. Suffice to say that my husband and I had unbridgeable differences in values. Among other things, I did not believe that open marriage—a trendy (and, in my view, kooky) belief popular at that time—was a good thing. By the mid-1980s, Quebec had already adopted no-fault divorce, and hearings of uncontested divorces were held quietly before a family court judge. We had been married more than a quarter of a century.

In 1994, *How To Live Alone Until You Like It ... And Then You Are Ready For Somebody Else*, my post-divorce book, was published. It dealt with the practicalities, not of going through divorce, but of taking charge of life after it, like the physical effort of moving two immense bronze sculptures all by myself (and my immense satisfaction after accomplishing that Herculean task):

> *... I tugged and strained and developed a method. If I pulled on the tail at a particular angle, I discovered that I could move one end in the direction I wanted to go just an inch or two. Then, if I moved the head and front legs to match, I could make another inch of progress. In this manner, I moved the bronze Foo Dogs, the Yin and Yang of my life, across the living room to the positions I desired.*
>
> *It took me two hours. I was so exhausted afterward that I spent the next two days, off and on, in bed just recuperating. But inside I felt strong. I knew that as a woman of my own generation, "the fifties", bred to depend on a male physically, financially, and emotionally, I had coped with what seemed impossible for my physical strength. Now the Foo Dogs were*

in position to protect me. In my first days in Toronto, I knew almost no one. So I gave my Foo Dogs a hug every time I came in. So what if my affection was wasted on two cold statues. They were my friends. They greeted me like immobile, oversize puppies.

There was a side benefit from my efforts. Although I had owned the oriental antique dogs (originally they guarded a Temple Palace in China) for seven years, I had never noticed before the gender of the bronze pieces. Lying there pulling them this way and that way from my floor position, the gender factor became obvious.

So my friends were a couple. In my imagination they became a symbol of what I wanted to attain. A male partner complementing my femaleness and standing side by side with me. Proud and tall and solid like the Foo Dogs.

That day I became a survivor. I was tackling my life. I was tackling the primary agenda.[1]

I agonized over trying to find out what was continually wrong with my car, a miserable experience almost as unnerving as the divorce itself. It was like taking a crash course without a helmet:

I wasn't car-smart enough at the time to realize that each major repair the car now needed was going to be followed by another one. At four years old, the car no longer had a guarantee. The car companies know when to quit. By the end of the year, as I attempted to avoid the expense of a new car, my station wagon had cost me 4,000 dollars in repair bills....

My experiences with the car were teaching me a lot. Especially, they were teaching me to yell a lot to get my point across. In the car business, they seem to regard women as fluffy non-people, unless they talk firmly. Firmly and soft didn't work. Firmly and loud did. Provided you are firm and loud repeatedly. Otherwise you are dismissed as hysterical. (A man who talks loudly with authority is considered forceful.)

However, with all this experience in assertiveness, I am now practicing being firm, forceful, authoritative, and softer in tone. Quiet authority works well for women once they are convinced they can take command of situations. If you can talk loudly when necessary without sounding like a fishmonger, you've got it made.[2]

Or the unforeseen difficulty of finding a job in my fifties:

After you receive five hundred or more letters that tell you how outstanding your qualities are, but that there is someone whose qualifications are more closely suited to the position advertised, you begin to think you may not get a post commensurate with your abilities. You contact all kinds of people and organizations who tell you your qualities are so outstanding, you should be a "big-C" consultant. You apply for jobs that do not demand the abilities you possess.

When you apply for a job as a saleslady at a fine jewelry store and hand them your professional résumé, *they think you're crazy. When you apply for a job as a secretary or receptionist, they raise their eyebrows at your graduate degrees and tell you that you're overqualified. You find yourself being interviewed by people half your age, or by someone who knows you could do his/her job and naturally won't hire you as his/her junior.*[3]

On the other hand, there was the sheer delight of temporarily trading my house in Canada for one with an unexpected rose garden in Paris. It marked a changing point in my life.

Everyone had cautioned me about trading my house. What if the visiting people wrecked it?.... I decided to take the chance and have some faith in human nature. I left everything "as is" and simply asked the visitors to replace anything they used. In Paris my hosts in absentia had done the same....

Since our funds were limited, [my daughters, Janet and Shelley, and I] decided early on to make all our meals at home and visit restaurants only for citron pressé *(lemonade) and coffee. From the local stores we bought our groceries, crusty bread and cheese and other supplies, and had delicious meals each evening.... My daughters knew several young people visiting France, so we invited them, too.... Every night we had a full table.*

It had been such an effort to get to Paris. It was the thought of making the trip [of using my reduced resources to maximum advantage], that had sustained me through that last year in Montreal while I was waiting for my divorce to become final. When I [finally] arrived in Paris, my children (who had preceded me by flying there the week before) picked me up at the airport in the car we had also exchanged with our French hosts. Then they drove me to the house in a green and beautiful suburb of Paris. The house was gracious, walled with wrought iron gates in the Parisian manner; but when I walked through the house and into the garden, I gasped in shock and pleasure. Tears rolled down my cheeks.

"Oh," I whispered. "Nobody promised me a rose garden, but it's here." The garden was blooming everywhere with quantities of magnificent roses. It was, indeed, a rose garden.[4]

Slowly my views of what was traditional and what was nontraditional were expanding to take in domestic situations I had never imagined, accentuated when I found an unconventional housemate to share expenses after my move to Toronto. He was young; he was male; and despite the speculation of my gossipy friends, we never "went out" as a couple and certainly never slept together.[5]

And, after I bought a new home in Toronto to help me feel rooted again, I exulted in the rescue of an abandoned husky, her long hair guaranteed to give me asthma, who couldn't bark to be my protector and companion. She was everything that was wrong for me, but the moment she kissed my hand, we were a match.

In my post-divorce years, I dated a number of men, and there were several marriage opportunities, but I did not find the "right" partner I had hoped for. Each time I came close to making a permanent commitment, I backed off. Probably I was afraid; possibly I was looking for the impossible. Nevertheless, those years were filled with personal and professional accomplishment, culminating in the Canadian Commemorative Medal that I was awarded in 1992. This honor attests to the significant contribution to Canada that its recipients have made.

Common wisdom suggests that people with stellar accomplishments, genius even, have singular focus. As an artist, I do not have a singular focus; my interest extends to all the arts. My cup, you might say, runneth over. Modesty aside, I am recognized as a fine actress, writer, editor, director. My husband and I owned a delightful Montreal art gallery for several years after the family business went down, and I supported myself in Toronto, post-marriage, as a private art dealer for a long time. Some of my friends kindly describe me with that left-handed compliment, a "renaissance" person, a considerable upgrade from artistic jack-of-all-trades. One of my latter day gentleman friends, however, a sales force development *guru* chided me ("You lack a killer instinct, Corinne!") for "zigzagging" in the arts, when I could have achieved greater heights by focusing on only one.

I may not have a singular focus, and my achievements are on a smaller scale than they might have been if I had not, for example, chosen the Mommy track so many years ago, although that excuse is probably a cop out, but I do feel singularly enriched, blessed really, to have seen such wonderful sights, to have experienced—and created—such marvelous things, to have such caring children.

In an earlier chapter, I wrote about my radio days. In my "second career," I became more interested in the societal benefits of dramatic exploration. I taught courses in how to use drama in education and to explore social issues at both McGill and Concordia Universities (although I was a lecturer, I enjoyed being addressed as "Professor") and did a great job.[i] For the Quebec Drama Festival, I initiated play readings of French-language plays in English translation ("Presenting Quebec Live," with the participation of the French-language authors, such as Michel Tremblay and Gratien Gélinas). The government was so pleased, it doubled the grant I had secured for the next year.

Hired to create a play on drug addiction for an international conference at McGill, I wrote, directed, and produced a bilingual play called *Metamorphose '77*, which had a duplicate cast of seventy drug addicts-in-treatment. It was so well received that I ended up working at the drug treatment centre (the only non-addict there, which presented its own challenges) as a drama therapist/sociocultural animator for two years, while we presented the play at universities, schools, prisons, and hospitals. It was the feature of Teachers' Convention, and the Quebec government honored us by presenting the play at the Quebec Pavilion of *Man and His World*. Then I was invited to Israel by Dr. Louis Miller, Chief Psychiatrist of the army, to give workshops

---

i   Grandma, this is Samantha. Do you think you need to write so much about the things YOU did. This book is supposed to be about my Mom and me. My teacher says that it is important to make POINTS and stay ON TOPIC.

to professionals at the Jerusalem Theatre on how to use drama in treating drug addiction. It was one of the peak experiences of my career.[ii]

Later, together with a French-language partner (who leaned to pro-separatist sentiments while I was a staunch federalist), and supported and housed by the International YMCA on a federal grant, I researched, created, and directed a powerful role-playing simulation on Canadian unity that we played in different locations in Montreal. It was an exhausting and rewarding experience for my partner and me, and for the fifty participants who took part in each "playout."

Stimulated by my dramatic experiences, the poetry poured out of me, and resulted in the publication of my first book, *Embrace/Etreinte*. It contained just thirty-six bilingual poems, culled from the four hundred or so I wrote at that time. Not only did it share my poeticized thoughts about the political situation in Quebec, which I considered a love/hate relationship between the English and the French, but, at another level, it expressed my conflicted feelings about my own marriage. It was my pre-divorce book.

I gave readings in various locations in Montreal and elsewhere in order to sell the book. While these projects were artistically very satisfying to me, they paid very little, and, I was fully aware that, if I had not had a husband supporting me financially, I would not have been able to undertake them.

*   *   *   *

My daughter, Janet, reminds me that I preceded the baby boomers by several years. I was born in the last years of the depression before World War II, not in the prosperity years after it. When that war ended in May, 1945, I was nine years old, with memories of an absent father, ration cards, recipes for eggless cakes in the newspapers, returning bottles to the grocery store, bringing wire hangers back to the dry cleaners, and tying up bundles of newspaper with string for collection. In Canada, skirts were cut short to save material; the well-dressed woman in wartime was said to need two suits and one dress; and, since silk stockings (silk came from our enemy, Japan, and nylon stockings were not yet on the market) were unavailable, young women put make up on their legs and drew black lines up the backs to simulate seams. The only alternatives

---

ii   Hi Samantha, this is Grandma. My POINT is that a mother can love her kids and grandkids and also do some good things in the world that make her feel proud. But maybe you are right, and I am DIGRESSING.

were heavy, baggy, lisle stockings. So, no, I am not a baby boomer, with childhood memories of rising prosperity.

As returning men took back the jobs their women had filled during the war, and women retreated to the home, they were both eager to build family life and economic security for their burgeoning families. Most of these children (the early boomers, now entering their sixties) grew up with an expectation of upward mobility and ever-increasing prosperity, whether they were to become plumbers, carpenters, contractors, doctors, lawyers, businessmen, engineers, or real estate developers. They grew up with a sense of entitlement. Over the next decades, the expectation of a house of your own with a garden could grow to become a McMansion by the end of the century. The two-car family became ubiquitous. By the 1990s, a million dollars of net worth was a commonplace expectation for many people. In the dot.com age of sudden billionaires, ten million—perhaps a hundred million—was required to truly be a millionaire.

With the advent of the feminist movement, women began to pound on the glass ceiling. As they advanced, women lawyers, women doctors, women scientists, or women business people, who now wore power suits, were likely to marry their male counterparts. Both singles and couples became known as "yuppies," savoring the fruits of economic prosperity. In order not to deter their advancement of the "good life," many of these couples either produced 1.3 children (so they could give them all the advantages), or they evolved into another new phenomenon, "Dinkies"—double income, no kids. Why have children at all when you can travel unfettered to Italy, China, Thailand, and West Africa?

Some of the early boomers have regretted this choice. And some of them haven't. The result, in any case, is that some of the best and brightest, both male and female, but particularly female, because males have a longer fertility timeline (and, with our current divorce rate, often have sequential wives), didn't reproduce themselves.

Late boomers, like my own children (born at the tail end of the boomer phenomenon), who are now in their late forties or entering their fifties, are a little different than their earlier counterparts. They have many of the same expectations, but they also experienced the financial and social consequences when the dot.com bubble burst, and they are conscious on a daily basis of an interconnected world. When terrorists destroyed the proud twin towers of the World Trade Center, when they saw the carnage so graphically portrayed on their television screens, my children's decade understood that material things can disappear in moments, and that what counts in the end is family, what counts are the people you love. They live with the specter of on-going warfare that may not end in their time, and they are scrambling to create a family life before it is too late.

As for myself, I realize that, even though the initial years of my growing up took place in a different era than that of my children, I have never really finished growing up. Maybe none of us do. After the birth of my children, I lived through the transformative decades that followed with them. Although I still retain my basic values because I believe they are good ones, there is no doubt that my views have altered very considerably over the years. You change, or you grow old. Hopefully, you grow wiser in the process.

When each of my children was born, all of them experiencing so idyllic a childhood, I could never have foreseen the different life paths each one has chosen, any more than I could have known in 1958, when I married, the route my own life would take. I could not have loved each of them more, then or now. Their life experiences have expanded my own views. I trust that, like my own, their growing processes will continue all of their lives.

*   *   *   *

Were the paths my children have chosen in life affected by their parents' divorce? Yes, I think so. They were affected, first of all, by the financial change in circumstances that our family had already suffered and, even though they were grown when it took place, by the divorce as well. By the time the divorce was final, I was fifty years old. My older girls, Janet and Shelley, were adults. They had already moved to Toronto, living together as they found their niches in the professional theatre there. My younger girls, Laura and Susan, were working during the day as waitresses in their uncle's upscale restaurant and attending university full time at night.

It's amazing how history seems to repeat itself in families. When I entered university at the age of sixteen, my father had suffered financial reverses, which almost precluded my going to college. When my twins were of college age, our family finances had also collapsed. Fortunately, it was possible for them to study at Montreal's Concordia University, which had a large evening campus catering to adult students, while working at the same time. As other strongly motivated students have done before them, that was the demanding route they undertook.

All my children have the resilient ability to frame events in a positive way. Laura and Susan look back at their college years as a marvelous experience. Unlike Janet and Shelley, who went to elementary school in an ethnically diverse, middle class suburb, the twins grew up as "rich kids" in a well-to-do neighborhood. In hindsight, Laura and Susan will tell you that working during the day gave them the opportunity to learn to get to know and to get along with diverse people from many walks of life. It also motivated them strongly to make sure that they succeeded in school, so that they didn't end up working as waitresses all their lives.

"We learned to organize our lives, to schedule our time," Susan says, "and we ended up as highly disciplined individuals filled with the joy of learning. We couldn't wait to get to our classes at night."

Not only did they do well at school, but they made adorable, efficient wait-resses. ("So cute," my friends would say, "that they are working in their uncle's restaurant!") They earned a lot of money in tips. Each of them brought home about four hundred dollars a week, and, with their combined income of eight hundred dollars weekly, they took an apartment together in an older building in Westmount, strategically located close to both work and school. It also happened to be a posh area of the city. They might have to work for a liv-ing to go to school, but they were still classy. The downside was that they had to relinquish the social aspect of college life. There was simply no time.

During those years, Laura was struggling with her sexual identity. From the time she was four years old, I had observed that she behaved differently in some ways than did Susan, her identical twin—or, better said, her similar twin from the same placenta. Laura liked to play with cars and trucks and "boy's toys." We participated in a fashion show organized by the Montreal Parents of Twins Club (I wrote their monthly newsletter) to raise money for medical research, but I had to fight to get Laura into a dress. Although both children were exposed to the same environment and influence, she was a "tomboy" who preferred jeans, T-shirts, and dirt on her face, while Susan was very "fem-inine," a girly girl who loved to wear pretty clothes and barrettes in her hair.

Both children were natural athletes, one of the reasons I was so happy to live in the Town of Mount Royal, which offered fantastic sports training and resources. Although my older girls had ballet lessons for years (graceful Shelley was immensely talented as a ballerina), Laura and Susan's forte was gymnastics and excelling in a host of other sports. Most of all, they enjoyed doing them together. Not only were the twins the star pitcher and catcher of the Little League baseball team for several years (with frequent newspaper notices of their stellar playing), but they were also actively involved in the swimming and ski teams.

As they got older, they participated in competitive athletic events—inter-provincial and even intercontinental events—that went far beyond the Town of Mount Royal. Both were members of the Montreal Irish Women's Rugby

Club (which no longer had any Irish ladies in it) until I had a call from the Massachusetts General Hospital informing me that Susan was recovering from a mild concussion. After her second concussion, she retired from the rugby team, but Laura and Susan continued playing a variety of other sports for several years and wound up with a roomful of medals from shot-put, track, basketball, and softball. Laura excelled in hockey, too. Both girls were on the ski team. Interestingly, although they were good enough, neither wanted to engage in individual competition. They loved team sports, probably because they could do them together.

When Laura was fourteen, she longed to buy black leather pants and a matching jacket. While I attributed this desire to her sports involvements, I already feared that Laura had unexpressed homosexual leanings. "It's a phase," I kept telling myself. "She'll grow out of it." So we went shopping, and I pointed out the difference in quality and softness between different leathers. "Your body," I told her, "is more suited to tailored clothes. I know you don't like ruffled things. You need to develop a style that suits *you*. Just make sure that what you choose is well made of good materials, and that it has good lines."

When we looked at shoes, she rejected anything with high heels. Then she looked at me and laughed, "Don't worry, Mom," she said. "When I buy a loafer, it'll have a ruffle."

At sixteen, she had her first romantic involvement with a boy. When Laura gives her heart, she gives it completely. This boy had problems and simply broke her heart when he stole money from her.

After completing three years of college, she took a year off to read voraciously in areas of her interest and consider her options. During that year, she also stepped back from her sports groups. As Laura puts it, "This was my 'What am I?' period." She was fighting, not only her lesbian yearnings, but also her own response to it. Eventually, Laura shared her feelings with her family. For the first time, she brought a lesbian girlfriend to meet us.

It was a difficult time for me. Intellectually I could accept the idea of a lesbian daughter, but emotionally was another matter. With my lips, I said that I understood, but, if my heart could have shaken its head negatively, that's what it would have done. Laura has always claimed to be bisexual in the sense that she can be physically attracted to men, but her emotional pull is toward women. That's why I was so annoyed when her counselor (a lesbian as well as a psychologist) suggested that she make a commitment to a woman for a year and see how she felt about it.

"Why didn't she suggest that you make a commitment to a man for a year?" I demanded.

"I like men, but when I have sex with a man, I would rather be reading a good book," she answered.

Knowing her identical twin was a lesbian, Susan, who is heterosexual, was deeply concerned for her sister's happiness. No one knows for sure how it happens that some identical twins have different sexual preferences. In the case of female twins, suggestions have been made in recent years that, as the mother's blood flows back and forth through the placenta, the twins may not receive equal amounts of estrogen, or that the second twin to be born is deprived of estrogen in the birth process.

In any case, as Laura puts it, "Susan tilts this way, and I tilt that way."

It was only when I viewed a controversial movie called *Forbidden Love* at a screening organized by Women in Film in Toronto that I really began to understand how important familial support is to lesbian women (and even more particularly to bisexuals, a category most lesbians don't accept, according to this film, and consider traitors). With tears in my eyes, I sat quietly at the back, not participating in the frank, emotional discussion, but truly listening to what the many lesbian women who had attended the screening had to say. Later, I discussed the content with my daughter and embraced her.

Laura returned to university, completed her BSc degree in Exercise Science, and graduated as valedictorian. It was a proud moment for our family. While working as a fitness specialist, she took further certification in Shiatsu and Swedish massage and studied osteopathic approaches. Then, concentrating on sports therapy, she opened her own practice. She accepted an invitation to the Wimbledon Championships to serve as a sports massage therapist with the Women's Tennis Association, a highlight of her career, until an injury forced her to abandon massage therapy and seek a new career in the sports equipment field.

With a committed partner, with whom she enjoyed a decade-long relationship, she moved across Canada from Montreal to Vancouver. She has recovered from her accident, lives happily in Vancouver, where she can enjoy the outdoors, including scuba diving and, more recently rock climbing. Naturally, being Laura, she already excels at them and is learning to be a rescue diver.

Laura's new partner, a loving person who is open to the world, has embraced our family, as we have her. A mature person ten years older than Laura, with a twenty-year old son conceived with the help of a friend, she works in the accounting field. Like Laura, she considers herself bisexual and lived with a man (not her son's father) for three years before she realized that she was happier as a lesbian.

"It never felt *right* to me with a man," she told me. "It feels *right* with a woman."

"God gives me everything," I confided to her a little ruefully. "With four daughters, I never expected to have a daughter-in-law—but I have one now."

Laura's twin, Susan, is a fun-filled dynamo whose view of life is expansive and embracing. While she is still a girly girl, who has converted my grand-daughter, Samantha, to her passion for upscale shopping, she is also a highly successful corporate executive. Her specialty is marketing. She brings both to her work and her personal life a vast creative capacity and a love of people.

Like Janet, Susan's biological clock has been ticking, almost to conclusion. She has been on fertility drugs for two years. With the guidance of the same top-rated doctor who helped Janet to conceive Samantha, she made nine unsuccessful attempts to conceive through artificial insemination. Nor did her tenth attempt using a different method, *in vitro* fertilization, succeed.

In vitro fertilization is a very serious endeavor. Even with the finest medical assistance at Susan's disposal, the risks of anesthesia, infection, puncture of the bowel or bladder, or hemorrhaging made the initial procedure (the retrieval of eggs from her ovaries) a surgical procedure not to be taken lightly.[6]

After the retrieval procedure, Susan continued a fertility injection and drug regime at home until she was ready for the second procedure: the implantation of five embryos in her womb. Multiple embryos increase the chance of at least one of them successfully implanting in the womb. The risk, of course, is that more than one embryo will take hold, so that a multiple birth, with all its pos-sible complications, might follow.

Then, after the implantation, Susan was sent home to guard the five fertil-ized embryos with bed rest for forty-eight hours. She had already signed a pile of legal papers, one of them giving permission for the eggs that were not fer-tilized to be used for medical research but not for the creation of life. Sadly, although she spent the next two weeks thinking positive thoughts in the hope of becoming blissfully pregnant, it was not to be. The outcome was devastat-ing for her, both emotionally and financially.

"Perhaps later you'll want to adopt," her sisters and I tried to console her. "The world is full of children who need rescue and love."

Somehow, after consulting her own doctor and going for a second opinion as well, she found the courage to try *in vitro* fertilization for a second time. The new doctor that she chose, Dr. V., who was originally trained in the Israeli medical system, suggested a longer drug protocol aimed at increasing, not the quantity, but the quality of her eggs. After retrieval, a shorter period of time between fertilization and implantation would enable the embryos to be in a natural environment as soon as possible.

Experienced *in vitro* implantation for twenty years, this doctor decided to implant some of the embryos in the fallopian tube on the day after retrieval, and, then, three days later, place the remaining eggs in the uterus. This procedure is called ZIFT (it stands for Zygote Intrafallopian Transfer).[7]

This double implantation seems to have had considerable success. "No one knows exactly why," the doctor told Susan, "although a minimum of six to eight 'good' eggs is necessary to undertake this procedure." In fact, the quality of the eggs is an all important factor. Another important factor is the skill of the anesthetist, who must keep the anesthetic light enough, a twilight sleep, so that the eggs are not too sleepy to wake up and do their part. Still another process, called "egg hatching" involves tapping on the eggs before they are fertilized to make sure they wake up and accept the sperm. In Susan's case, a single sperm was injected into each egg to accelerate the fertilization process.

Susan has a strong success drive, and, obligingly, on this eleventh try, she produced eggs that the doctor pronounced not only "A," but "A plus." There was only one "B" egg. The longer protocol, along with the best available medical expertise, and the depletion of her financial resources, had done its work. And, unbelievably, this time Susan got pregnant.

Her battle has not ended yet. Susan's pregnancy is considered high risk, due to her age and her high blood pressure, which will have to be carefully monitored to avoid preeclampsia, a condition that can endanger both mother and child. In order to maintain a receptive environment in the womb, she continued fertility injections, which had already left her bloated and heavy, for a critical twelve weeks. An early ultrasound determined that she is carrying only one child; a multiple birth would have entailed the risk of prematurity.

Through a CVS test, which takes a tiny snip from the placenta, the little embryo was screened for Down's syndrome and other genetic problems associated with older mothers, and, thank God, the testing showed that Susan's baby did not have any of these things. At this early stage, the baby's gender was also determined. So it looks like our family will soon have another Cryo kid—another little girl—to bring us joy.

There are days when I think that my children's generation of men and women has thrown out the baby with the bathwater. Literally.[iii] But then I

---

iii This is your computer speaking, the one that makes it possible for you to get all those Internet jokes floating around. Did you hear this one? A few decades from now, if a baby is actually born naturally, the doctors will be flummoxed. Ha, ha, ha, ha, ha.

think of my daughter, Susan—a career woman who waited almost too long, and her rugged determination to have a child—and, with reborn optimism, I believe once again that our twenty-first century world will sort it all out. We are just transitioning.

♦

10

TRANSITIONING

Although arranged marriages were at one time traditional in most cultures, contemporary Western cultures see love as a prerequisite to marriage. In other cultures, such as India and parts of Southeast Asia, where arranged marriages still predominate, respect, not love, is considered a prerequisite to marriage, with the idea that love can grow during the marriage.

Family relationships are presently in an accelerating state of flux all over the world. From single women who choose to have children, to married couples who choose not to have children, to couples who live together without tying the knot, the times they are a' changing. "There are fathers and mothers in serial marriages," writes Alvin Toffler. "Monogamy won't go away, but polygamy may gain wider acceptance."[1] Gay civil unions and gay marriage are contentious issues. To reiterate the oft-stated obvious, change is scary.

♦

In seven decades, I have experienced quite a few transitions. The first transition of note was moving from my parents' home to the one I would share with my husband. Like most girls of my era, I did not have the experience of living on my own before entering a marital state. Next came the awe-invoking transition to motherhood. When the children were grown, and after almost three decades of married life, there was the heartbreaking and scary transition to divorce and the single life, re-lived. All of these transitions involved changes in my emotional state. Then there were the geographic transitions, in which old friends and associations were left behind, and new ones needed to be forged. I moved from Montreal to Toronto for personal (my kids were urging me to come because they were there), political, and economic reasons. The move involved cultural changes as well. I loved Quebec, but I loved Canada more. I was sad to leave the place where my immigrant forebears had found refuge, where three generations of my family had attended McGill University, where I had so many friends. I could not bring myself to publish a poem reflecting these feelings, which I wrote at this time of contemplated leave-taking in 1984. Even the title, "*Au Revoir*," lacks finality.

Lands where my fathers cried
brought me to birth
on rich free man's soil
where each one has worth.

Quebec, how I love you,
rivers flow through my mind,
Quebec, how I'll miss you,
shall I leave you behind?

Your green forests encircle,
binding me close ...
lest I grow to feel alien
in my very own house.

Quebec, how I love you,
you sing in my soul.

I was fortunate to live in Toronto during that city's intense growth in what seemed to me every avenue—economically, culturally, and in terms of an expanding, diverse population. It was becoming, indeed had become, a world class city (Montrealers could no longer boast that the only good thing about Toronto was the road to Montreal), and I was lucky enough to be part of that adventure. My two older children and I "re-nested" there, as I rented an apartment on the third floor of a grand, old building (close enough to the 401 highway so that I could drive to Montreal to visit their younger siblings, Laura and Susan, with ease), and, a year later, Janet and Shelley rented one on the first floor. It felt safe; we were luxuriously happy as we ran up and down the stairs to reach one another, sharing thoughts, dinners, theater, and creating new memories. Shelley was making substantial strides as an actress. Janet became a sought-after stage manager before transferring her skills to the film industry, already booming in Toronto.

As for myself, I started my art business by selling art and antiques at Toronto's lovely Harbourfront, and then, as I made contacts, began to ply my trade as a private art dealer. Until I found my own apartment in that zero-vacancy rate market, I stayed with my kids for a couple of months in the somewhat seedier apartment they were renting when I first arrived. I slept on their living room sofa and organized a large exhibition of animation art at the Ontario Science Centre from their kitchen table. At my children's urging, I began to act professionally again on a modest scale, mostly in television commercials, and directed a slew of plays for community theatre. And again I became active in the Jewish and general community. I made many new friends, some close ones. I was happy. Toronto was the place to be.

And Toronto was good to me. There were so many projects over the years. I am proudest, though, of two that took place in Toronto.[i] One was *Altar Pieces*, a collection of my stories and poems that had taken me several years to put together and polish. I narrated them on camera, together with my daughter, Shelley, while Janet directed the filming on video. Roland Pirker, our cameraman and a friend of Janet's, had an international reputation and many awards but only a day and a half at his disposal before he left for an assignment in Africa. So that was all the time we had to shoot *Altar Pieces,* intended to be half an hour in length when it was finished. I had a small government grant to produce it, but our budget allowed for only one take for each scene, so every detail had to be meticulously planned beforehand. The shooting experience was a throwback to my old radio days when I had to perform live—one shot with no mistakes! It certainly generates a sense of excitement in the performer.

Roland did not have the time to travel to Toronto; instead, we met him in Ottawa at a friend's borrowed townhouse. Since it was completely empty, we

---

i   Grandma, are you digressing again?

enlivened the bare, off-white walls with plants we purchased at the nearest market. Fortunately, a few of her family's fabled collection of Group of Seven artists were still stored in one of the cupboards. These Canadian impressionist paintings, worth hundreds of thousands of dollars, decorate the walls of our low budget, quickly filmed production.

Despite the time constraints—perhaps our collective talents were enhanced by the frenetic energy of that pressure cooker atmosphere—we did it well. The video was intended to honor the memory of my war veteran father. A religious theme demonstrating the importance of sacred rituals in our everyday lives interconnected the four stories portrayed, which were interspersed with poems. The people who later viewed it across Canada found it touching and meaningful.

Actually, the video was originally planned to be a promotion to raise funds to produce a large, coffee table version of *Altar Pieces*, so when I sent it to Vision TV, a respected, national Canadian television network that focuses on religious and educational themes, it was a long shot. To my amazement, the network's director called me within a week of receiving it. They viewed it; they liked it; and they bought it. *Altar Pieces* was aired nationally to critical acclaim about twenty-five times. The purchase fee was small, but I didn't care. The intention was to honor my late father. My daughters say that in business, I give away the store.

The second project is a story to tell at another time in more detail.[ii] In short, with my professional background in art and long experience as a volunteer in the Jewish community, I was asked to coordinate an international art exhibition, to bring Jewish art treasures from Yugoslavia—it was not yet the former Yugoslavia—to the West.

The Yugoslavian Jewish art treasures have a very different history from the larger, better known Czech collection. The Czech treasures were confiscated from Jewish institutions and people by the Nazis during World War II. They were methodically itemized, tagged, and stored, with the intent to create a museum of an extinct people after the war. The Yugoslavian Jewish art treasures were similar religious items, ranging from large ceremonial objects to the keys to synagogues in Spain prior to the inquisition that had been secreted and passed down from generation to generation. These treasures had been hidden from the Nazis by individuals who buried them and kept them hidden during the Communist regime as well. They had been buried for fifty years when the emergence of the Czech collection stimulated an interest in gathering the

---

ii   Yes, Samantha, I am having fun remembering. That's what Grandmas do.

treasures from various localities in Yugoslavia to form a Yugoslavian collection. There were many problems involved in doing so, the foremost amongst them legal and diplomatic: to whom did the "collection" belong—the families that had hidden them, the Jews of Yugoslavia, the Jews of the world, the Yugoslav government?[2]

I was invited by my longtime friend, the Honorable Kalman Samuels, a Montreal lawyer[3] who served as Honorary Consul to Yugoslavia, to attend a meeting in New York City. Here I met colleagues from the Central Museum in Zagreb and the Jewish Museum in Belgrade (which was funded from New York), as well as others with whom I had been establishing a trust relationship since 1984, when a first organizing meeting with Dr. Salomon Gaon was held at Temple Emmanu-el in Montreal. Later, back in Toronto, I would meet Dushka Cohen, whose ancestors originally owned the Sarajevo *Haggadah* (the family's children colored on some of the pages, and there were some wine stains as well!), the star of the collection, but sold it to the National Museum in Bosnia in 1894 because they desperately needed the money. She had produced a video telling the story of the *Haggadah*.

In New York, I stayed at the lovely apartment of Mary Levine, President of the American Association of Yugoslav Jews, an admirable, elegant woman, who for many years had been broadcasting for the *Voice of America* at the United Nations. She was instrumental in smoothing the way for the collection to come to New York and would help bring it to Canada as well. Kalman would facilitate the legal and diplomatic channels to make it possible. Security issues were discussed.

At this New York meeting, I was formally asked to find a suitable venue in Toronto to mount an exhibition of the treasures there. It would be called "Jewish Life in Yugoslavia: Treasures of Two Millennia."[4] Finally, after my presentations to the board of directors of the magnificent Beth Tzedec synagogue—for whom security concerns were a huge consideration—the curator of the synagogue's jewel of a museum, Judith Cardozo, a jewel in her own right, agreed to hold the exhibition there.[5] Communications were difficult with Yugoslavia, whether to Zagreb or Belgrade. Fax machines were rare there, and even if computers had been readily available, e-mail did not yet exist. The time difference of six hours meant that I had to make phone contact in the middle of the night, and worry about the success of the diplomatic, legal, and security "channels" kept me nail-biting (and I am not a nail biter) until the artifacts finally arrived safely.

To say that the exhibition was splendid is an understatement. The staff of the Beth Tzedec museum outdid themselves. The synagogue itself is a magnificent structure, with bronze, sculptured walls, and marble floors. Ancient altar man-tles hung not only in the museum, but also from the high ceilings of the syna-gogue and the sanctuary. The exhibition continued quietly from October 20 to December, 23, 1990. We had started to organize it in 1984.

I was briefly joyful to obtain a grant from the City of Montreal to bring the exhibit to a *Maison de Culture* there, but it was circumvented when hostilities broke out in Yugoslavia. The Jewish Museum in Belgrade requested that the treasures be sent back immediately, not to the Central Museum in Croatia, but to Belgrade. It was my understanding that, although some localities wanted their own artifacts back for another round of safekeeping, from Belgrade the treasures could be sent to Israel. There are many pieces of the puzzle that I don't know and didn't want to know then. What I do know is that the Jewish art treasures, including the Sarajevo *Haggadah*, are all safe.

It had been a long haul, bringing the exhibition to Toronto. It involved my cooperation with individuals and groups in Yugoslavia, Montreal, Toronto, and New York. In gaining the trust of the Jewish community of Belgrade, I was also involved in other projects, such as helping to arrange the first free Yugoslav art exhibition in Montreal and selling thirty-two, space-age paintings (previously exhibited at the Ontario Science Centre) by a celebrated Yugoslav architect, George Petrovic, to a large corporation in Toronto. I also helped the Canadian Representative of the Friends of the Simon Wiesenthal Center in Toronto to cir-cumvent attempts by an organized group of Holocaust deniers to prevent the Ontario Science Centre from holding a festival of Yugoslav films. The protest-ers objected to the screening of two Yugoslav films documenting Jasanovac, a concentration camp that had incarcerated Jews and others during the Nazi regime.[6] Even before "Jewish Life in Yugoslavia" came into being, I was both exhausted and exhilarated by the adventure into the art business that had begun with my husband when we opened a Montreal art gallery in 1981. As my friend, Lucienne, who had worked with the French resistance during World War II, was fond of telling me, "If I knew when I started what I was getting into, I would never have done it."

During the years I worked on bringing the Yugoslav art collection to Toronto, I no longer had a husband to support the luxury of following artistic pursuits with such noble goals, and so I had to pursue my "day job" and work on the exhibition at night, odd hours, and on the weekends. Literally, I was working day and night to make it happen.

One interlude I will never forget not only revitalized my energy, but it also revalidated my artistic purpose in life. In the summer of 1990, I was awarded a grant which came in the form of an invitation to be a guest artist in residence—

a resident writer—at the Leighton Artist Colony of the famed Banff Center for the Arts in Alberta. Unfortunately, the funds no longer exist to maintain this program in the form it was at the time I was there.

During my stay, I was given my own architect-designed cottage in the woods. Windows opened on all sides to the trees, so that little animals visited me all day like a Disney scene from Bambi or Snow White. My food and whatever supplies I needed were all free. I simply presented my card, like a credit card, and that's all there was to it. Smart cards were a brand new innovation then, and this was my first one. It seemed like a miracle. I was being given a credit card I didn't have to pay for because I was a valued artist! There was only one thing I was required to do: have the freedom from care to create whatever I wanted. And I did. I wrote the manuscript of *How To Live Alone Until You Like It ... And Then You Are Ready For Somebody Else* that summer.

I also spent a lot of time getting to know my fellow guest artist, a Chinese musician who composed in his head like Beethoven. Even though there was a grand piano in his forest studio, he would sit at the table and set down notes on his composition papers with the fluidity of a skilled writer composing a letter. He heard it in his head. This was a skill he had developed while he was interned for twenty years in a labor camp in Northern China.[7]

During my summer in Banff, with the mountains shielding us from the outside, the only sense of what was happening outside that microcosmic world came through the morning's dire newspaper headlines predicting that the first Gulf war was impending, or through my phone calls either to my children, or to make sure that the exhibition schedule was on track. I recall only one day in this temporary dream world when a hail storm seemed to mirror the world outside, and I wrote:

> *Today's bold headlines, honed in*
> *humanity's ugliest image,*
> *permeate this peaceful retreat,*
> *stratify the morning mist with*
> *conflict's ominous shadow,*
> *blaspheme this sacred rock.*
>
> *Here, amidst primeval peaks, a*
> *prophet's prescient sorrow*
> *waters the pure, thin air, and,*
> *frozen, trembling,*
> *shudders the perceptive earth in*
> *persistent, icy warning.*

Here, shades of ancient strife
hover over full-grown children of
freedom, sharing transitory
pleasures while war portends,
unaware destruction beckons
a new generation, again
apple-cheeked and honey-haired,
to become its bride and groom.

Then the hail storm stopped, and it was the dream world of Banff once more. When I returned home, a happier poem that I had written, "Never Say Good-bye," remained in Alberta. Printed in the Leighton Artist Colony's newsletter in August, 1990, it reflected my feelings about this still-treasured, other-worldly experience, one of the best gifts anyone ever gave to me:

Oh, Alberta, where the sky is my friend,
and double rainbows, triumphant,
circle the sun ...

where a community of artists
co-create, painting in tongues,
making music with words,
writing in sound, rhythmically
blended in the nestling curve
of mountainous arms ...

where memories of craggy rockfaces
etch themselves in my eye's lens,
arch imprints of tomorrow's
vision, wherever, transported,
it may be newly invoked ...

where I pass from this cameraed,
heady air without leaving because
its eternal fragrance wafts within
me and the soaring snowpeaks stand,
believing, there.

Shortly after I returned from Banff, the Judaic artifacts were scheduled to arrive from Yugoslavia in mid-October, and it was time to plunge into the minutiae of exhibiting "Jewish Life in Yugoslavia: The Treasures of Two Millennia." But once the exhibition was behind me, I felt somewhat empty. I had lived with it for so long. Nevertheless, it was back to business for me in Toronto. In 1991, the recession put into motion by the 1987 stock market crash had already impacted Canada very badly. Jobs were being cut everywhere, and the writing was on the wall that art sales would take a back seat for some years to come.

Cyberspace was new. I conceived of having a portable office on the Internet and plunged into the exciting possibilities of the new technology. That is how my writing and editing business, Timesolvers (www.timesolvers.com), came into being. Although now it focuses mainly on creative projects, at the beginning it concentrated on helping middle-aged business people, who had been laid off, re-create themselves with business concepts, business plans, *résumés*, promotional material, speeches, and presentations. I had young clients, too, who no longer believed in the permanence of their jobs and were organizing businesses of their own "on the side." Everyone was working long hours. I spent ten or twelve hours a day (and night) on the computer.

If I look back at the course of my life, I realize that I tend to reinvent myself every twenty years or so. I write, I act, I direct, I organize art exhibits, and then the circle starts again. In my writing and editing business, I help people put their best foot forward, just as I did with developmental drama. I nurture children and grandchildren, perhaps my greatest strength. Maybe I could have achieved more. In my next life, if there is one, perhaps I will be able to maintain a singular focus, but in this life, my multiple foci have given me a life that is rich in love and friendships and rewarding in scope and content. I tell myself that, in this technological age, all the arts are combining anyway. Singular focus has changed to multi-media.

*　　*　　*　　*

Meanwhile, things were changing all around me. My oldest daughters were leaving Toronto. Although Shelley met her husband, Ira, in Toronto, eventually they left for California, where he planned to make his way in the music industry. As I recounted earlier, Janet and her husband, Cameron, had moved to Winnipeg, and when they divorced, Janet took a job back in Montreal. Alone in Toronto, I felt the urgent need to re-root myself, and, just as the burgeoning house market was at a standstill to make room for an on-coming recession, I bought a lovely house with "character" and a large garden backing onto a quiet park. It needed a lot of work, but it was mine, and it had an apartment I could rent out to alleviate my expenses.

When my father passed away after a lengthy, debilitating illness that reduced him to a vegetative state, I brought my elderly mother from Montreal to live with me, so *Grand'mère* lived in Toronto for the last ten years of her life. We had so many happy times in Toronto. (I wrote an entertainment column for two Jewish newspapers, *Jewish Life* and *The Jewish Tribune*, mostly because I got free tickets to theatrical performances. Once I calculated that I had taken her to fifteen hundred dollars worth of plays that year.) Emotionally, however, she remained attached to Montreal.

Perhaps it is always so. We are permanently attached, umbilical-cord-like, to the places where we are born. Cutting the cord that ties us to that place is painful. The moves we make after that first wrench come more easily. At least, that has been my experience.

After more than a dozen years of re-rooting myself in Toronto, once again because my children had preceded me and were urging me to join them, and again integrating myself into the community and setting up a business, I moved not to another city in Canada, but to a friendly country in the same continent. I exchanged motherhood for the doubly joyful experience of grand-motherhood.

Why did three of my children and I move to California (the fourth, Laura, moved to Vancouver to be in the same time zone) when we were all proud Canadians? We still have Canadian social consciousness deeply ingrained in us. So why? *Don't blame Canada*; blame it on Hawaii. A trip to that paradisiacal group of islands was a gift from my children to celebrate my sixtieth birthday. We all decided to go, meeting in Honolulu from our various locales: Shelley traveling from Los Angeles, where she already lived, Janet and Laura voyaging from Montreal, and Susan and I from Toronto.

It was January in Canada, with an outside temperature of almost forty below, if you included the wind chill. A raging snow blizzard was doing its best to prevent our respective airplanes from lifting off to make the trip. Then, miraculously, we were up, up, and away, traveling to a destination we would reach when it was pitch-black and transferring to the little plane that would take us to Kauai.

When we awoke in the morning, the sky was blue, with mountains and tall trees framing the foaming ocean. The temperature was balmy as we breakfasted on the patio overlooking the sea. Everywhere we looked, turning ourselves around 360 degrees, there were fragrant flowers, a breathtaking view. No bugs, no little things that jump out at you everywhere, like Florida.

"Why do we live in the ice and snow?" we soon-to-be-expatriate Canadians asked ourselves.

"I told you so," Shelley replied with her newly sunny, Californian expertise.

My four daughters rationalized that they were yet to purchase homes, to settle down and raise families—and they wanted to do it together. When Janet left Cameron and returned to Montreal, she had moved in with Laura and Susan. "In getting closer to us," Laura remembers, "she realized how much she missed Shelley." So, at that breakfast table in Kauai, we decided that we did not want to be scattered, like most of the families we knew, with various members living in different cities, different countries. In Kauai, on that heaven-sent morning, we recognized the value of an extended family and especially one with the geographical proximity to help one another out. How extended our family would turn out to be, we did not yet know! We just knew that we wanted to live near one another, to be closely connected.

Janet posed the question thoughtfully: "Then why not do it in a place with a hospitable climate?" On consideration, although Hawaii was drop-dead gorgeous, we all sensibly realized that, with our long-ingrained, urban inclinations, we would probably get rock fever if we stayed in Hawaii for more than a couple of years. After all, this paradise is three thousand miles from anywhere else. If you are not born into it, how much paradise can you take? And there was still the practical need to make a living.

So we settled on California, with its astounding geographical variation, and specifically on sunny Los Angeles as a compromise. Each of us would make our way there individually. Shelley and Ira were already living there. In all, it took ten years for Janet, Susan, and me to accomplish that goal. Laura is still waiting for her visa number to come up. After a great deal of thought, and after my three little American grandchildren were born, Shelley, Ira, Janet, and I all became American citizens, too.

My family and I have all become experienced in uprooting and re-rooting ourselves, in transplanting ourselves.[iii] Transplantation. Transition. Transformation. *Transism*, to coin a new word—a developmental life-skill for

---

iii   This is Samantha speaking. I am an American kid who lives in Encino, California. Did you know that a lot of people in Southern California think it's paradise? Except for the traffic. This summer I went to Aloha Camp, right on the beach of California, and I learned to ride a boogie board. What's better than that? (I'm only allowed to go in the waves to my waist, though.) Mom says that I should put in that I like Canada, too. This summer I took a plane to visit Auntie Laura in Vancouver, and we walked across the Capilano Bridge. It was fun, eh?

enriching our individual and collective futures. Our connective future. A rolling stone gathers no moss? That ancient proverb needs an amendment, it seems to me, in this technologically connected world. When, post-divorce, I moved to Toronto, I knew almost no one, apart from my family, and so my first point of connection was nature. "Homage to a Veteran," the poem I wrote, in that moment of branching out, has stood me in good stead ever since. It helps me remember that my roots are intact, wherever I go. My roots are my family. My roots are this wondrous world around us—in all of its forms.

> *I found a tree that feels like me,*
> *all flame and autumn fire,*
> *dark branches reaching fine-honed*
> *fingers to hold the wistful sky.*
>
> *I touched a tree whose roots go deep,*
> *proudly placed by sturdy stones,*
> *moistly loved by velvet earth,*
> *tall grown to sanctify this day.*
>
> *I touched a tree whose time has come,*
> *whose color gladly bares herself*
> *to winter's gutsy grasp and*
> *guards her blazing power ...*
> *transplanted in the night*[8]

◆

11

MY INTERNATIONAL KIDS

Throughout these centuries of human history, can we pinpoint the most important ingredients of family life? Have these ingredients varied in different cultures, religions, races, and ethnicities? Have they changed over time? Do they change from generation to generation or from household to household? As each new generation arises, does the "old" generation worry that family values are being eroded?

What is a family?

While I was waiting for the necessary papers enabling me to join my daughters in California, the issue of what constitutes a family took on global dimensions for me. Maybe because, in my salad days, my theatrical family was like an extended family, maybe because when I was Samantha's age, my mother had to be a single parent while my absent father served in the military overseas, I've always liked to have extended family around me, whether by blood or "adoption." So, in Toronto, in the absence of my children when they headed for the American southwest, I "adopted" a surrogate family.

♦

For two years, I consecutively hosted what I called "my international kids," a "family" of students from a variety of countries. They arrived with student visas that had been arranged in their countries of origin. Each of them stayed with me for two months, while they took daily, intensive English classes at a private language school. I gave them my hospitality, my love, and my guidance in a strange land. I provided great meals for them, and they cooked for me, too. I used the money I got from the school to take them to plays and concerts. From each of them, I learned more than they learned from me. During those two years, they helped me continue the process of transplantation in the beautiful house-on-the-park in Toronto.

Then, soon after I had transplanted myself once again to California—living now with Janet and infant Samantha—I received an e-mail message from Khaled. He was one of the international students who had lived with me in Toronto. It was 2001, and the 9/11 disaster was filling the world's television screens.

"How are you, Mummy? Are you okay? How is your family?"

I noted that the return address on the e-mail was blank but replied immediately. "Yes, we are all okay in Los Angeles. Where are you, Khaled?"

"I am still in Toronto, Mum," he answered. "I am trying to finish my studies."

"I am glad that we had a chance to get to know and love one another in Toronto," I responded calmly. "Let us hope for peace in the world, despite this madness."

The last e-mail I would receive from him read, "They are crazy, Mummy. They kill everything, even peace."

It was a sparse exchange, but the subtext spoke of many things. Khaled was not the first of the students who occupied a bedroom in my home. It had been a difficult time for me. My mother, who lived with me, was blinded overnight by a stroke to the visual cortex of her brain; she was both incontinent and suffering from dementia. I had finally been able to secure a place for her in a nursing home. Each day when I visited her, the hardest part to bear was the similar condition of the other "residents." Although they were well cared for, it was clearly a place where people waited for death.

Hosting international students during the two years my mother lived at the nursing home filled my own home with life, with young people who had hopes and dreams for the future. For me, in the years 1998 and 1999, it was a good antidote to despairing thoughts. On occasion, some of the students even visited the nursing home with me; they offered smiling faces and gentle words to my mother.

There was Lily, a spunky, "poor-little-rich-girl" from Taiwan who had spent most of her growing up years in boarding schools and said the best thing about her stay in Canada was me. "I brought myself up," she would say.

But her eyes sparkled. She was filled with curiosity about life in North America and wanted to see and know *everything*. The students all shared comments about their respective hosts, and Lily's reports about me were so glowing that several of her fellow students from Taiwan made my house their meeting place on many evenings. The language school encouraged its host "families" to act like parents, even held meetings where we could get to know one another and share helpful observations, and so here I was—a surrogate Mom whose own children were, at that point, living in other cities, making their way in the world. When one of my own daughters visited while Lily was living with me, she was surprised to hear Lily (and sometimes her friends) calling me "Mom."

My daughter was also amazed that her new Taiwanese "siblings" always asked for "North American food." Hot dogs and hamburgers were their preference, so they were very easy to please in the epicurean department. Most of them had lived their young lives in luxurious circumstances, catered to by housekeepers and maids, and had never learned to cook themselves. They delighted in helping me clear the table and put the dishes in the dishwasher. Sometimes I helped them with their homework.

When they arrived in Toronto, all the Taiwanese girls spoke a precise English, fluent in varying degrees, but they were anxious to talk like "native speakers." I was really upset that their elite language school was teaching them "American-style" English, so that they would "fit in": to say (and write!) things like "gonna" and "wanna" and "coulda" and "ya" instead of "going to," "want to," "could have," and "you."

Lily was fascinated by the new idioms she was absorbing on a daily basis. One evening, she graphically demonstrated her latest idiomatic acquisition to me. Opening her mouth wide, she repeatedly moved her fingers back and forth inside this moist cavity, as if she were vomiting.

"Do you know what that means?" she cried excitedly.

"Tell me," I said faintly.

"It sucks!" she pronounced proudly.

"They're ruining your English," I wailed.

She was not as impressed by the rooms of my home, though, as she was by her acquisition of English idioms. Although Lily was amazed at the spacious lawns that surrounded many of the homes in my Toronto neighborhood—in Taiwan, such exterior space is limited—she considered her bedroom at my home "small," in comparison to the spacious room she enjoyed in her parents' grand apartment in Taiwan.

The Christmas card she sent to me when she returned home in 1999 bore a triumphant "Joy" on its cover. Inside was this message in carefully inscribed block letters:

> *WISH YOU ALL THE BEST ON THE SPECIAL SEASON! SINCE WE MET ON LAST SUMMER, YOU'VE BEEN AN IMPORTANT PERSON IN MY LIFE. TO ME, YOU'RE A THOUGHTFUL MOMMY, A LOVELY FRIEND. A WISEFUL TEACHER. YOU'RE EVERYTHING!!! PLEASE REMEMBER ME, THE GIRL WHO ADMIRE YOU SO MUCH.*
>
> *LILY*

I still cry every time I come across her message, which I keep stashed with my photo albums. Dear Lily, I wish I could have given you a bigger room.

I learned, however, that perception of space is culturally conditioned when Mariko followed Lily as the next student I hosted and found the small bedroom that Lily had occupied *huge*. Mariko was from a middle class family in Japan, where interior space is compact. In fact, she had never before called a room her own. At night, her family unrolled their *tatamis*, spread them on the floor, and slept in the same multi-purpose room together. In the morning, they simply rolled them up again. She kept her few belongings in a small chest.

After Mariko, I took a little break for a while, as I usually did between students, either to visit my own children, or for them to visit me, or just to relax a little. There were my mother's ongoing needs to consider. She had adapted to the nursing home, but there were little crises from time to time, and I still spent a lot of time there.

And then Danilo came to live at my house. Tall and handsome, with hazel eyes that belonged on a film screen, he was my first Brazilian student, my first male guest, and a breath of fresh air every time I came home after visiting my mother. We got along so famously, it was like having an eighteen-year-old son live with me. (They're so happy when you feed them well!) He wouldn't let me lift finger to do anything that he could physically help me with.

He explained to me that the degree of poverty experienced in Brazil is almost unimaginable for a Canadian. It is nearly impossible for poor people to have any upward mobility. If you are born poor, you die poor. Even though I certainly did not consider myself a rich person, Danilo would point to my dishwasher, or to my washing machine and dryer, or the décor in my living room and pronounce gravely, "You are a very favored person" in the English he was rapidly learning.

The next student to enter my home came through the door with the largest suitcase I have seen in a long time—almost the size of an old-fashioned steamer trunk—and behind him slipped in a second someone who appeared so furtively that, for a moment, she appeared to be a shadow.

"I am expecting one student," I said. "Not two." It was two in the morning. I had expected my Yugoslavian student to arrive by midnight, and I was already in my night gown and bathrobe.

"No," the shadow cried dramatically, her feet firmly planted in my hallway. "We cannot be separated."

"You are from Yugoslavia?" I inquired. "Students at the language school?"

He nodded vigorously, as his female companion in the hallway answered rapidly in understandable, heavily accented English.

"Yes, and we have been assigned to different homes. No! No! We must remain together."

"Why did the school place you in different homes?" I asked, trying to assess the situation. The school's rules did not require that hosts keep students assigned to them if they did not find the students suitable to their home environment.

"We are not married," she told me. "They say that we can only stay together in the same house here if we are married. But we live together in Yugoslavia. We are like one!"

"I see," I replied. I knew that many of the host families had young children, and the language school had set the rule in order to prevent embarrassment to the families.

"It's very late," I continued. "I can't contact the school now. I do not have young children, and I have no objection to you sharing a room, since you have apparently been living together for some time, but I have only one room to offer you. It does have a double bed." I thought for a moment about Lily and Mariko and their different space perceptions. "I think the room is big enough, but you might find it too small for two people."

"Oh, thank you, thank you," the girl replied, tears filling her eyes. *"It does not matter if it is a single bed. The room will be big enough."*

When I opened the door to what would be their bedroom for the next two months, they gasped with happiness.

"It is wonderful. Thank you, thank you."

"We'll talk in the morning," I said, summoning up a pleasant smile. I could hardly keep my eyes open. "Welcome to Canada."

After a myriad of morning "thank yous," they began the task of hauling the huge suitcase up to their new room, where they somehow stashed it in the clothes closet. Olga and Llazlo were a team not only in regard to hauling a suitcase, but when it came to language skills as well. They were a totally complementary couple. She could speak English but not read or write it (Cyrillic script is very different from the English alphabet), and he could read English but not speak it. Their intention was to reverse the situation at the language school. She hoped to learn to read and write, and he wanted to learn to speak English. Meanwhile, together they could communicate in a strange land.

During the few weeks they were with me, gradually they told me a lot about their life in Yugoslavia. They marveled at the variety and plentitude of food that stocked the shelves of Toronto's supermarkets. "We earn salaries," Olga said sadly, "but we can't buy anything with them. The shelves are empty in my country." In comparison to the other students I had hosted, their concerns were so serious, so concentrated on basic needs.

At my anything but empty table, they greedily filled themselves with food. Olga was a tiny brunette, but it was amazing how much food she could hold. And Llazlo was a big boy, a professional hockey player in his home town, who was always hungry. They ate everything at every meal. It was as if they wanted to make sure they were full in case another meal was not forthcoming.

One day, as Olga grew closer to me, she showed me the contents of their still bulging suitcases. They contained mostly food. "Look," she gestured grandly, "Dried soups, smoked sausages, sardines, crackers, enough for a long time." They had stocked themselves up for a disaster.

After Olga and Llazlo, I took a break from hosting for a while. My mother was failing, and I was beginning to contemplate moving to California. My first grandchild was on the way.

But it was lonely living by myself when I had gotten used to bustling activity, company for meals, and youthful enthusiasm. So I agreed to host Jade, my first visitor from mainland China. A rather plain, somewhat awkward girl from a rural area, Jade had a business mind like a steel trap. Her father ran a shoe factory in China and had sent her to study English, so that she could help him do business with the West.

When I looked at the solid, clumpy shoes that Jade wore, I realized that indeed she had a lot to learn in the area of shoe design, if her father's factory was to please Western tastes. Jade, however, was a fast learner, a sponge, in fact, absorbing everything. She was thrilled to be in Canada, so excited at the prospect of learning, and honored to have the responsibility with which her father had entrusted her at an early age. Although her English was very halting at the beginning, she progressed quickly. With her inquisitive mind, she analyzed everything she saw around her. Unlike the other Asian girls whom I had hosted, Jade was lacking in charm and polish, and she was smart enough to realize it. She extended her course of study for another few months.

I was now alternating between spending a lot of time with my mother at the nursing home (where I also sat on the Resident's Care Committee), attending to my writing and editing business, and quick trips to California to see my children, my first grandchild, Joshua, and the new grandchild-to-be, who was growing steadily in my daughter's tummy. More and more, I was facing the prospect of my mother's demise sooner rather than later and considering selling my house, so that I would be free to join my children when the time came.

And then I got another call from the language school. "Please, Corinne," the administrator almost begged me. "Please. We can't find anyone else who will take him."

His name was Khaled. He would be my last student—and I would love him most of all. Like my own son. Khaled was from Saudi Arabia, and I was Canadian. He was Muslim, and I was Jewish. Like the other students I had hosted, he had come to Canada on a student visa to study at the private school catering to international students who wanted to learn English.

"You are so good with the students," the coordinator cajoled. "If you're not happy, just call us, and, somehow, we'll place him elsewhere."

Only Khaled didn't know that he was coming to a Jewish home when he arrived at my home, fresh off the plane, and obviously agitated because his luggage had apparently been lost and would be delivered to him later by immigration authorities. Every few minutes he kept stepping out of my house to nervously puff on a cigarette—the school had advised him that he couldn't smoke on my indoor premises. He was bareheaded at the time and wearing the business suit, white shirt, and tie that were his usual garb during his more formal, first days in Canada. Sweat was glistening on his dark-skinned face, and his eyes darted nervously around, hesitant to look at me directly. His small mustache quivered above his compressed lips. He was twenty-six years old.

I didn't know then that I was the first unveiled woman, apart from his mother and sisters, with whom he had ever been alone. Or that he had never before met a Jew.

I had struggled with my own doubts about accepting him as a resident in my home when the school had almost begged me to take him in. "We have such trouble in placing Saudis," the harried housing coordinator explained.

"People don't want to take them because most of the Saudi students who come to us are from very rich families and tend to be somewhat arrogant. They treat the people who house them like servants." She told me about one Saudi prince who was furious when the father of the hosting family asked him to limit his time on the only computer in the house. "The prince stamped out angrily," she confided, "and came back a little later with his own newly purchased lap top."

Khaled was not a prince. He had not traveled internationally. The only places he had ever visited, outside of Saudi Arabia, and then only briefly with his father, a music teacher, were the United Arab Emirates and Bahrain. He came, he said, from a "middle class" family in Saudi Arabia.

When he sat down on my white-tiled kitchen floor to mix the rice for the meal he had offered to cook for me, it brought home to me the enormous chasm that separated our cultures—Khaled who called me "Mummy." The worst day in his own mother's life was the one she was too sick to make her husband lunch and forgot to phone him not to come home for it. "He loved her so much," Khaled said with pride, "that he didn't beat her."

◆

PART III
THE SIBS

"Having a child is an act of faith."

—Rabbi Ed Feinstein
Valley Beth Shalom, Los Angeles

"Family is family, wherever you find it."

—Grandma (1936–?)

12

DISCOVERY

New scientific advances create the possibilities for both great benefits and great risks. What does "benefit" mankind can, of course, be interpreted by various cultures or individuals in benign or malevolent ways. That's why ethical and religious issues need to be sorted out.

New methods of conception imply radical changes in concepts of parenthood, especially fatherhood. The creation of a human being without intimate relationships implies the destruction of the nuclear family, yet the nuclear family itself created radical change in an earlier society—one that anticipated the continuation of extended families, with members that more or less stayed put in a particular place and helped one another through the multi-generational ups and downs of living. The nuclear family is not dead, true, but it appears be only half alive as what we used to think of as a family unit diversifies.

How do we adhere to our values in a futuristic concept?

♦

I guess by now you're glad to hear from me again. My grandma has lots of memories, and sometimes she forgets she already told them to you and tells them again. I even know some of them by heart, but she says, that's good, because I'll be able to tell them to my children.

I have something very exciting of my own to tell you: it's kind of a discovery. It's a family tree. My teacher, Ms. P., gave our first-grade class a project about the numbers that are important in our lives, like the date you were born, and phone numbers, and your address. That's pretty easy. I already did that when I was four years old in Pre-school. So my grandma said, "Why don't you make it more interesting? There are lots of birthdays in your family. You could make a family tree, with the birth dates of all the people in your family."

I really liked that idea. Just to keep Ms. P. happy, I cut out a picture of a telephone from the pile of magazines grandma helped me find. Then I pasted it on the *big* poster board with three sides that we bought at the art supply store and wrote my phone number beside it. I found an envelope addressed to my right name but the wrong address. So I pasted that on the poster board and put my correct address underneath it. I pasted on a birthday card that someone gave me that had a big seven on it, and a cartoon of a girl jumping up and down with joy, and a picture of me blowing out eight candles (one for good luck) at my birthday party.

And then I drew a family tree. An apple tree with lots of apples on it. I drew the apple tree with crayons and cut out little apples for each member of my family and pasted them on the tree, and very, very carefully, in each apple I wrote the birth date—my grandma helped me find them all—for my four great-grandparents (*Grand'mère* was the first one, of course) and my Mom, and my Grandma, and my Grandpa who lives in Montreal, and Aunt Shelley and Uncle Ira, and Auntie Sue and Auntie Laura, and for my two cousins, Joshua and Rachel. Now here comes the surprise. I also cut out little apples with the birthdates of my eight half-siblings. That is the *discovery*. My Mom discovered them: two little half-sisters called Andrea and Lucy, and a half-brother called Tim. There are also a set of twins and a set of triplets. The twins are boys called Bernard and Edward, so they are my half-brothers, and the triplets are two boys and a girl, so they are my two-half-brothers and a half-sister.

Including me, we are nine half-siblings, at least so far, because Mom says it's possible that more half-siblings may turn up one day.

I didn't learn fractions in school yet, but the reason they are halves and not wholes (like the half-notes or whole notes you play on the piano) is because we all have the same donor father but different mothers. I am the oldest kid, the first one to be born from my donor father (who doesn't donate any more because he's getting married and wants to have his own kids with his wife). I always wanted to have an older sister, but my Mom says that she's the oldest sister in her family, and so was my Grandma, and the oldest sister usually gets more privileges, like staying up late, so I guess it's okay to be an older half-sister.

It was a real discovery to find my siblings, like finding pirate treasure. I think when I grow up, I may be an archaeologist or geologist and find things under the earth or in rocks. But my half-siblings were not under rocks or buried in ruins. They were right there on the Internet.

For a long, long time, it was a very big secret who the donors are that help people like my Mom have babies. They have something called an *identity* (this means who they are) that is strictly guarded (which means it is kept secret). The biological fathers are a secret, and the kids born from their sperm are a secret. We have an identity, too.

My Mom says that in the last couple of years, the California Cyrobank and other people started sibling registries because they thought it would be nice for the kids to know if they had any half-brothers or sisters. Then, if they wanted to, they could get in touch with one another. "It's kind of an extended family," Mom explained, "even though it's different from most other kinds of extended families. We won't live in the same house and not even the same city, but it's very nice to know about one another."

When I'm older, my Mom says, if I like them and want to get to know them better, I can. In the meantime, we're going to meet some of them this summer. Did you ever hear of a discovery like that? It's as good as gold.

By the way, Ms. P. thought my project was too complicated, and that I could cut some of it out and be just like the other kids when we share our projects. So my Mom cut off the side boards of the poster and made it real simple (like Pre-school), and Ms. P. liked it better. But my Grandma said that she is glad that I was accepted into a Magnet School for Gifted Children next year because I am *not* like the other kids. I am very special. My Aunt Sue says that every child is special.

*   *   *   *

In a way, it's a relief to find out that we are not so unique, after all, and that a growing number of mothers of other donor-assisted children like my daughter, Samantha, have searched the new sibling registries, just as I did, and found one another. According to correspondent Steve Kroft, approximately thirty thousand children like Samantha are born in the United States annually. "Now, with the help of sperm bank records and the Internet, some of them are finding half-brothers and half-sisters they never knew they had, who were sired by the same anonymous donor, forging family ties they never knew existed.[1]"

A lot of credit for the discovery of these new family ties goes to Wendy Kramer,[2] who had the foresight and determination to create an online data base called the Donor Sibling Registry. It was on this "world-wide registry for donor-conceived people"[3] that I found a message posted by "Lawyer Marn," the mother of Andrea and Lucy, Samantha's half-siblings. I had earlier answered a message from a "Marnie Z.," searching for other children born to donor 57590 on the donor sibling registry established by the California Cryobank (which takes great pains to preserve donor anonymity, but had recently decided to establish a sibling registry). Although I checked back with the site repeatedly, my response continued to be unanswered. Later, it turned out that Marnie had started using Kramer's Donor Sibling Registry instead. In 2007, there were a reported 7,000 members of this site—including me.

Members "send in their contact information," says Kramer, along with the name of the sperm bank that was used, and the donor number. The Web site collates the information, allowing donors, their offspring, and half-siblings to contact each other."[4] According to Kramer, more than 1,600 people have connected through her site, finding what my mother calls "cyberspace mishpocha," the Jewish equivalent of biological family.[5]

It seems that many other people, like Marnie and me, have first connected on the Internet with e-mails back and forth, and are then, Kramer says, "flying all over the country to meet.... It's redefining family. It's family where there was none."[6] As my mother is fond of saying, "You build the family tree."

Some of these family trees can be considerably larger than the family tree that Samantha drew for her school project. According to Kramer, some donors have fathered as many as twenty children. That's why, after Lucy was born, Marnie bought up every one of the remaining vials of donor 57590, already "retired" as a sperm donor. She didn't want the family tree to grow so big it might be cumbersome—so she cornered the market. She is hoping that all the siblings will find and get to know one another. Bless you, Marnie.

Well, I did find "Lawyer Marn," and through her, Samantha's other half-siblings who had earlier registered on the DSR site, but it took some doing. I answered her posting on the DSR site, and, just to make sure that "Lawyer Marn" was the same person as the "Marnie Z." who had listed with the California Cryobank, I searched for every "Lawyer Marn" and "Marnie Z.," on the Internet, and, surprisingly, came up with five e-mail addresses. Four of them did not have a donor-conceived child. The fifth one did! I had found "Lawyer Marn/Marnie Z." and, through her (bless her again!), Samantha's other half-siblings, whose mothers had earlier registered on the DSR site— and with whom Marnie had already had contact.

Not only did Samantha have two half-siblings, one called Andrea, age six (a year younger than Samantha), and the other named Lucy, age four, but she also had a half-brother in Burlington, Vermont (a lot closer to Andrea and Lucy than California) called Tim, also age six. In addition, she had twin brothers (five and a half-year-old Bernard and Edward) in Connecticut and a set of six-year-old triplets (two boys, Gerry and Elliot, and a girl called Rhonda) in Phoenix, Arizona. Samantha, at seven years of age, appears to be the oldest half-sibling.

Prior to the discovery of Samantha's own half-sibs and their Moms, my mother and I were thrilled to switch on the TV one evening and discover a personable pediatrician, thirty-four year old Dr. Matthew Niedner of Ann Arbor, Michigan, on the screen. He was sharing his role as a donor in an updated, widely screened CBS News rebroadcast of a segment previously aired on Sixty Minutes. *The original segment also featured the twenty-four kids the doctor had sired through donor insemination. Just as we did the first time we viewed it on March 19, 2006, we had tears of joy in our eyes. So did the group of siblings and half-siblings gathered together before a TV screen in another location to watch their fantasy Dad take shape on the screen as a good-looking, intelligent, caring person, happy that he had helped to bring them into this world. He did not consider the two dozen kids to be his own children, but rather the children of the mothers (and fathers) who would raise them, who would nurture them in their own environments.*

Will he feel the same way in the future? Since the televised interview, the doctor and his wife, Nicole, have just had their first child. He is now filling a parental role with his own child. One can only speculate how this couple will feel about meeting his donor-conceived children as they have more children of their own, as their own children grow older. How will their children feel? Will they be resentful? Will they be curious? Will they be welcoming?

Will Dr. Niedner and his family want to meet the half-siblings when they reach eighteen and have a legal right to request a meeting, if he agrees to it? He has no legal, moral, or financial obligation to do so. The answer remains a question mark. How can he know now what the future holds? How can he know how he—or his own family—will feel in a decade or two? None of us do.

*   *   *   *

At the outdoor pool at the Calabasas Swim Club this summer, a landscape serenely surrounded by majestic mountains, Samantha encountered three water-winged, dark-haired beauties, all her own age. As they splashed around together, chortling happily, Samantha commented, "You look a little bit the same, but a little bit different. Are you sisters?"

"We're triplets," one of the sisters announced. "I'm Holly, that's Polly, and that's Molly. Do you have any sisters?"

"I have three half-sisters," Samantha answered proudly. Their names are Andrea, Lucy, and Rhonda."

I had explained to Samantha carefully about her sibs—I've always been really honest with her, in a kid-friendly way, since she was old enough to have questions. This past year, she had been asking a lot about her father and wanting to have siblings. So the timing seemed appropriate to tell her that she had some. She was pretty mixed up for about the same amount of time as me. Mostly she was concerned that she wouldn't have to go and live with any of her "other" family and have to leave me.

Like the pediatrician on the TV screen, we had already arranged our own meeting, not with twenty-four products of one man's semen, but with two of the little half-sisters I had discovered on the Donor Sibling Registry, "Lawyer Marn's" kids. Not a virtual meeting on television, but for real. In person. With both exhilaration and a degree of trepidation, Samantha, my mother, and I voyaged from California to White Plains in upper New York State to meet our Samee's half-sisters, Andrea and Lucy.

I will always hold in my memory the image of the three little half-siblings, so happy to find one another, posing for their group picture, which was then digitally transposed on T-shirts. They immediately donned the T-shirts and sported them proudly. Underneath their pictures was the banner "Sisters, 2007."

I will always remember six-year-old Andrea and Samantha running around, hand-in-hand, chattering away to one another, while four-year-old Lucy tried to keep up. When we first met, Samantha was very protective of Lucy, cuddling her and placing her head atop the younger child's in a motherly embrace. By the second day, however, she was treating her much like her four-year-old cousin, Rachel. "You can't play that game with us," she said. "You're too young."

When we first encountered one another in Marnie's huge, fairy tale of a garden, the atmosphere was almost surreal. I felt as if I were outside myself, witnessing our meeting from afar, even though I was inside it as well. I was so glad when Samantha's "older sister," comment to Lucy brought our relationship to normalcy. They were sisters. Half-sisters. Sibs.

And Marnie and I? We had become comfortable with one another, almost by osmosis, from the first moment of meeting. From elated, prospective "family" members chatting excitedly first on the Internet, then on the phone, then arranging the practical matters of timing, airline, hotel, and what we would do together when we did meet, we evolved to one big family sharing the necessary chore of cleaning up glass that had shattered all over Marnie's patio.

She had taken such pains to prepare meticulously for our arrival: making sure the house was in order; preparing the food for the cookout; inviting her mother, a gregarious woman almost jumping out of her skin with the delight—and apprehension—of meeting us for the first time; and asking a few supportive friends to drop in for that all-important, first meeting. Then, the final touch: she inserted an umbrella into the large, glass-topped patio table in order to ensure the shaded comfort of her guests as they shared a meal together. Unfortunately, the umbrella would not cooperate, and only moments before our momentous arrival, the glass top shattered, scattering its sharp splinters all over the patio.

So that is how we got to be a family, with brooms and dustpans cleaning up the glass and setting up TV tables around the garden. And after the initial tension was over, we had a good laugh together. Not everyone has such a shattering introductory meeting.

We were all well prepared for this first gathering in Marnie's garden, though. The kids had exchanged messages with lots of e-mail "smiley faces" and little birthday gifts. Thrilled to know that they had half-sisters, they were looking forward to meeting one another with high anticipation. They hit it off from the word "go," hand-holding, hugging, talking non-stop, and playing together animatedly through the afternoon. The next day we had lunch together; we went to the mall; and we went swimming at our hotel's lovely pool.

Marnie watched from poolside as I frolicked in the water with Andrea and Samantha, who can both swim a little. My mother floated Lucy around the shallow end. We wound up our time together with dinner at a nice restaurant followed by kisses, hugs, and promises to meet again.

Marnie had become "the hub" of the family long before we met. In fact, she had been amazingly diligent and proactive about initiating contact with all the 57590 Moms who had registered on the DSR and sharing information and photographs of all the sibs. Although my first and only contact for a while was with Marnie, soon after we exchanged e-mails and phone calls, she sent me the e-mail addresses of the other sibs' mothers: Eileen, Dahlia, and Cecilia. So before Marnie, Eileen, and I ever met face-to-face in Marnie's garden, I had already corresponded and held telephone conversations several times with all of the other Moms, too. As Marnie put it, "this wonderful family is growing so nicely." Who would have EVER thought this contact possible?

As a matter of fact, when Marnie told me about Eileen—and then Eileen was the next one to contact me—I was completely freaked out for a week. "I'm so unbelievably grateful," I wrote to Eileen. "I've not communicated with the other Moms yet, and I'm very pleased to make contact with you." We exchanged photographs of our children. "I recognized Samantha's eyebrows," Eileen wrote back excitedly.

In an e-mail, I poured out what was in my heart to Eileen. "It really is a redefinition of what family is, and certainly what ours will be. I'm looking forward to getting to know you and your son and hopefully staying connected through the years, so that our children will be able to develop whatever their sibling relationship might hold in store for them as they get older. I'd LOVE it if you would join us at Marnie's in July."

With some trepidation, Eileen did travel from Vermont to meet us in Marnie's garden, but, to our disappointment, she didn't bring Tim with her. An attractive, feminine redhead, with a bubbly personality that surfaces the moment you meet her, Eileen is very cautious. She works full time as a Physical Education teacher at a high school in Burlington, where she lives. "I only recently told Tim about his biological father," she explained. "I didn't think he was "ready" to meet his siblings." So she came to scout out the sibs herself.

As we began to enjoy being with one another in a relaxed way, she confided ruefully, "I'm so sorry now that I didn't bring him." When she passed around the many photos she had brought of her son, we could see that, like all the other sibs, he was very good looking. A handsome lad.

We live so far from one another. On the other hand, Eileen works mainly in a school setting and has the summer off each year, as well as Christmas and spring vacation. Maybe one day she'll accept our invitation to visit us in California. Maybe we'll get together elsewhere.

What is so fascinating about the mothers of Samantha's half-sibs is that we all have such different backgrounds and situations. "So many questions!" I wrote to them. "Are you married? Partnered? Single? Straight? Gay? Do you work? If so, how do you handle it all? Were you hoping to find siblings?"

Eileen is forty-two and lesbian. She is not Jewish, but to Sylvia, her partner at the time Eileen conceived Tim, having a child of Jewish background meant a great deal. That was one reason why they chose Adam as donor, and then Sylvia adopted Tim. Eileen and Sylvia lived together for ten years, but, when Tim was three, they decided to part. Each took her responsibility to Tim seriously, and they arranged their lives so he could have easy access to both of them. "Sylvia and I share our son. We live minutes from each other, so it works," says Eileen. "In fact, I couldn't imagine doing it alone. Sylvia's parents are also a big help.

Tim is my only child, and both Sylvia and I feel SO GRATEFUL to have him. While I would love to have another, I am managing to come to terms that it is not likely in my future."

Marnie had already met Dahlia, the twins' mother. She reported that Dahlia is a delightful person, and that Edward and Bernard are extremely bright and good looking. For reasons that were not genetic, but rather the result of complications of the pregnancy, Bernard was born with some serious medical problems. After a series of delicate operations, he is doing well. Perhaps because of his medical ordeal, he exhibits a maturity and brilliance beyond his years. It has been a long, hard struggle, but, fortunately, like Cecilia, Dahlia is surrounded by a large and loving family.

Like Marnie and Eileen, Dahlia is a lesbian. She and her partner had previously adopted a baby girl from another country, so Edward and Bernard have an older sister as well. "The Moreno family is heading south to visit relatives this summer," she wrote, expressing regret that they could not join Marnie, Eileen, and me, and, of course, our kids in White Plains. I hope to get together with them on another occasion.

Cecilia, the mother of triplets Gerry, Elliot, and Rhonda, is the youngest of the group at thirty-six and heterosexual. Her complex story is quite different from the other Moms. Her first husband agreed to a vasectomy during a prior marriage that produced three children in short order, but when this marriage broke up, and he subsequently wed Cecilia, she wanted to have children of her own—enter the donor sperm bank. Triplets were the result, and so was a divorce. Cecilia is now married to a "wonderful" second husband, who fathers the triplets lovingly. They have recently opened a business together and are working very hard to promote it.

She wrote to me with great enthusiasm, commenting on the family photos that we had all passed around by e-mail. "Dahlia's twin boys are almost identical to my two boys," she exclaimed, projecting her excitement by e-mail, "and the twins are exactly four weeks younger than my kids." Cecilia's huge extended family makes Christmas a lot of fun; and, of course, her triplets also have an older step-brother and step-sister, the year-apart children of their first Dad that precipitated his "snip."

Like Eileen, Cecilia is Christian, but she intends to teach her triplets about their donor father's Jewish heritage. "We have not directly told them about the donor," she wrote, "since they have a Daddy, but they do know about the other brothers and sisters. They have not figured out yet how to make brothers and sisters!" Unfortunately, Cecilia's family had already made other summer plans—the triplets were enrolled in camp—and were unable to join us in

White Plains for the encounter with Marnie and Eileen. One day, we plan to get together in Arizona, where Cecilia and her big family live, but obviously, much like Dahlia, they do not—at least not at the present time—have the need to connect in person with an even greater extended family of half-siblings.

In terms of sexual orientation, of all the Moms so far, three (Marnie, Eileen, and Dahlia) are lesbian. Marnie and Eileen have both separated from their former lesbian partners, but Marnie's partner did not adopt Andrea and Lucy. Andrea expressed her upset at the change in their household. Who would she make a Father's Day gift for in the future? "Joyce was LIKE a Daddy," she repeated several times. "But she moved out."

Two of the Moms (Cecilia and me) are heterosexual. Cecilia is married for the second time, and I was married and divorced before I conceived Samantha as a single mother. Eileen whispered in my ear, "You were the smartest one, Janet. You had Samantha all alone."

Whew! It's a lot to absorb.

After an exhilarating weekend, it was time to leave our new extended family, time to go back home. At the thought of parting with Andrea and Lucy, Samantha was sad, as were the other little girls. She wiped away Andrea's tears and promised to write. She hugged Lucy close. But somehow Samantha managed to put the experience into perspective all by herself. As we packed the next day before checking out of the hotel, I reminded her, "Your cousins, Joshua and Rachel, will be so happy to see you when you get home."

Samantha threw her arms around me and exclaimed, "I miss Andrea. I miss her already. I don't want to forget her."

"Why would you forget Andrea, Samantha?" I asked her softly.

She replied matter-of-factly, "Because she is not the actual sister that I was born with." With that, she rolled up her p.j.s, her bathing suit, and other belongings, and stuffed them firmly into her suitcase. She was going home. With me, with my mother. To our real family.

Yet, when she did return home, she was so proud to show off her "Sisters" T-shirt to her aunts, cousins, and all her friends, so deeply satisfied to tell new friends encountered in a swimming pool, who were themselves triplets born through in vitro *procedures, "I have three half-sisters and five half-brothers."*

She will always be my only child, but she has sibs.

*   *   *   *

CHARTING A NEW MAP:
Samantha's Known Sibs and their Mothers

Mothers	Marital Status	Sexual Orientation	Donor-Conceived Children	Medical History	Other Children
Janet, 48	Divorced, Single Parent. Live-in Grandmother.	Heterosexual	Samantha, 7	Healthy	No. Close relationship with cousins. Large extended family.
Marnie, 47	Partner left and will not participate.	Lesbian	Andrea, 6 Lucy, 4	Healthy	No. Grandmother, relatives nearby.
Eileen, 42	Separated. Partner adopted child. Shared custody.	Lesbian	Tim, 6	Healthy.	No
Dahlia, 43	Partner	Lesbian	Twins: Bernard, 5 1/2 Edward, 5 1/2	Bernard overcoming birth complications. Edward is healthy.	Older, adopted daughter. Large extended family.
Cecilia, 36	Married (second husband)	Heterosexual	Triplets: Gerry, 6 Elliott, 6 Rhonda, 6	All healthy.	Three step-children from second husband. Large extended family.
Other mothers unknown					Marnie bought remaining vials.

With this visit, the veil of anonymity that had enveloped us until we mothers and sibs discovered one another, was gradually lifting. To my great surprise and delight, the hidden and closely guarded identity of the biological father was gradually dissolving as well.

That was the BIG, BIG NEWS that Marnie had sent me in the course of the e-mails we exchanged. After she registered on the Donor Sibling Registry, it was not only the mothers of the half-sibs that answered her request for information. Our common donor, Adam, responded too! Engaged now to the woman he wanted to marry, he had discovered the existence of the DSR. Just as I did at a later date, he found Marnie's message, and, just as I was, he was both elated and rather apprehensive about contacting her. His purpose? "I told my fiancée about my stint as a sperm donor when I was in university," Adam wrote, "and we will soon be getting married and want to have our own children, but, before we do, we'd like to know that all the children resulting from my sperm are well and in good circumstances." Incredibly, Adam gave Marnie his real name and told her where he was living. He also made it clear that, while he was concerned, he still wanted to keep his distance. He had his own life and a wife-to-be to think about.

"I was so astounded," Marnie said, "that he had actually revealed himself to me so openly. It took a lot of courage. Although Adam did tell his father when he contributed his sperm while he was at college, he had never told his mother. To this day, she doesn't know. So I'm sure it took courage to tell his fiancée, too. She must be a very special person."

Marnie and Adam corresponded by e-mail several times, and he even helped her fix her computer problems from afar. As he had hoped to do, he had combined his interest in both bio-medicine and computer technology by working for a bio-tech firm, and he was doing very well in a line of work he loved. That was how he met his future wife. Marnie sent Adam photos of Andrea and Lucy, described their personalities, and Adam responded with photos, not only of himself as a child and at the present time, but also of both his parents, his stepmother, his sister, and even his maternal grandmother, who was still alive and well.

As Marnie made contact with Dahlia and Cecilia, she forwarded Adam's family photos to both these women. Like Marnie, they were ecstatic. It made a huge difference. The shadowy "father unknown" no longer existed. The mothers and the sibs could see what he looked like. He was Adam, their biological father. Not a Daddy who lived in their homes, but a father.

Marnie also forwarded photos of the sibs to Adam by e-mail, but she guarded his e-mail address carefully, and Dahlia and Cecilia forwarded their messages to Adam via Marnie. They assured him that they were all financially and emotionally in good shape and did not need or want anything from him. The mothers were so grateful to have the photographs of Adam and his family. It was so kind, so empathic of him, to send them.

But, by the time Eileen and I contacted Marnie, perhaps he had grown a little apprehensive. Although she sent photos and news of both Samantha and Tim to Adam's e-mail, he was no longer responding. I felt that I should respect his privacy and wait for him to contact me, if he so desired. On the other hand, I hoped that his e-mail address was still valid, and that the photos of Samantha that Marnie had forwarded had reached him. I wanted him to know that he had sired such a beautiful child, to whom he had imparted not only his intelligence, but also his capacity for human kindness. And I was glad, so glad, that Adam had cared enough to want to know how his biological off-spring were faring. As a retired donor, he now had photos of all his sperm bank kids, or at least the ones we knew about.

I never realized how important it would be to me to see the tangible visual evidence that the biological father of my child had a family, to see the face of the grandmother who lived in Montreal, to try to identify the parts of Samantha that looked like Adam—or his father, or his mother, or sister. It was important to me to show this biological family to Samantha and to my Mom.

"Hmph!" my Mom, sniffed, even though she was studying the photos of Adam and his family with great satisfaction. "She gets a lot from my family, too. I think Samantha looks more like my side of the family. Look at her eyes."

Samantha giggled. "Oh Grandma, everybody says I look just like my mother."

"And I look a lot like Grandma," I smiled. Somehow that has nothing to do with my mother's multi-colored hair which is now varied shades of grey. I got out of the habit of calling her Mom. It's usually "Grandma" now, for both Samantha and me. Her soft face, unwrinkled except for the laugh lines accenting her green eyes, looks like a woman twenty years her junior.

"Can I tell you a secret?" Grandma asked me after Samantha was safely in bed. She hesitated for a moment, and then what was on her mind spilled out. "You know, BEFORE we met Samantha's siblings, it seemed so important to find them, to travel across the country to meet them. It seemed so cruel not to know Adam's identity, because he is part of Samantha's biological self. But now that we've met Marnie and Eileen, and the kids, and now that we know who Adam is, it doesn't seem so earth-shaking any more. We know. It was nice to meet. We'll meet again, and we'll be glad to do it. I'd like to meet the other

sibs and Cecilia and Dahlia in Arizona and Connecticut, but, somehow, I don't feel the need to go rushing off to do it. All in good time."

"I feel the same way," I whispered. "It's just hard to say out loud. We've built a good life for Samantha. I like what we have here in our nice little house in Encino."

Grandma was lost in her own thoughts for a few moments, and then she mused aloud, "The sibs, the Moms, Adam—they've become part of the fabric of our lives. We just have to digest it all for a while." We sat silently for a long time. "Maybe one day Adam will be brave enough to contact you," Grandma added. "Somehow that doesn't seem so important anymore either."

"But it may be very important to Samantha," I countered.

♦

13

NEW TERRITORY

Life is full of polarities. While it may seem as if everything is changing all around us, our basic human needs, our drives remain the same. *Plus ça change, plus c'est la meme chose*. There is nothing new under the sun, right? Everything is already here in our universe, the good and the bad; it exists, we have only to discover it. Do you believe that? I do. In some ways, everything changes, and, in some ways, everything remains the same—a concept at once contradictory and complementary. It all depends on our time frame.

One of the marital problems we face today is the mixed blessing of medical advances: we live longer; we don't have to look too far back to find the time when women frequently died in childbirth, and the widowed husband took another wife. Now, as life expectancy increases, it seems to be getting harder for some people to contemplate living with one mate for the rest of their lives. So they don't. Serial monogamy is not a joke; it is a fact.

So what makes a family a family?

What is most important in creating the foundation for a good family life— whatever its format—is not inheritance, alliances, money, success, social status, higher education, the multiplicity of "things" we can give our children, or even security, but rather the quality of our loving relationships.

♦

CRYO KID

It's Grandma again. Most writers don't know how to finish their books, and
this one is no exception—because who knows where we are going with all
these biological changes? How is it all going to end? So I'm not sure if what I
want to say is: here is the last chapter of a book written straight from the gut;
or, this is an epilogue to put the final gloss on a finished work; or, and I suspect this is the case, the beginning of another book still to be written over time.

Initially, I was motivated to write *Cryo Kid* by my daughter Janet's discovery of the half-siblings on the Internet and, through Marnie Z., of Samantha's
biological father. Although I did construct an outline to guide me through the
morass of my memories and the events that stimulated them, these episodes
seem like only a small part of the story that has emerged, is still emerging, is
still what I think about when I go to bed at night. Originally, I had a different
title, *My Cyberspace Mishpocha*, with the intention of introducing a humorous
note (*mishpocha* means extended "family" in *Yiddish*): we think we're so
smart with all our innovations, but maybe someone up there is playing a big
joke on us. It's not a joke, though. It's for real. As individuals, as families, as a
society, we have been in a continual state of transition throughout the past century and now almost a decade into this one. We don't know yet what we are
transitioning *to*, and that's what makes it so difficult to be truly transformed.

I began the book with the concept of continual change and, because I will
always be a romantic, with the ideal of enduring love. Only as my story began
to grow and flow and essentially write itself, did I realize that what I was writing about did not so much concern single women and their donor-conceived
children, as it did the family in the process of transformation. My family, your
family, all our families. We are all in the process of becoming something else.
Like reaching for the divine, we can only see where we are going through a
glass darkly.

Only one of my very bright, extremely personable, and highly accomplished daughters has what might be called a normal marriage pattern, even
though it is located in the midst of the hectic Los Angeles music industry.
Shelley is heterosexual, has been married to one loyal mate, Ira, for more than
fifteen years, and has known him for twenty. It's rather ironic that Shelley,
who was the most rebellious of my kids as a teenager, should be the one to
have a traditional marriage. The two delightful children her marriage produced, my grandchildren, Joshua and Rachel, are gifted children and can rival
in intelligence, physical attractiveness, and social attributes the best of
"designer" babies that any of the sperm bank alliances can boast.

This is also not surprising, considering the fact that their mother, Shelley,
trained for three years to get her black belt in karate at the venerable age of

forty-six! She can run in the sand on the beach for two miles, create her own artistically-inspired karate forms, and then climb and rappel down a mountain in no time flat, emerging from all of this physical activity spiritually tuned-in. Fortunately, Ira has a black belt, too. He designs professional sound systems, and Shelley, who works from home, designs residential interiors. For this day and age, they have a traditional marriage, with traditionally conceived children. She loves making *Shabbat* dinner on Friday night.

Is this the procreation pattern that I am most comfortable with? To be perfectly honest, yes. And yet, given Janet's circumstances, at the end of the day—at the end of this book—I find myself comfortable with the procreative choice of my eldest daughter as well, and certainly with the product of that choice, my grand-daughter, Samantha. Both Janet and Shelley have gone forth and multiplied in their different ways, and I find it good.

For her own reasons, and despite the fact that about half the women who have donor-conceived children are lesbian couples or single women,[1] my daughter Laura has chosen not to bring a child into her alternative lifestyle. She visits her sisters and nieces and nephew often, dedicated to the role of a loving aunt. Now that her identical twin, Susan, has become pregnant through *in vitro* fertilization, Laura is ecstatic. "I'll be a genetic parent," she crowed in happiness when she heard the news. "Not just an aunt. I'm going to be the godmother. Do you think she'll have more than one?"

Societally, we have come a long way, baby, since Aldous Huxley shocked the *literati* with his science-fiction predictions of test tube babies in *Brave New World*. Maybe it's because I'm on the lookout for it, but it seems to me that ever since the "layout" of the human genome was uncovered, every other day a new development is reported in reproductive-assisted technology or in stem cell research. Now Japanese scientists have found a way to create an artificial "womb" to speed the growth of *in vitro* eggs. They have developed miniscule "chips," which, in providing a "bed" for the embryos, simulate the conditions of a natural womb. "Fresh IVF embryos are slipped into the chips, which rest on a membrane of cultured uterus cells. Once they are ready to attach themselves to the uterus wall, the eggs are reinserted into the mother's womb."[2]

The headlines abound. It's a hot topic. "Baby-making at a crossroads"[3] informs us that, although the effects of aging can't be reversed, doctors worldwide have made great strides in helping infertile people have a family through fertility drugs. In the United States alone, over the last twenty-five years, at least four hundred thousand babies have been born with the help of improved assisted-reproduction techniques.[4]

The same article explains that, when doctors, using the IVF method, transfer fertilized embryos to the mother's womb, the challenge is to select embryos with the genetic capability to develop further—in other words, to choose the cream of the crop. Apparently, the key to IVF success is the quality of the embryo. Although there is still a knowledge gap, doctors are constantly trying to improve the IVF process to make it more tolerable for the women who undergo it. They anticipate that this knowledge gap will be filled in the next five to ten years. New developments like embryo evaluation and egg freezing may help birth rates increase. Uterine transplants are another experimental route being explored. In a further distant future, doctors may even be able to use stem-cell technology to produce sperm and eggs in the lab, "allowing a man or woman who otherwise can't reproduce their own biological children to do so. Experiments have shown that human egg and sperm can be artificially grown, though no babies have been created."[5]

Who knows? Maybe one day, the biblical Garden of Eden "curse" of laboring to have a child will be lifted. Maybe one day babies will be able to grow and develop completely outside the mother's womb by simulated means. No papas, no mamas? Will this be a good thing if it happens? I don't know. There are a lot of "I don't knows" involved in continued, exponential change. "Don't be too open-minded," a joke recently passed around the Internet cautioned. "Your brains will fall out." On the other hand, as *Looking for Normal*, a play performed in 2007 at the Geffen Theatre in Los Angeles, so poignantly asked, "What's normal?"[6]

How far, for instance, is too far to go to follow your dream of having a child? Should you try to have one on the cheap by going to a foreign country, like Cape Town, in search of less expensive IVF treatments or donor eggs or surrogates? An article called "Crossing borders for fertility treatments" explores these choices, which are not merely future possibilities but routes to fertility available now.[7] Who knows if such "medical tourism" (apparently, some people shop internationally for cataract or hip surgery also) is a good thing or a bad thing? There is as yet no international body that regulates foreign IVF clinics or donor consent.

Other journalists play further on the sensational aspects of assisted reproductive technology by asking questions such as "Will science render men unnecessary?"[8] It turns out that women might not be so essential to the reproductive process either. On another day, I click onto the Internet and find that a mom has frozen her eggs (through a process called vitrification) for a period of twenty to twenty-five years so that her daughter (born with Turner's syndrome, which rendered her sterile) will be able to have a child one day. Seang

Lin Tan, director of the McGill Reproductive Centre, terms this an ethically permissible procedure, similar to donating a kidney to your own child.[9]

Other ethical questions make the news. Deaths occasioned by terrorism, acts of war, or accidental deaths raise an agonizing dilemma. Should children be conceived when a parent dies? The Israeli army, for example, allows soldiers, who so desire, to deposit their frozen sperm in sperm banks before they go off to battle. Should the sperm go to the widow? Or a girlfriend? "An Israeli court ruled that parents of a deceased soldier could use sperm taken right after his death to impregnate a woman he never met."[10] In the aftermath of Iraq, the U.S. army is also considering guidelines for such issues: "Long after her husband died in Iraq, Maria Sutherland has a baby—using sperm he froze before he deployed."[11] Arthur Caplan, Ph.D., suggests that it's time for some legal limits on posthumous reproduction, as he poses the following hypothetical question: as technology evolves, if both parents are dead, would it be permissible to remove both the sperm from the man and the egg from a woman "to create a child, a sibling, or grandchild?"[12]

There are a lot of "who knows?" and "don't knows" that remain at the conclusion of this book. In societal terms, we have still to define our ethical boundaries, not just for North America, but also globally. And that globalization, that world of expanded connections that we live in today affects us individually. It affects us intimately. Samantha's extended family is a microcosmic reflection of what is happening in the macrocosm.

In the next years of this century, we will need to reach some sort of consensus on how babies may or may not be born. As the traditional marriage ceremony proclaims—because whether we like it or not, we are married to change—whatever happens will be "for better or worse," and we'll stick it through, hopefully together.

Global contexts aside, the question that has been bugging me through the writing of this book is this: just how non-traditional *is* my North American family in this first decade of the twenty-first century? I am wondering if perhaps the variations we have experienced in our family structure are not exactly ho-hum but are gradually slipping into the mainstream. I open the daily newspaper and see the smiling picture of the Vice President of the United States, Dick Cheney and his wife, Lynne, proudly holding their sixth grandchild. The baby, Samuel David Cheney, has been born to his daughter, Mary, who is a lesbian and her female partner of fifteen years (who, incidentally, will have no legal obligations toward the baby).[13]

In vitro fertilization has already become the subject matter (fertilized donor eggs are mixed up and implanted in the wrong wife) of a popular televised soap opera, *The Bold and the Beautiful*. In a segment called "Wombs for Rent" on Oprah Winfrey's widely televised show, I watched Oprah and Lisa Ling interview women who shopped for surrogates in India—a new kind of outsourcing. The surrogates were also shown, as well as Alexis Stewart, the forty-two-year-old daughter of Martha Stewart, who discussed her own infertility problems and outlay of 28,000 dollars per month in the attempt to have a child. Later, I clicked on the Web site to catch the responses that women were posting.[14] I'm right. Innovative ways of having children have gone mainstream.

A single woman of my acquaintance, a professional in her mid-forties, has so far been unsuccessful in her attempts to adopt a child. In the hope that she will be able to do so, she is currently foster-parenting a two-year-old girl, whose birth-mother the court has decreed must get her act together in order to get her child back. Other friends, desperate in their longing to have children, have adopted babies from China and Guatemala. That also costs a lot of money. The world of conception, of parenting as I once knew it, of what constitutes a family, has already changed. What makes up an extended family has also changed.

As I think about my own children, I often wonder how my international kids, my "adopted" Toronto family, are faring. Are Llazlo and Olga, the inseparable couple for whom no room was too small, who would gladly share a single bed to remain together, still a team? Are their biologically-induced chemicals still flowing? And Lily? My guess is that, after traversing the world for a while, she would opt to marry the well-heeled, classy suitor her parents favored, one who could give her a spacious apartment in Taiwan. I suspect that she will not send her children away to boarding school, as her parents did with her. She will be at home with them when they are young.

Mariko knew that she was too "Western" for most Japanese men, so I imagine that she soon became the principal of the Japanese school that teaches English to foreigners and married the Japanese suitor educated in the United States, who, on her behalf, hand-delivered a plastic Japanese rice-maker, made in New Jersey, to me in Toronto. I hope that Danilo married his Brazilian sweetheart, and, that while they were raising their family in relative luxury in Brazil, they also did something to alleviate the poverty in which so many families live in that country.

Khaled had already decided to avoid paying the "bride price" demanded for a Bedouin bride in Saudi Arabia by marrying the Chinese student he fell in love with in Toronto. Also, because the Bedouins, from whom he originated, tend to marry their cousins, he hoped to circumvent the genetic sickle cell disease that plagued his family by marrying "out." As for entrepreneurial, sharp-as-a-tack

Jade, I would hazard a guess that she quickly became a prime footwear entrepreneur in China. She likely put marriage and family on the back burner, delaying having children until her career goals were met.

It may be true, as Jacqueline Stenson asserts, that the availability of fertility treatments have made women falsely confident that they would be able to conceive in later life; they have placed their careers first. "Statistics [in the United States] show that as more women have entered the workforce since the mid-1979s, the percentage of first births to women ages 30 and up have increased fourfold."[15] Apparently, this situation applies in a wider context than the United States.

Sometimes I think that, despite my own flexibility and adaptability, this is all becoming too post-post modern for me; at other times, I think that next week I might switch on the television set and find that it is my family in an episode or two or three or four on *The Bold and the Beautiful* or on *Oprah*; or, I will be holding my newly-born, donor-conceived grandchildren proudly and smiling from the pages of a newspaper.

I have a feeling, though, that the upcoming generation of young women and young men—the echo boomers—will profit by their boomer parents' experience. I think they will realize that career time and upward mobility don't necessarily coincide with biological time and parenting. Even if you can freeze your eggs and mix them with sperm at a time of your choosing, you can't beat the clock, and, if you try, it can prove very expensive. Although marriage patterns may continue to vary, I'd like to believe that, generally speaking, the next generation will choose to marry earlier, to have children earlier, and perhaps take a fresh look at commitment to marriage. I really hope so, because when push comes to shove, I guess I'm still a traditionalist— whatever it is that traditionalist means—at heart. I'll still take that Neolithic couple in enduring embrace as my romantic ideal. Amid all the "don't knows," that's something I do know.

What I also know is that in the process of writing this book, I have examined my own feelings exhaustively; I have learned a lot, and I have been personally transformed and enriched. I hope that all of you who read this book, my labor of love, have a similar experience.

But, as ball player, Yogi Berra, famously said, "It ain't over 'til it's over."[16] Just as I was beginning to believe that I had arranged my thoughts tidily, Janet at last received an e-mail from Samantha's biological father, Adam. It had been forwarded to her by the Donor Sibling Registry. What he had to say, and her response, speak volumes for themselves. Like the pediatrician on TV, Dr.

Niedner, Adam was taking a big risk. Maybe he thought about his biological children when he went to sleep at night.

Hi,

I am CCB 57590. My real name is Adam, but I am somewhat apprehensive of getting too close to the recipients of my donation (both parents and children). I'm sure you can understand.

I have recently gotten married to a beautiful woman, and I have shared with her about my once alter ego of CCB 57590. She is very interested to see how the children are growing up, personalities, what they look like, etc.

Let me know if you would be willing to share some of those things with us, and I would be happy to share some things about me that I have also shared with some of the other mothers/parents of 57590.

Kind Regards,

Adam

Janet was thoroughly delighted to receive his message, and she responded quickly:

Hi Adam,

I'm so glad to hear from you. Congratulations on your marriage! You must have a wonderful wife. I guess we are all redefining this type of family-making in the twenty-first century. I can understand both your reluctance and your curiosity to have some sort of contact—I feel pretty much the same as you probably do, but I'm open to communicating and sharing with you. I'm sure you never expected to have produced so many offspring, or that you would ever be in touch with any of us.

My name is Janet, and I have a gorgeous daughter, thanks to your generosity. Her name is Samantha and she is seven, the oldest of your offspring, healthy, smart, and beautiful.

Thank you for having some GREAT genes! When you and your wife decide to have kids, they will likely be gorgeous!

I've been in contact with all the other mothers (wow, this must be very freaky for you ... but you are a wonderful man for making contact). Just a few weeks ago, my daughter met two of her half-siblings who live in White Plains (Andrea and Lucy). Their mom is Marnie. We also met Eileen, who lives in Vermont (mom to Tim) but she felt it was too early to introduce her son to half-siblings. None of us are sure how these relationships will or will not evolve, but it seemed to feel right for our kids to feel some connection. They did recognize physical traits in each other and got along very well and very naturally.

Marnie did share your e-mail address with me when we met, but I was reluctant to make uninvited contact with you, as I was aware that you had recently gotten married, so thank you for getting in touch with me. Marnie has sent me pictures that you shared with her—of you as an adult and of your folks and grandmother. She also sent a picture of you as a young boy. My daughter, who I had always thought looked just like me, is also the spitting image of you as a child—I think you'll see the resemblance when I send you the pictures. Of course, I'd love to have any additional information that you are willing to share.

I'm in London, UK, right now, on business, but I'll be happy to send you pictures of Samantha when I get back into town. We live a very happy life, in Encino. I just turned forty-eight (!), a single working mother—a corporate executive—making a good living and able to provide Sam with a really good life. I'm not married, but I date, and won't marry unless I find someone who can be a good father as well as a husband. We are Jewish, and part of the reason I chose you as a donor is that you are Jewish. I'm originally from Canada (lived in Montreal till I was thirty-six) and also liked the fact that you had lineage from Montreal.

Samantha knows about you and the gift that you gave, so that she could have a life, and is proud to have you as her biological father. The information that you have shared (that Marnie passed along) has made an enormous difference to her—just made her feel kind of the same as other kids—she knows she has a biological father who doesn't live with us, has seen your pictures, and understands that you have your own life. She knows all about what is in your profile and is proud to share your genes and many of your traits.

She is tall, slim (and gorgeous!), very bright and has been accepted to a high ability/gifted program next year. She loves music, sports, math, is reading at a Grade Four level while only in Grade One, seems to have an aptitude for science and wants to be a geologist or a veterinarian at this point (except she won't work with skunks). Insectology was high on her list until about two weeks ago. Bugs are now out of the picture. She's a good cyclist and razor-scooter. She's learning to rollerblade.

Right now, she's kind of lanky, but getting her coordination together (still skins her knee every few days), and is a decent swimmer, too. She is on a growth spurt and grows out of her shoes every month or so! She has an ebullient, energetic personality, a great sense of humor, and an intelligence beyond her years. We laugh a lot.

I'm kind of going on, but I'm so very pleased to hear from you. In terms of health, she is really healthy, but has had one serious allergic reaction that has not been identified. It may have been fertilizer from the dog park. Don't know if you have ever had any serious allergic reactions, but if so, I'd appreciate if you could let me know.

I'll send you pictures. Thanks again for getting in touch. I'm happy to keep our communication as open as we both feel comfortable with, and we can take it from there.

Thanks again. And wow!

Janet

And the very next day Adam replied:

Hi Janet,

Thank you for your thoughtful reply as well as your great stories about Samantha. I wanted to get back to you in a timely manner, but I also want to respond with as much thought as you put into your e-mail. I am currently very busy with work and will reply to you soon. Hope your trip in the UK is going well.

Kind Regards,

Adam

In a subsequent exchange of e-mails, he wrote, "I never dreamed ten years ago, when I was a sperm donor, that it would engender such happy, loving relationships." "Yes," Janet answered, "but if we should decide to meet at some future time, it would have to be carefully thought out. Once we open a door, there is no going back."

So what does the future hold? "*Que sera, sera,*"[17] as Doris Day sang so well when I was growing up. Now Dora the Explorer teaches her young listeners to follow The Map in both English and Spanish. It looks like these kids, my grand-daughter, Samantha's generation, will have to create one of their own as they grow up. There are no rules in the new territory, but it offers a fascinating opportunity to be explorers. Again.

♦

ABOUT THE AUTHOR

Corinne Heather Copnick

Born in Montreal, Canada, and now living in Los Angeles near her children and grandchildren, Corinne Heather Copnick, C.M., M.A., is a multi-talented writer and performer. Her career in the arts has spanned radio, television, film, and stage.

A recipient of various grants and awards, Corinne served as resident writer at the Leighton Artist Colony, Banff Center for the Arts, Alberta. She also designed a role-playing simulation on Canadian unity called *Future Directions*. The Canadian Commemorative Medal (1992) recognized her substantial contribution to Canada. In 1998, the National Council of Jewish Women (Montreal Section) honored her as a woman of distinction.

Her literary works include *Altar Pieces*, screened nationally many times on Canadian TV, *Embrace*, bilingual (English/French) love poems, and the humorous *How To Live Alone Until You Like It ... And Then You Are Ready for Somebody Else*. An acclaimed play that she wrote for drug education purposes, *Metamorphose*, was featured at Montreal's *Man and His World*. Her play, *In the Quiet of a Saturday Night*, was presented for National Canada Book Week in Toronto.

She is currently working on *Middle of the Air*, a screenplay; *Cindy's Daddy*, a companion book to *Cryro Kid* for children aged four to eight; and a new collection of stories, *Tales of Laughter and Inspiration*. In addition, she is the founder of Timesolvers Writing and Editing Services (www.timesolvers.com).

Corinne received both her bachelor (honors English) and master (English: developmental drama) of arts degrees from McGill University. She earned a Ph.D. in adaptabilty, which has taken her seventy-one years to complete.

♦

END NOTES

PROLOGUE

1   "Revolutionary wealth—a tour d'horizon of the future with Alvin Toffler," *European CEO*, July-August, 2007, 17.

PART I FERTILITY FOREVER

CHAPTER 1 THE BOOK OF JANET

1   Characterized by the rise of farming, the Neolithic period of the New Stone Age came to an end when metal tools became widespread.

2   Associated Press, "Archeologists find prehistoric Romeo and Juliet," http://www.theglobeandmail.com/servlet/story/RTGAM.20070207.WROMEARCH0207/bnsTOR (accessed February 8, 2007). Even death did not dissolve their bond. The archaeologists who found them did not separate the couple.

3   Disseminated by the Associated Press from Rome (February 8, 2007) and published in Toronto's *Globe and Mail* (February 8, 2007).

4   If ever there was evidence that romantic love is not an invented concept but instead unites human experience, it is the stunning image of love between these two people captured in time. Of course, we do not know if this couple was married, or if a form of marriage even existed in unrecorded time. At least until the archeologists give us more information, we can only imagine. It is known that in ancient times a young wife was likely to have been captured, without choice, because women of child-bearing age were in scarce supply. The men of her family were likely to seek revenge, and often the young couple had to go into hiding to escape the warriors. Was that the story here? Or was there a famine in the land, and the lovers died embracing one another?

5   They were impressionistic Canadian painters who became famous for painting
    the Canadian landscape outdoors, in *plein air*, instead of indoor subjects

6   Corinne Copnick, "Sutton," *Etreinte, Embrace: A Love Story in Poetry* (Montréal:
    Guy Maheux Edition, 1981), 85.

7   My own recollections have been refreshed by an account of that distressing time
    found in: Wikipedia, http://en.wikipedia.org/wiki/October _Crisis, 1-5 (accessed
    March 14, 2007). When the Montreal Stock Exchange was bombed in 1969 by
    the sovereignist "cells" of a Quebec nationalist group calling themselves the
    Front de libération du Québec (*FLQ*), twenty-seven people were injured. The
    public was terrorized by their continued threatening *communiqués*, and although
    twenty-three FLQ members were already in jail by 1970, it was discovered that
    other members of the group planned to kidnap the Israeli consul. Quantities of
    firearms and explosives for that purpose were discovered at a home in the
    Laurentian Mountains. In October 1970, this situation came to a head with events
    that were considered to be "the most serious terrorist attack on Canadian soil in
    modern times." (4)
        The British Trade Commissioner James Cross was kidnapped by members of
    the *FLQ* and kept hooded by the kidnappers for sixty days. The kidnappers'
    demands included the broadcasting of their Manifesto on all French-and English-
    speaking media. The Vice-Premier and Minister of Labour of the Province of
    Quebec, Pierre Laporte, was also kidnapped and later "executed" by strangling
    with the gold cross he wore around his neck. His body was found stuffed in the
    trunk of an abandoned car.
        The October Crisis accelerated when the Quebec government by unanimous
    vote asked for the assistance of the federal government and formally requested
    the Canadian army to intervene. In response, separatist speakers mounted their
    opposition at the *Université de Montréal*, and students sympathetic to the FLQ
    cause demonstrated at a large rally.
        I well remember that the politically-oriented labor unions and even the main-
    stream *Jean Baptiste* Society took out supportive ads in the newspapers. The
    Canadian public was terrified that a revolution was in the making. On October 16,
    1970, at the request of the Premier of Quebec, Robert Bourassa, and the Mayor of
    Montreal, Jean Drapeau, Prime Minister Pierre Elliot Trudeau invoked the con-
    troversial War Measures Act. Several members of the *FLQ* cells were rounded up,
    but not until they had negotiated their safe passage to Cuba. The remaining mem-
    bers were finally arrested on December 27 and charged with the kidnapping and

murder of Pierre Laporte. My children were later to attend the high school named in his memory, the Pierre Laporte High School.

Although the War Measures Act was initially welcomed by the Quebec and Canadian public, in later years its use was berated by intellectuals and academics (some of whom had also been rounded up by the police, because they were sympathetic to the separatist cause) as being an overreaction. They charged that the police abused their power. Trudeau, they claimed, had used an elephant gun to shoot fleas.

8   My own vivid memories have been augmented by the following sources: Claude Bélanger, "Language Laws of Quebec: Quebec History," http://www2.marianopolis.edu/quebec_history/readings/langlaws.htm, 1-4 (accessed March 14, 2007); and "Charter of the French Language," http://en.wikipedia.org/wiki/Charter_of_the_French_Language, 1-7 (accessed March 14, 2007).

In 1974 the Liberal government of Quebec Premier Robert Bourassa, trying to appease the French-speaking voters—who were insulted by an earlier Bill 63 proposed by the conservative *Union Nationale* party—and with an eye on the next election in 1976:

> proclaimed French the official language in Quebec (*Loi sur la langue officielle*), set up a *Régie de la langue française* to supervise the application of the bill, mandated that all public institutions had to address the public administration in French, made French the official language of contracts, forced corporations to give themselves a French name, and to advertise primarily in French in Quebec, as well as to seek a certificate of francization that could only be obtained when it was demonstrated that the business could function in French and address employees in French. On the subject of schools, it maintained the freedom of choice for the language of instruction, but subjected the entrance into English schools to those children that a test showed had a knowledge of English (Bélanger, 2).

So, under Bourassa, Anglophones could keep their English schools, and, if requested in writing, business contracts could be in English. This legislation pleased neither the English nor the French, and, in the next election in 1976, the English protested against the Liberal government by voting for the *Union Nationale*, which didn't stand a chance. As a result, the separatist *Parti Quebecois* was swept into office. There were shock waves when the *Parti Quebecois* promptly passed the *Charte de la langue française* in 1977 (the infamous Bill

101). In an attempt to make Quebec a largely unilingual province, this bill affected every area of daily life.

> ...the bill required that all advertising on billboards be done in French only and that all commercial signs in business establishments be in French alone. All public administrations and businesses had to address their employees in French. All government agencies were directed to use the Official language in their dealings with corporations and other governments in Canada. Government Ministries and Agencies, as well as professional associations in Quebec, were to be known by their French name. The laws of the province were to be enacted in French although an English translation might also be made.... English education was to be restricted mostly to those already in the system, their siblings, those temporarily posted in Quebec or whose parents had themselves received an English elementary education in the province (Bélanger, 2)

Some of these restrictive laws were later challenged in court and have since been softened.

CHAPTER 2 LOVE, MARRIAGE, NO BABY CARRIAGE

1   Sam Roberts, "To be Married Means To Be Outnumbered," *New York Times*, Oct. 15, 2006.

2   Blaine Harden, "Numbers Drop for the Married With Children," Washington Post, Sunday, March 4, 2007.

3   "Greek Words for Love," http://en.wikipedia.org/wiki/Greek_words_for-love, 1-2 (accessed February 11, 2007).

4   Kimberly Powell, "Your Guide to Genealogy: Romance through the Ages," http://genealogy.about.com/ca/timelines/a/romance_history.htm (accessed February 11, 2007).

5   Norine Dresser, *As You Aren't: Celebrating Events in the New Cultural Diversity* (Lanham; New York; Boulder; Toronto; Oxford: M. Evans Edition, 2006), 29.

6   Dresser, *As You Aren't*, 29.

7   Quoted by Dresser. *As You Aren't*, 25

8   Jacqueline Stenson (Contributing Editor), citing statistics noted by the American Fertility Association, "Baby-making at a crossroads: Doctors see new hope on the fertility front even as success rates level out," June 13, 2007, http://www.msnbc. msn.com/id/17937812/print/q/displaymode/1098 (accessed June 27, 2007).

9   Lisa Palmer quoting Dr. Ravinder Dhallan, "Safer Babies," *Fortune Small Business*, October 2007, p. 52.

10   Stenson," June 13, 2007 (accessed June 27, 2007).

11   Margaret Atwood, *The Handmaid's Tale* (New York: Anchor Books, an imprint of Random House, 1998).

CHAPTER 3 *THE BOOK of ADAM*

1   Constance Holden, "Paleoanthropology: Ancient Child Burial Uncovered in Portugal," www.sciencemag.org/cgi/content/full/283/5399/169b?ck=nck (accessed March 24, 2007). See also *Science 8*, vol. 283, no. 5399, 169.

2   "World Events, 1999," http://www.infoplease.com/year/1999.html (accessed March 24, 2007)

3   Norman Mailer, *The Castle in the Forest*. (New York: Random House, 2007) 155-210

4   Joel Garreau, Washington Post Staff Writer, "Honey, I'm Gone: Abandoned Beehives Are a Scientific Mystery and a Metaphor for Our Tenuous Times, *Washington Post*, Friday, June 1, 2007:C01

5   David Plotz, "The Genius Factory: My Short, Scary Career as a Sperm Donor," *Slate Magazine*, http://www.slate.com/id/2119998/,2 (accessed April 18, 2007). See also David Plotz, *The Genius Factory: The Curious History of the Nobel Prize Sperm Bank* (New York: Random House, 2005). His book resulted from a series of articles called "Seed" that were printed in *Slate* magazine and found a fascinated readership. Founded by millionaire Robert Graham, the Repository for Geminal Choice's philosophy had overtones reminiscent of the Nazi era. It opened in 1980 with a great deal of fanfare and lots of applicants and closed quietly in 1999.

6 "About the Genius Factory," http://www.thegeniusfactory.net/about.php.1 (accessed April 17, 2007).

7 "A Global Guide to Baby-Making." *The Hamilton Spectator,* http://www. hamiltonspectator.com/NASApp/cs/ContentServer?pagename=hamilton, Dec. 23, 2006 (accessed April 20, 2007).

8 "Calls to Customer Support Drive Sperm Bank Deposits," Sunday, March 11, 2007, New *Delhi (AFP),* http//thewelltimedperiod.blogspot.com/2007/03/calls-to-customer-support-drive-sperm.html (accessed April 20, 2007).

9 G. Pascal Zachary, *Wall Street Journal,* Friday, January 7, 2007, http://sfgate/cp./cgi-bin/article.cgi?file=/examiner/archibe/2000/01/07/NEWS7186 (accessed April 20, 2007).

10 Although what I am writing about this cryobank is based on Janet's personal experience, a very extensive history of the California Cryobank and its multiple services and methods, from which some of this material is derived, as well as the history of sperm banking, can be found on the company's Web site. See Sonia Fader," Sperm Banking: A Reproductive Resource," http://www/cryobank.com, 1-9 (accessed March 28, 2007).

11 Fader, "Sperm banking," http://www/cryobank.com, 1-9 (accessed March 28, 2007). Although the brochure is out-of-print, the information is available on the Web site.

12 "Donor Insemination—The Long Road to Acceptance," California Cryobank, http://www/cryobank.com/banking.cfm?page=2&sub=126, 2 (accessed March 28, 2007).

13 "Company Overview," California Cryobank, http://www.cryobank.com, 1-2 (accessed March 28, 2007).

14 California Cryobank, http://www.cryobank.com/donorinfocfm?page=43 (accessed March 28, 2007).

15 "Genetic Screening," These genetic screening tests are donor requirements at the California Cryobank, http://www.cryobank.com/gen_tests.cfm?page=44, 1-3 (accessed March 28, 2007).

CHAPTER 4 *THE BOOK of SAMANTHA*

1   The English word "love" can be interpreted in many debatable ways. Love can embrace romantic, sexual, platonic, religious, and familial relationships, as well as casual or pleasurable activities, http://en.wikipedia.org/wiki/Love, 1-7 (accessed February 11, 2007).

2   Love was not always the basis of Western marriage requirements. Scientific views of love refer to love in purely biological or chemical terms, http://en.wikipedia.org/wiki/Love, 1-7 (accessed February 11, 2007).

3   Helen Fisher, "Why We Love: A Nature and Chemistry of Romantic Love (New York: Henry Holt and Co., 2004). See also "Scientific Views: Biology of Love," http://en.wikipedia.org/wiki/Love (accessed February 11, 2007).

4   According to Torah scholar, Dr. Steve Marmer, Jacob was allowed to enjoy Rachel as his second bride a week after he married Leah, because this was the start of the next seven years he had to work.

5   Sheri and Bob Stritof, "Your Guide to Marriage: History of Marriage," http://marriage.about.com/cs/generalhistory/a/marriagehistory.htm (accessed February 11, 2007). The concept that a couple must consent to marriage stems from the ninth century C.E. teachings of the Catholic Church.

CHAPTER 5 *I NEVER MET MY DADDY*

1   "Genesis," (1:28; 9:1), *The Bible.*

2   Corinne Copnick, Excerpt from "Who," *Altar Pieces*, a collection of Corinne Copnick's stories and poems screened many times nationally on Vision TV, a Canadian national network, 1992.

PART II MY TRANSFORMATIONAL FAMILY

CHAPTER 6 *A FAMILY IN PROGRESS*

1   Stephanie Coontz, as quoted by Elizabeth DiNovella, "Last Comes Love," *The Progressive*, Sept, 2005, 1, http://www.findarticles.com/p/articles/mi_ml1295/is_9_69/ai_nl5397773, 1 (accessed February 11, 2007). See also Stephanie

Coontz, *Marriage, A History From Obedience to Intimacy or How Love Conquered Marriage* (New York: Viking, 2005).

2   Barbara Kingsolvers, "Stone Soup," from *High Tide in Tuscon: Essays from Now or Never*, 1995. Reprinted by permission of Harper Collins Publishers. In *My Father Married Your Mother: Writers Talk about Stepparents, Stepchildren*, ed. Anne Burt (New York: W.W. Norton & Co., 2006), 270.

3   Kingsolvers, "Stone Soup," 270.

4   Coontz as quoted by Elizabeth DiNovella, "Last Comes Love," http://www.findarticles.com/p/articles/mi_ml1295/is_9_69/ai_nl5397773, 2 (accessed February 11, 2007).

5   Joe Palca, "Opposum Genome May Answer Human Questions," NPR, May 19, 2007; Will Dunham, "Opposum's genetic map sheds light on humans," Reuters, May 10, 2007, 1, www.globeandmail.com (accessed May 11, 2007).

6   Ray Kurzweil, *The Singularity is Near* (New York: The Penguin Group, 2005).

7   "The Bones and Bird Art of Sarah Perry and Joyce Cutler Shaw," Fisher Gallery, University of Southern California, Spring, 2007.

8   Dresser, *As You Aren't*, 25.

9   Dresser, *As You Aren't*, 43.

10   Perry Bacon, Washington Post Staff Writer, "Romney reaches to the Christian right," *Washington Post*, Sunday, May 6, 2007: A04.

11   Kingsolvers, "Stone Soup," 270

CHAPTER 7 *LAND of REFUGE*

1   "Greek Words for Love," http://en.wikipedia.org/wiki/Greek_words_for-love, 1-2 (accessed February 11, 2007).

2   Copnick, "The Story of Pearl," *Altar Pieces*, 1992.

3   I read the full text of this story in concert reading to an enthralled audience in
     Toronto in 1992.

4   Popular song during World War II circa 1944. My mother played the piano, as my
     sister and I sang to the sheet music. Words and music by Sammy Cahn and Jules
     Styne. Sung by Dinah Shore in the film *Follow the Boys*.

5   Irving M. Abella's and Harold Troper, *None Is Too Many: Canada and the Jews
     of Europe (1933-1948)* (Toronto: L. and O. Dennys, 1986). This excellent book
     documents this time.

6   Words and music written by Eily Beadell and Nell Tollerton in 1945. Won a pub-
     lic song-writing competition in the U.K. Nineteen weeks on the Hit Parade of the
     Lucky Strike program in 1949.

CHAPTER 8 *THE MOMMY TRACK*

1   "Religious Views," *Love*, http://en.wikipedia.org/wiki/love, 2007 (accessed
     February 11, 2007).

2   "Song of Songs," (2:16), *The Bible*

3   Stephen Spender, "I Think Continually of Those Who Were Truly Great," *Oxford
     Anthology of English Literature*, *vols. 1-2*, ed. Frank Kermode and John
     Hollander, (London: Oxford University Press, 1973), 1:22-26.

4   Many thanks to Brian Ferstman for the genealogical data he meticulously gathered.

5   A popular song recorded by many artists, including Judy Garland, celebrating the
     1904 Louisiana Purchase Exposition, better known as the World's Fair, which
     was held in St. Louis. In the public domain.

6   In 1958 in Canada, there was only one ground for divorce, adultery. The divorce
     had to be approved by the Senate, a lengthy process.

7   Copnick, "Icicle," *Embrace/Etreinte: A Love Story in Poetry*, 17.

CHAPTER 9 *MY FOUR KIDS*

1   Corinne Copnick, "The Foo Dogs," excerpted from *How To Live Alone Until You Like It...And Then You Are Ready For Somebody Else*, (Toronto: La Magie de L'Art, 1994) 16-17. Reprinted in *Jewish Life*, Toronto, 1994.

2   Copnick, "Taking a Crash Course without a Helmet," excerpted from *How to Live Alone,* 32-34. Reprinted in *Jewish Life*, Toronto, 1994.

3   Copnick, "How to Apply for 500 Jobs and Still Smile," excerpted from *How to Live Alone*, 59-60.

4   Copnick, "The Rose Garden," excerpted from *How to Live Alone,* 72-73. Reprinted in *Jewish Life*, Toronto, 1994.

5   Copnick, "The House Mate," *How to Live Alone,* 41-45. Reprinted in *Jewish Life*, Toronto, 1994.

6   With extensive fertility treatment, including a host of prescription drugs and injections in the belly with a long needle four to six times a day, the patient's ovaries are stimulated to produce multiple follicles. During this time, she is carefully monitored with blood tests and ultrasound until the eggs are ready to be retrieved. During the retrieval, the liquid from the follicles is aspirated with a straw-like needle inserted into the vaginal cavity and put into a test tube for later use in the fertilization process. Eggs of varying sizes are then retrieved from the follicles and graded. Attempts are made to fertilize these eggs with the sperm in a Petri dish. Eggs that are successfully fertilized are incubated until they are ready to be implanted into the woman's body. The remaining eggs may be directly injected with a single sperm in order to help them become embryos that develop the desired six to eight cells.

7   The ZIFT procedure is threefold: first the eggs are retrieved, and the patient is sedated during the retrieval. Next, a laparoscopic surgery is performed, one that requires small incisions and a skillful surgeon with cosmetic sensitivity, with the patient under anesthetic. Selected fertilized eggs (now called zygotes) are placed in the fallopian tubes, where they warm themselves and begin their journey into the uterus. The final procedure places the remaining eggs into the uterus.

The four or five extra days that the eggs implanted in the fallopian tubes spend in the natural warmth of the mother's body can turn a "B" egg into an "A" egg.

Meanwhile, the implantation into the uterus of the eggs warmed in the incubator begins to create a receptive environment in the womb. The quality of the eggs implanted immediately into the fallopian tubes is unknown, though, and cell division has not yet taken place when they are implanted. Only on the third day can it be seen how well the remaining eggs—the embryos destined for the uterus—have developed. If the eggs are "A" eggs, chances are the ones already placed in the fallopian tubes will be "A" eggs as well. If they have grown the desired four to eight cells, preferably eight, it is likely the ones in the fallopian tubes are doing well, too.

CHAPTER 10 *TRANSITIONING*

1   Alvin Toffler, "Revolutionary wealth—a tour d'horizon of the future with Alvin Toffler," *European CEO,* July-August, 2007, 17.

2   As late as 1984, the Jewish community of Belgrade, terrified that the treasures might be taken from them, was denying to the Chief Sephardic Rabbi, Dr. Salomon Gaon, who visited the community as an emissary from the West (specifically a group in which I was involved in Montreal), that these treasures even existed. Eventually they were unearthed, gathered together, and sent to Croatia for exhibition at the Central Museum. The Sarajevo *Haggadah,* a beautiful, illuminated, fourteenth century manuscript that survived the Spanish inquisition (the Cohen family fled to the Balkans carrying the *Haggadah* with them) and the Nazis (the *Haggadah* was hidden during the Nazi regime behind a brick wall in the home of a Muslim cleric), had long been secreted in Bosnia and was said to be in need of repair. With hostilities between Serbia and Croatia continually accelerating, the horrific conflict that eventually took place was feared, and the various Yugoslav groups involved became more amenable to sending the "collection" to the West. Before I became involved, a first attempt to bring it to the Jewish Museum in New York was aborted when the Yugoslav government intervened. Mounts for the collection had already been made in New York, and a catalogue was published, and then the exhibition had to be cancelled. The result was that other large museums did not want to chance holding an exhibition that might be cancelled at the last minute, leaving them in the lurch. When the collection finally arrived in New York, after extensive diplomatic negotiation, no museum was available to exhibit it.

3   In a legal capacity, he assisted the Canadian government with various projects, including a satellite communications project in Yugoslavia.

4   This was no small task, partly because the major museums were aware that the Yugoslav government had cancelled the exhibition in New York. In Toronto, Canadians of Croatian origin and those of Serbian origin held permitted demonstrations on a main street every weekend. They took turns: one week it was the Canadian Croats demonstrating, and the next week it was the Canadian Serbs. On the multicultural radio talk shows, they hurled insults at one another on a daily basis. The museums didn't want trouble.

5   It was possible because this museum already housed the famed, large Cecil Roth collection of Judaica, only part of which could be shown at any one time. Thus if, at the last minute, the Yugoslav exhibit should be cancelled, the museum would still have more than enough to exhibit. The Board stipulated, however, that the exhibit be publicized privately: to the membership of synagogues, Jewish schools and institutions, and to invited guests. It would not be publicized to the general public. This restriction did not please the Yugoslav consul in Toronto. He was hoping for the good publicity the event would generate to counteract the bad impression created by the weekly demonstrations, which were well covered by the media. Dr. Salomon Gaon made his own stipulation: the Sarajevo *Haggadah* would not travel from Bosnia to the West for exhibition because he considered the 600-year-old manuscript to be too fragile. In 1992, the Sarajevo *Haggadah* was again to survive another catastrophe, this time the shelling of the National Museum in Bosnia. The museum's Muslim director, Enver Imamovic, and three volunteers disregarded their own safety to break into the museum vault and remove the *Haggadah*. They took it to the National Bank where it was kept safely in an underground vault through the conflict—buried again. After a visiting delegation from the American Jewish Joint Distribution Committee viewed it, with the help of the UN, the *Haggadah* was spirited away to the Austrian Academy of Fine Arts in Vienna for repair by conservator, Andrea Pataki, who stabilized the binding but left the wine stains for history.

6   This is another story to be told. The protesters, Canadians of Croatian origin, objected to the screening of two Yugoslav films documenting *Jasanovac*, a concentration camp that had incarcerated Jews and others during the Nazi regime.

7   A musical prodigy, he had been brought to Beijing to study music at the age of eleven, but when he attended university, he made the mistake of becoming involved in a student protest. Labor camp was the result. He was forbidden to compose or play music, so for twenty years he composed in his head. Eventually he was allowed to conduct the provincial orchestra in North China. At the end of

the twenty years, he was returned to Beijing and allowed to resume his musical career, as if nothing had happened in between. He was tall for a Chinese man, a handsome man, and after he married the director of the Beijing opera, he was sent by his government to competitions in Europe, which he won. When I met him, he was composing a symphony to be played at the Lincoln Center. If you asked him about anything even slightly political, however, he would give the same reply, "I do not understand the question." Twenty years had done its job.

8   Copnick, "Transplantation," *Altar Pieces*, 1992.

PART THREE THE SIBS

CHAPTER 12 *DISCOVERY*

1   Steve Kroft, "Sperm Donor Siblings Find Family Ties,", June 24, 2007, http://www.cbsnews.com/stories/2006/03/17/60minutes/printable_1414965.shtml (accessed July 1, 2007)

2   Wendy Kramer, www.donorsiblingregistry.com (accessed July 1, 2007).

3   Kramer, www.donorsiblingregistry.com (accessed July 1, 2007).

4   Kroft, quoting Wendy Kramer, "Sperm Donor Siblings" (accessed July 1, 2007).

5   Kroft, quoting Kramer, "Sperm Donor Siblings" (accessed July 1, 2007).

6   Kroft, quoting Kramer, "Sperm Donor Siblings" (accessed July 1, 2007).

CHAPTER 13 *EPILOGUE: NEW TERRITORY*

1   Steve Kroft, "Sperm Donor Siblings" (accessed July 1, 2007).

2   Tan Ee Cyn, "Japan Scientists devise 'womb' for IVF eggs," *External Womb*, 1, July 27, 2007, http://news.Yahoo.com/s/nm/200700727/sc-nm/japan_womb.dc_1; *New Scientist Magazine*, no. 2614, July 26, 2007, 28.

3   Jacqueline Stenson, Contributing Editor, "Baby-making at a crossroads: Doctors see new hope on the fertility front even as success rates level out," June 13, 2007,

MsNBC.com, http://www.msnbc.msn.com/id/17937812/print/1/displaymode/1098)
(accessed June 27, 2007).

4   Stenson, "Baby-making at a crossroads," June 13, 2007 (accessed June 27, 2007).

5   Stenson, "Baby-making at a crossroads," June 13, 2007 (accessed June 27, 2007).

6   Jane Anderson, *Looking for Normal*, produced at the Geffen Theatre, Los Angeles,
2007. The play was published by the Dramatist's Play Service, Inc. in 2002.

7   Susan Wilson, "Crossing borders for fertility treatments: 'IV' tourism touts
cheaper chance at baby, but critics see a downside, June 13, 2007, Special to
MSNBC,   http://www.msnbc.msn.com/id/19100571/print/1/displaymode/1098)
(accessed June 27, 2007).

8   Brian Alexander, "Will science render men unnecessary? The possibility seems
real but don't drop your guy just yet," MSNBC contributor, June 27, 2007,
http://www.msnbc.msn.com/id/17937813/print/1/displaymode/1098/) (accessed
June 27, 2007).

9   "Mom freezes eggs so daughter can have child: If girl chooses to get pregnant, the
child will be her half-sibling," Reuters, April 19, 2007 (accessed June 27, 2007).

10   Arthur Caplan, "Should kids be conceived after a parent dies? It's time for some
legal limits on posthumous reproduction." MSNBC contributor, June 27, 2007,
http://www.msnbc.msn.com/id/17937817/print/1/displaymode/1098/. (accessed June
27, 2007).

11   Linda Kramer, "He Looks Just Like His Dad: Long after her husband died in Iraq,
Maria Sutherland has a baby—using sperm he froze before he deployed," *People*,
September 10, 2007, 111-112.

12   Caplan, "Should kids be conceived after a parent dies? June 27, 2007 (accessed
June 27, 2007).

13   Times Wire Reports. "Washington, D.C.: Mary Cheney gives birth to a son," *Los
Angeles Times*, Thursday, May 24, 2007, A 15.

14 "Re: Lisa Ling Investigates: Wombs for Rent," www.Oprah.com/Community/thread, Oct. 11, 2007 (accessed Oct. 14, 2007).

15 Jacqueline Stenson, Contributing Editor," Have kids? Sure…someday: Not just careers, but complacency, delay the pregnant pause," June 6, 2007. http://www.nsnbc.msn.com/id/17937795/print1/displaymode/1098/ (accessed June 27, 2007).

16 http//yoggiberra.com (accessed Sept. 27, 2007). The ball player was famous for his "yogi-isms."

17 *Que Sera, Sera*, lyrics by Ray Evans and Jay Livingston and music by Bernard Herrmann, won the 1956 Oscar for Best Song. Later became the theme song for the Doris Day show.

978-0-595-47834-7
0-595-47834-4

Printed in the United States
100863LV00005B/1-132/A